Netscape Composer™ Fe

MW00675858

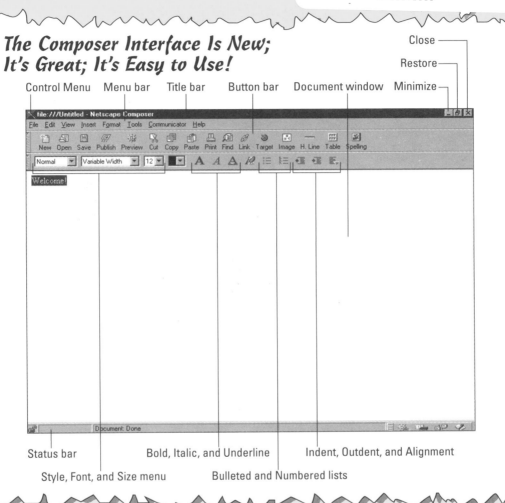

The Composer Interface Is New; It's Great; It's Easy to Use!

Control Menu · Menu bar · Title bar · Button bar · Document window · Minimize · Restore · Close

Status bar

Style, Font, and Size menu

Bold, Italic, and Underline

Bulleted and Numbered lists

Indent, Outdent, and Alignment

Useful Info to Obtain about Your Internet Service Provider

Technical support info (phone/e-mail) _____

Web page address (URL) _____

FTP address (if needed) _____

Address for online documentation for Web services provided by your ISP _____

The type of doughnuts ISP staff likes _____

Other information volunteered by ISP (when prompted) _____

_____

...For Dummies: #1 Computer Book Series for Beginners

Netscape Composer™ For Dummies®

Cheat Sheet

Some File Formats You'll Likely Encounter

Extension	Use	Purpose
.HTM, .HTML	Web pages	Used for Web pages.
.GIF	Images	Used for simple line art or transparent or interlaced images. Recognized by all graphical Web browsers.
.JPG	Images	Used for photographs or complex images, particularly when size or quality is a key factor. Recognized by most newer graphical Web browsers.
.AIFF	Audio	Used for audio files. Recognized by most newer Web browsers.
.AU	Audio	Standard audio format for Sun computers. Variable quality, but often not as good as .AIFF. Recognized by most newer Web browses.
.WAV	Audio	Standard audio format for Windows computers. Recognized by most Windows-based browsers with the help of an additional plug-in or program.

Composer's Really Useful Buttons

 Publish — Lets you publish your Web pages.

 Preview — Lets you view your page in Navigator.

 Find — Lets you find text within the current Web page.

 Link — Lets you easily link pages to other Web sites and pages.

 Target — Lets you easily create a link to a place (target) within a Web page.

 Image — Lets you easily add an image to your Web page.

 H. Line — Lets you — you guessed it! — add a horizontal line.

 Table — Lets you easily add and format Web page tables.

 Spelling — Lets you run a quickie spell check of your Web page.

Ten Steps to a Great Web Site

1. Analyze your readers.
2. Organize your topics.
3. Develop Web site contents.
4. Determine Web site theme.
5. Select images.
6. Develop navigation tools.
7. Polish your pages.
8. Publish your pages.
9. Submit your site to search engines and directories (so folks can find your site).
10. Maintain your site.

...For Dummies: #1 Computer Book Series for Beginners

NETSCAPE COMPOSER™ FOR DUMMIES®

by Deborah S. Ray & Eric J. Ray

IDG
BOOKS
WORLDWIDE

IDG Books Worldwide, Inc.
An International Data Group Company

Foster City, CA ♦ Chicago, IL ♦ Indianapolis, IN ♦ Southlake, TX

Netscape Composer™ For Dummies®

Published by
IDG Books Worldwide, Inc.
An International Data Group Company
919 E. Hillsdale Blvd.
Suite 400
Foster City, CA 94404
www.idgbooks.com (IDG Books Worldwide Web site)
www.dummies.com (Dummies Press Web site)

Library of Congress Catalog Card No.: 96-79275

ISBN: 0-7645-0075-9

Printed in the United States of America

10 9 8 7 6 5 4 3 2 1

1O/RT/QY/ZX/IN

Distributed in the United States by IDG Books Worldwide, Inc.

Distributed by Macmillan Canada for Canada; by Transworld Publishers Limited in the United Kingdom; by IDG Norge Books for Norway; by IDG Sweden Books for Sweden; by Woodslane Pty. Ltd. for Australia; by Woodslane Enterprises Ltd. for New Zealand; by Longman Singapore Publishers Ltd. for Singapore, Malaysia, Thailand, and Indonesia; by Simron Pty. Ltd. for South Africa; by Toppan Company Ltd. for Japan; by Distribuidora Cuspide for Argentina; by Livraria Cultura for Brazil; by Ediciencia S.A. for Ecuador; by Addison-Wesley Publishing Company for Korea; by Ediciones ZETA S.C.R. Ltda. for Peru; by WS Computer Publishing Corporation, Inc., for the Philippines; by Unalis Corporation for Taiwan; by Contemporanea de Ediciones for Venezuela; by Computer Book & Magazine Store for Puerto Rico; by Express Computer Distributors for the Caribbean and West Indies. Authorized Sales Agent: Anthony Rudkin Associates for the Middle East and North Africa.

For general information on IDG Books Worldwide's books in the U.S., please call our Consumer Customer Service department at 800-762-2974. For reseller information, including discounts and premium sales, please call our Reseller Customer Service department at 800-434-3422.

For information on where to purchase IDG Books Worldwide's books outside the U.S., please contact our International Sales department at 415-655-3200 or fax 415-655-3295.

For information on foreign language translations, please contact our Foreign & Subsidiary Rights department at 415-655-3021 or fax 415-655-3281.

For sales inquiries and special prices for bulk quantities, please contact our Sales department at 415-655-3200 or write to the address above.

For information on using IDG Books Worldwide's books in the classroom or for ordering examination copies, please contact our Educational Sales department at 800-434-2086 or fax 817-251-8174.

For press review copies, author interviews, or other publicity information, please contact our Public Relations department at 415-655-3000 or fax 415-655-3299.

For authorization to photocopy items for corporate, personal, or educational use, please contact Copyright Clearance Center, 222 Rosewood Drive, Danvers, MA 01923, or fax 508-750-4470.

is a trademark under exclusive license to IDG Books Worldwide, Inc., from International Data Group, Inc.

About the Authors

Deborah S. Ray and **Eric J. Ray** are the award-winning authors of *HTML For Dummies Quick Reference* and *Dummies 101: HTML,* as well as other computer books. Together, they own RayComm, Inc., a technical communication consulting firm, where they spend their time on HTML-related development, training, consulting, and writing about other cool stuff — when they're not writing books, that is.

Deborah, a hard-core writing type, has been involved with computer and Internet projects for the past four years. She has very diverse experience, including creating computer and engineering documents and teaching technical writing to college students. Her areas of emphasis include writing, designing, and illustrating documents to meet various audiences' information needs. Deborah is accomplished in technical communication, having received numerous regional and international awards from the Society for Technical Communication as well as awards from previous employers for her achievements in the field.

Eric has been a hard-core techno geek for years, including contributing thousands of hours of overinvolvement to the Internet, running a mailing list for technical writers (TECHWR-L), and generally just putzing around with computers and calling it work. Eric has made numerous presentations and published several papers about HTML and online information. His technical experience includes a wide range of technical support and Internet-related projects. As a technical communicator, Eric has received many regional and international awards from the Society for Technical Communication as well as awards from previous employers for his contributions to technical communication projects.

When not glued to their computer monitors, Deb and Eric spend their days enjoying their daughter, Ashleigh, whose first real word, not surprisingly, was c*aaaa*t. (It was either that, or comp*uuu*ter.)

ABOUT IDG BOOKS WORLDWIDE

Welcome to the world of IDG Books Worldwide.

IDG Books Worldwide, Inc., is a subsidiary of International Data Group, the world's largest publisher of computer-related information and the leading global provider of information services on information technology. IDG was founded more than 25 years ago and now employs more than 8,500 people worldwide. IDG publishes more than 275 computer publications in over 75 countries (see listing below). More than 60 million people read one or more IDG publications each month.

Launched in 1990, IDG Books Worldwide is today the #1 publisher of best-selling computer books in the United States. We are proud to have received eight awards from the Computer Press Association in recognition of editorial excellence and three from *Computer Currents'* First Annual Readers' Choice Awards. Our best-selling *...For Dummies®* series has more than 30 million copies in print with translations in 30 languages. IDG Books Worldwide, through a joint venture with IDG's Hi-Tech Beijing, became the first U.S. publisher to publish a computer book in the People's Republic of China. In record time, IDG Books Worldwide has become the first choice for millions of readers around the world who want to learn how to better manage their businesses.

Our mission is simple: Every one of our books is designed to bring extra value and skill-building instructions to the reader. Our books are written by experts who understand and care about our readers. The knowledge base of our editorial staff comes from years of experience in publishing, education, and journalism — experience we use to produce books for the '90s. In short, we care about books, so we attract the best people. We devote special attention to details such as audience, interior design, use of icons, and illustrations. And because we use an efficient process of authoring, editing, and desktop publishing our books electronically, we can spend more time ensuring superior content and spend less time on the technicalities of making books.

You can count on our commitment to deliver high-quality books at competitive prices on topics you want to read about. At IDG Books Worldwide, we continue in the IDG tradition of delivering quality for more than 25 years. You'll find no better book on a subject than one from IDG Books Worldwide.

John Kilcullen
John Kilcullen
CEO
IDG Books Worldwide, Inc.

Steven Berkowitz
Steven Berkowitz
President and Publisher
IDG Books Worldwide, Inc.

Eighth Annual
Computer Press
Awards ≥1992

Ninth Annual
Computer Press
Awards ≥1993

Tenth Annual
Computer Press
Awards ≥1994

Eleventh Annual
Computer Press
Awards ≥1995

IDG Books Worldwide, Inc., is a subsidiary of International Data Group, the world's largest publisher of computer-related information and the leading global provider of information services on information technology. International Data Group publishes over 275 computer publications in over 75 countries. Sixty million people read one or more International Data Group publications each month. International Data Group's publications include: **ARGENTINA:** Buyer's Guide, Computerworld Argentina, PC World Argentina; **AUSTRALIA:** Australian Macworld, Australian PC World, Australian Reseller News, Computerworld, IT Casebook, Network World, Publish, Webmaster; **AUSTRIA:** Computerwelt Osterreich, Networks Austria, PC Tip Austria; **BANGLADESH:** PC World Bangladesh; **BELARUS:** PC World Belarus; **BELGIUM:** Data News; **BRAZIL:** Annuário de Informática, Computerworld, Connections, Macworld, PC Player, PC World, Publish, Reseller News, Supergamepower; **BULGARIA:** Computerworld Bulgaria, Network World Bulgaria, PC & MacWorld Bulgaria; **CANADA:** CIO Canada, Client/Server World, ComputerWorld Canada, InfoWorld Canada, NetworkWorld Canada, WebWorld; **CHILE:** Computerworld Chile, PC World Chile; **COLOMBIA:** Computerworld Colombia, PC World Colombia; **COSTA RICA:** PC World Centro America; **THE CZECH AND SLOVAK REPUBLICS:** Computerworld Czechoslovakia, Macworld Czech Republic, PC World Czechoslovakia; **DENMARK:** Communications World Danmark, Computerworld Danmark, Macworld Danmark, PC World Danmark, Techworld Denmark; **DOMINICAN REPUBLIC:** PC World Republica Dominicana; **ECUADOR:** PC World Ecuador; **EGYPT:** Computerworld Middle East, PC World Middle East; **EL SALVADOR:** PC World Centro America; **FINLAND:** MikroPC, Tietoverkko, Tietoviikko; **FRANCE:** Distributique, Hebdo, Info PC, Le Monde Informatique, Macworld, Reseaux & Telecoms, WebMaster France; **GERMANY:** Computer Partner, Computerwoche, Computerwoche Extra, Computerwoche FOCUS, Global Online, Macwelt, PC Welt; **GREECE:** Amiga Computing, GamePro Greece, Multimedia World; **GUATEMALA:** PC World Centro America; **HONDURAS:** PC World Centro America; **HONG KONG:** Computerworld Hong Kong, PC World Hong Kong, Publish in Asia; **HUNGARY:** ABCD CD-ROM, Computerworld Szamitastechnika, Internetto online Magazine, PC World Hungary, PC-X Magazin Hungary; **ICELAND:** Tolvuheimur PC World Island; **INDIA:** Information Communications World, Information Systems Computerworld, PC World India, Publish in Asia; **INDONESIA:** InfoKomputer PC World, Komputek Computerworld, Publish in Asia; **IRELAND:** ComputerScope, PC Live!; **ISRAEL:** Macworld Israel, People & Computers/Computerworld; **ITALY:** Computerworld Italia, Macworld Italia, Networking Italia, PC World Italia; **JAPAN:** DTP World, Macworld Japan, Nikkei Personal Computing, OS/2 World Japan, SunWorld Japan, Windows NT World, Windows World Japan; **KENYA:** PC World East African; **KOREA:** Hi-Tech Information, Macworld Korea, PC World Korea; **MACEDONIA:** PC World Macedonia; **MALAYSIA:** Computerworld Malaysia, PC World Malaysia, Publish in Asia; **MALTA:** PC World Malta; **MEXICO:** Computerworld Mexico, PC World Mexico; **MYANMAR:** PC World Myanmar; **NETHERLANDS:** Computer! Totaal, LAN Internetworking Magazine, LAN World Buyers Guide, Macworld Netherlands, Net, WebWereld; **NEW ZEALAND:** Absolute Beginners Guide and Plain & Simple Series, Computer Buyer, Computer Industry Directory, Computerworld New Zealand, MTB, Network World, PC World New Zealand; **NICARAGUA:** PC World Centro America; **NORWAY:** Computerworld Norge, CW Rapport, Datamagasinet, Financial Rapport, Kursguide Norge, Macworld Norge, Multimediaworld Norge, PC World Ekspress Norge, PC World Nettverk, PC World Norge, PC World ProduktGuide Norge; **PAKISTAN:** Computerworld Pakistan; **PANAMA:** PC World Panama; **PEOPLE'S REPUBLIC OF CHINA:** China Computer Users, China Computerworld, China InfoWorld, China Telecom World Weekly, Computer & Communication, Electronic Design China, Electronics Today, Electronics Weekly, Game Software, PC World China, Popular Computer Week, Software Weekly, Software World, Telecom World; **PERU:** Computerworld Peru, PC World Profesional Peru, PC World SoHo Peru; **PHILIPPINES:** Click!, Computerworld Philippines, PC World Philippines, Publish in Asia; **POLAND:** Computerworld Poland, Computerworld Special Report Poland, Cyber, Macworld Poland, Networld Poland, PC World Komputer; **PORTUGAL:** Cerebro/PC World, Computerworld/Correio Informático, Dealer World Portugal, Mac*In/PC*In Portugal, Multimedia World; **PUERTO RICO:** PC World Puerto Rico; **ROMANIA:** Computerworld Romania, PC World Romania, Telecom Romania; **RUSSIA:** Computerworld Russia, Mir PK, Publish, Seti; **SINGAPORE:** Computerworld Singapore, PC World Singapore, Publish in Asia; **SLOVENIA:** Monitor; **SOUTH AFRICA:** Computing SA, Network World SA, Software World SA; **SPAIN:** Communicaciones World España, Computerworld España, Dealer World España, Macworld España, PC World España; **SRI LANKA:** Infolink PC World; **SWEDEN:** CAP&Design, Computer Sweden, Corporate Computing Sweden, Internetworld Sweden, it branschen, Macworld Sweden, MaxiData Sweden, MikroDatorn, Nätverk & Kommunikation, PC World Sweden, PCaktiv, Windows World Sweden; **SWITZERLAND:** Computerworld Schweiz, Macworld Schweiz, PCtip; **TAIWAN:** Computerworld Taiwan, Macworld Taiwan, NEW ViSiON/Publish, PC World Taiwan, Windows World Taiwan; **THAILAND:** Publish in Asia, Thai Computerworld; **TURKEY:** Computerworld Turkiye, Macworld Turkiye, Network World Turkiye, PC World Turkiye; **UKRAINE:** Computerworld Kiev, Multimedia World Ukraine, PC World Ukraine; **UNITED KINGDOM:** Acorn User UK, Amiga Action UK, Amiga Computing UK, Apple Talk UK, Computing, Macworld, Parents and Computers UK, PC Advisor, PC Home, PSX Pro, The WEB; **UNITED STATES:** Cable in the Classroom, CIO Magazine, Computerworld, DOS World, Federal Computer Week, GamePro Magazine, InfoWorld, I-Way, Macworld, Network World, PC Games, PC World, Publish, Video Event, THE WEB Magazine, and WebMaster; online webzines: JavaWorld, NetscapeWorld, and SunWorld Online; **URUGUAY:** InfoWorld Uruguay; **VENEZUELA:** Computerworld Venezuela, PC World Venezuela; and **VIETNAM:** PC World Vietnam.
3/24/97

Dedication

To our parents . . . you know who you are . . . thanks.

Authors' Acknowledgments

We need to thank a bunch of people for helping make this book the best it could be. First, we'd like to thank our project editor, Melba Hopper, for helping us keep track of this amorphous project and for helping us write a quality book in a timely manner. Thanks for all your hard work and dedication to this project. Our e-mail box misses you . . . it's lonely.

Second, we'd like to thank some other folks at IDG. We'd like to thank Joyce Pepple, Kevin Spencer, and Mark Kory for their help with the CD. Also, thanks to Cindy Phipps and the folks in IDG's production department for turning our manuscript into cool-looking pages. Oh, and thanks, as always, to Gareth Hancock, acquisitions editor, for his continued confidence in us.

A big thanks also goes to the technical editor, David Karlins, for doing an outstanding job in making this book as accurate and complete as possible.

Finally, thanks to Janet Rowe (hi, Deb's mom!) for providing some of the photos used in this book. And, of course, thanks to our favorite veterinarian, Malcolm Jacox, for (unknowingly) providing the inspiration for the examples.

Publisher's Acknowledgments

We're proud of this book; please send us your comments about it by using the IDG Books Worldwide Registration Card at the back of the book or by e-mailing us at feedback/dummies@idgbooks.com. Some of the people who helped bring this book to market include the following:

Acquisitions, Development, and Editorial

Project Editor: Melba Hopper

Acquisitions Editor: Gareth Hancock

Media Development Manager: Joyce Pepple

Associate Permissions Editor: Heather H. Dismore

Technical Editor: David Karlins

Associate Technical Editors: Kevin Spencer, Mark Kory

Editorial Manager: Mary C. Corder

Editorial Assistants: Jody Kennen, Chris H. Collins, Jerelind Davis

Production

Project Coordinator: Cindy L. Phipps

Layout and Graphics: Steve Arany, Lou Boudreau, Maridee V. Ennis, Drew R. Moore, Brent Savage

Proofreaders: Henry Lazarek, Renee Kelty, Christine Berman, Joel K. Draper, Robert Springer

Indexer: Liz Cunningham

Special Help

Publication Services, Inc.

General and Administrative

IDG Books Worldwide, Inc.: John Kilcullen, CEO; Steven Berkowitz, President and Publisher

IDG Books Technology Publishing: Brenda McLaughlin, Senior Vice President and Group Publisher

Dummies Technology Press and Dummies Editorial: Diane Graves Steele, Vice President and Associate Publisher; Judith A. Taylor, Product Marketing Manager; Kristin A. Cocks, Editorial Director

Dummies Trade Press: Kathleen A. Welton, Vice President and Publisher

IDG Books Production for Dummies Press: Beth Jenkins, Production Director; Cindy L. Phipps, Manager of Project Coordination, Production Proofreading, and Indexing; Kathie S. Schutte, Supervisor of Page Layout; Shelley Lea, Supervisor of Graphics and Design; Debbie J. Gates, Production Systems Specialist; Tony Augsburger, Supervisor of Reprints and Bluelines; Leslie Popplewell, Media Archive Coordinator

Dummies Packaging and Book Design: Patti Sandez, Packaging Specialist; Lance Kayser, Packaging Assistant; Kavish + Kavish, Cover Design

♦

The publisher would like to give special thanks to Patrick J. McGovern, without whom this book would not have been possible.

♦

Contents at a Glance

Cartoons at a Glance

By Rich Tennant

page 11

page 203

page 49

page 293

page 223

page 131

page 319

Fax: 508-546-7747 • E-mail: the5wave@tiac.net

Table of Contents

● ●

Introduction

● ●

*T*he most difficult part of this whole information age is that just when you think you are getting the hang of the latest-and-greatest technology, developers come up with something new. Well, they've done it again. (Hey, they're just doing their jobs, right?) But the good news is that Netscape Composer — the star of this book — is truly an outstanding tool that makes it easy for you to develop, design, and publish Web pages on the World Wide Web.

Netscape Composer is part of a larger package — that is, Netscape Communicator, which is a one-stop-shop for using the Internet; you can send and receive e-mail, browse the World Wide Web, read and post newsgroup messages, and even conference over the Web (notice we dropped the "World Wide" business, which we'll continue to do throughout the book to conserve paper, ink, and typing fingers). And as if all this isn't enough, you can use Netscape Communicator to publish hot-diggity-dog Web pages, which is what this book is about.

About This Book

Netscape Composer For Dummies. Hmmm. Had there been more room on the cover, the title might have been really long-winded, like *Learn How To Use Netscape Composer To* <breathe> *Develop Kick-Butt Web Pages And* <breathe> *Publish Your Stuff On The World Wide Web* <breathe> *For Dummies.* Good thing there wasn't more room on the cover, huh?

Anyway, just as the existing title is apparently crammed full of information, so is this book (can't you tell it's bulging at the spine?). You'll find the following:

- ✔ Information about using Netscape Composer to publish pages on the World Wide Web: You'll find the how-to's of using Netscape Composer as well as tips and tricks to help make your life easier as a Web publisher.

- ✔ Information about designing A+ Web pages: You'll find essential information on creating attractive Web pages that keep readers glued to their monitors. (Technically, nobody is going to grade you on your Web pages, but if you follow the information in this book, you'll get an A+. We're sure.)

> ✔ Information about creating and publishing fabulous Web sites: You'll find information that will help you develop attractive, usable Web sites that readers will want to visit again and again.

You might be wondering why we've included so much information about design and publishing. Well, even though Netscape Composer does make Web publishing easier than ever — heck, it practically does the work for you — you still have to use your noggin. For example, even though you don't have to type pages and pages of code or shuffle 17 different programs to do one little Web page, you still have to plan your site, design pages, select suitable graphics, develop content, and create intuitive navigation. For this reason, we've included essential design and publishing information that will help you make your Web pages and sites the best they can be.

Why You — Yes, You! — Need This Book

Aside from being fun to read and easy to understand, this book does the following:

> ✔ This book includes all the information you need to use Netscape Composer to publish great Web pages. You find out what all those buttons and menus do, how to edit and view your pages, and how to let Netscape Composer do the grunt work for you.
>
> ✔ Besides covering the standard Web topics, such as making headings, paragraphs, lists, and links, this book covers all the hot Web topics, including these:
>
>> • Graphics and imagemaps
>>
>> • Tables and forms
>>
>> • Colors, backgrounds, patterns, and sounds
>>
>> • JavaScript, Java applets, and frames
>
> ✔ This book provides information about creating *effective* Web pages and sites. Armed with a little information about design and publishing, you can create pages and sites that your readers can easily use and will want to return to.
>
> ✔ This book provides invaluable tips and tricks that will let you achieve the design you want. Hey, there's more than one way to skin a cat — er, um, create a nifty design — and these tips will help you out!
>
> ✔ This book comes with a handy-dandy CD that includes sample Web pages, image-editing software, and sample HTML editing programs, as well as sample graphics, animated GIFs, and cool sound files — many of which you can use or modify to use in your own Web pages and sites.

Who Are You?

We want to get something straight before you buy or use this book — we're not going to treat you like a *dummy* because we know you're not one. Instead, we're going to treat you like someone who just happens not to be an expert *(yet)* in using Netscape Composer or in publishing on the Web. You may not be brimming over with confidence *(yet),* but that's not a biggie either. You're probably more interested in doing stuff than reading all the latest jargon about it. You may have a lot of computer experience, or maybe you don't. You may have an eye for design, but maybe not. You may be a closet-computer-geek, but we'd never tell anyone. The point is that you are certainly capable of taking on Web publishing using Netscape Composer — and our goal is to help you do that. There. We're glad we got that straightened out.

So, just what kinds of computer skills do you have? Well, you may be a computer novice or someone who has only vaguely heard of the Web. Or you may be a frequent computer user who also frequently surfs the wild, wild, Web and understands jokes about the "World Wide Wait." (All of you will get the joke by the time you finish this book.) You may even be a total computer geek . . . or a computer geek wannabe . . . or . . . well, you get the idea. No matter what your computer proficiency, you'll find this book invaluable if you want to use Netscape Composer to design great Web pages or to publish an entire Web site.

You should have a basic familiarity with some computer lingo and procedures, though. For example, you should have an idea of which end of the mouse to use and be able to click and double-click without a problem (or at least be practicing hard!). If you're not too familiar with Windows or MacOS or UNIX, you can still use this book to create Web pages, though you will probably also want to refer to other resources (we point you to some good ones along the way!) to cover the specific Windows- or Mac- or UNIX-related issues.

Last but not least is figuring out what computer equipment you need. You don't even need the latest and greatest computer equipment; you can use Composer on Macs, Windows 3.1*x*, Windows 95, and several flavors of UNIX. If your computer has one of these operating systems and about 15MB of free hard disk space, you're okay. Of course, the faster your computer is and the more memory it has, the happier you'll be. Also, if you want to publish your Web pages on the World Wide Web, you need an Internet connection and either an account with an Internet Service Provider (ISP) or an accommodating boss.

What Are Webs, Web Pages, and Web Sites?

We're assuming that you have some familiarity with Webs, Web pages, and Web sites, but just for a brushup, here's the skinny.

A *Web* is, technically speaking, a glob of information that is generally published on the Internet and connected by *links* that allow you to jump from topic to topic. The links take you from miniglob 1 to miniglob 2, or 8, or 17, or 462. If you draw a picture of all those globs and draw lines to show the links, you'll see something that looks like a Web — perhaps a Web made by a spatially-impaired spider, but a Web, nonetheless.

The most common Web is the *World Wide Web*, which basically is one big Web that contains many, many smaller Webs and individual globs (henceforth called Web pages or documents). You may also be familiar with some smaller Webs, such as your company's internal Web, on which you can publish your own Web pages and Web sites.

Web pages and Web sites are closely related. A *Web page* is a single document that is published on a Web. A *Web site* is similar to a Web page, but a site typically includes a collection of related documents rather than just a single document.

The World Wide Web resides on the *Internet*, which is a mammoth network of computers. A company's internal Web probably resides on an *intranet*, which is a companywide network of computers designed to promulgate internal corporate-type information. Intranets are very much like the Internet, only drier and more boring.

Why Should You Create Web Pages and Sites?

You can create Web pages and sites for a variety of reasons. You might think it's fun; you might like seeing the fruits of your work published for all to see; you might just be doing it because your boss tells you to. Whatever your reason, you're probably creating Web pages and sites to either provide or gather information (or perhaps a combination of the two).

Probably the most common use of Web pages and sites is to *provide* either personal or business-related information. For example, suppose that your family is bugging you to send them snapshots of your little one. You can create a Web page and include the latest and greatest shot of your tot. (Or you could create a Web page that states, "I'll send you the &**# photos when I get around to it," but that would probably be less effective.)

Or suppose that your company wants to tell the world about its new MidgetWidgetFidget-izer product. You can create Web pages that provide information about the product, demonstrate how to use it, show updated price lists, and even let people order one (or more!) online.

The other primary reason for creating Web pages and sites is to *gather* information. You can gather information from your readers by letting them e-mail you directly from your Web site, or you can even provide an online form for them to fill out and return to you. For example, suppose that at the MidgetWidgetFidget company, you want to compile demographic information about the people who shop for your products online. You can provide an online form that lets interested people fill out their names, contact information, region of the country (or world), age group, and the like. Then all they have to do is click a button, and — depending on how you set it up — they can send information right to your e-mail box. No fuss; no muss. No paper; no pencils; no post office. The end; *das ist alles;* a donkey's behind; the south side of a north-bound horse.

Web Tools to Hammer Away On

Web pages and sites are created using a combination of tools: HyperText Markup Language; an editor; a Web browser; and, optionally, a Web server. We'll take these one at a time.

HyperText Markup Language (HTML) is the language that makes Web pages work. Web browsers read HTML and translate it into the Web page display you see on your computer screen. HTML consists of tags and attributes that allow you to include text, graphics, colors, sounds, and more in your Web pages. You might hear the phrase Web page and HTML document interchanged because the HTML document is the basis for the Web page.

An *editor* is just a word processor for your HTML document. The editing part of Netscape Communicator is called Composer, named so because you use it to compose Web pages. From within Composer, you can enter text, apply formatting, insert links and images, and generally reign masterfully over your Web site. Occasionally, the HTML editor is just a little too specialized, so you may have to use a plain text processing program, such as Notepad (for Windows), Simple Text (Macintosh), or vi or pico (UNIX) to accomplish some of the nuances.

A *Web browser* is what you use to view your HTML documents. The Web browser in Netscape Communicator is called Navigator, named so because you use it to navigate through Web pages and sites. No, we don't know why they didn't call it Surfer.

A *Web server* is what you use to put your HTML documents "out there" on the Web. You don't technically have to put the documents anywhere — you might keep them on your own little computer for yourself, in which case, you don't need a Web server at all. If, however, you plan to take your Web pages and slap them out on the Internet so that all and sundry can see your skill and creativity, you'll need to use a Web server. That generally means just taking advantage of services offered by your ISP.

What's in This Book

If you've heard it once, you've heard it — well — once. "This book contains thus and so that will help you create fabulous and entertaining snorts and grunts using only your nose, hands, and pits." Well, maybe you didn't hear that, exactly, but we bet you're familiar with the "This book contains the following sections" concept. So, here it is. This book contains the following seven parts and a cool CD.

Part I: Getting to Know the Web Publishing Parts of Communicator

This part introduces you to Netscape Communicator and its Web tools (Composer and Navigator), shows you how to start the software, tells you a bit about its functions, and shows you how to toggle between Composer and Navigator. Even if you're familiar with earlier versions of Netscape, you might check out this information for the scoop on new features and functions related to Web page development.

Part II: Creating Awesome Web Pages

This part is a must for anyone interested in creating solid, functional, usable Web pages and sites. This part shows you how to use templates and wizards and how to apply formatting to your Web pages.

Part III: Connecting Your Web Pages and Including Goofy Pictures

This part is where the fun starts. Here you'll see how graphics can add vim and vigor to your Web pages. You'll find out how to include graphics in your Web pages and discover tips and tricks to make your graphics even more snazzy. And you'll find out all about links and navigation, as well. Knowing how to include graphics and links is — by today's standards — essential, but knowing how to include these elements *effectively* is a bonus. Read this part for the full scoop.

Part IV: Making Your Web Pages Scream, Jiggle, Gyrate, and Whir

This part shows you how to turn an average, everyday Web page into one that sings, "I Did It Myyyyyyyy Way!" In this part, you'll see how to create neat effects such as colors, backgrounds, and patterns, as well as how to create imagemaps, add sound, and change alignment. More important, you'll see how and when to use these effects for maximum results.

Part V: Grad School Stuff: Activity, Interactivity, and Hyperactivity

This part delves into the world of creating forms and frames and using JavaScript and even Java applets. Don't be scared off by the big buzz words, though! The basic principles of HTML apply here, too, and they pay off in spades. This is where you can get your boss to exclaim "Oh, wow!" when she sees your new site.

Part VI: The Part of Tens

Yup. You even get a part of tens — ten steps to a great Web site; ten design tips for a great Web site; nearly almost sorta ten cool things about Netscape Composer; and ten sites for the latest information on the Web. One little, two little, three little tidbits, four little, five little, six little tidbits . . . Whew!

Part VII: Appendixes

This part wraps things up with a glossary and some handy — but not essential for using Composer — information. For example, you'll find instructions for installing Netscape Communicator (in case, you haven't already) and information about what's on the CD. Are we good to you, or what?

Conventions Used in This Book

Just to make your life a little easier so that you can concentrate on the task at hand, we've included a few conventions, described in the following sections.

Check out these text conventions

A text convention is not a bunch of words gathered at a fancy hotel to discuss grammar. A *text convention* is just a way of consistently showing certain words in a certain format so that you can recognize what we expect you to do based on how the words appear.

For ease of reference, we've shortened several long-winded phrases, for example:

✔ New words or terms appear in *italics* the first time they're used. You then see definitions of the words or terms that, in most cases, are followed by examples.

✔ If you're supposed to use an option from the menu bar, you see instructions such as "Go to File⇨Open Page," which means to go to File in the menu bar and choose Open Page from the resulting menu.

✔ Shortcuts (for those of you who like the keyboard more than the mouse) are indicated by underlined letters. For example, to use the keyboard shortcut for File⇨Open Page, hold down the Alt key while you press F (Alt+F), and then press O. If you're a Mac user, hold down the ⌘, press F, and then press O.

✔ If you're really into avoiding the mouse, you'll also notice that we've stuck little things like Ctrl+S into the text here and there. In this particular case, holding down the Ctrl key, you press S and then release both keys. This action saves your document without you ever having to see a menu or use the mouse.

✔ Within regular paragraphs, anything you are asked to type appears in **bold**.

✔ URLs (Web addresses), e-mail addresses, and short pieces of HTML code that fall within regular text are all shown in monospace font (for example, `http://www.raycomm.com/`).

✔ Larger segments of code appear on a line (or lines) separate from the text, like this:

```
This will help you see the code better.
```

✔ If you're working through an example, adding a line or two of code at a time, the new line(s) of code to add appear in bold, like this:

```
First, there was one line.
Then, there was this other line.
And here's the line you're supposed to type now.
```

✔ Generally, the first step in instructions are something like, "In your HTML document, do yada yada yada." In saying this, we're assuming that you have your HTML document open in Composer and ready to go. We know, we know. Don't tell us about assuming. We'll do it anyway.

Meet the icon crew

The icon crew is here for your convenience and to draw your attention to important information and helpful hints.

Indicates issues that depend on how your system administrator has set up the Web server. Just because we direct you to your administrator doesn't mean that a task is difficult or time-consuming. It just means that he or she is the only person who has the information you need. We can't predict how your system administrator set up the server any more than we can predict what you're having for dinner next Thursday. (We'd guess pizza, but could be wrong.)

Indicates more serious information that you shouldn't forget — for example, your toddler used the kettle in the sandbox, and you'll need to wash it before you boil water.

Indicates a time- or frustration-saving technique or idea — for example, water boils faster if you put the lid on the pot and don't watch it.

Indicates interesting but nonessential information. Don't confuse technical stuff with boring stuff! This information is often interesting to the most nontechie readers, but it isn't completely necessary for you to "get it."

Visit the "running example"

To help illustrate the concepts and instructions, we've provided a sample Web site that you see throughout this book. This Web site (much of which by the way, you also find on the CD) is for Malcolm's Animal Clinic, a fictitious veterinary clinic. Through this example, you'll see how concepts are applied and the multitude of effects you can create. You also get a sampling of some solid page layouts and designs.

How'd It Go?

This book can help you develop A-#1 Web pages and sites in no time at all! We have every confidence in you! Let us know how it goes — either while you're working on your pages or when you're done. You can contact us at debray@raycomm.com and ejray@raycomm.com, or you can visit our Web site at http://www.raycomm.com/. We'd love to hear your comments and suggestions. In the meantime, good luck!

Part I

Getting to Know the Web Publishing Parts of Communicator

The 5th Wave   By Rich Tennant

"THIS IS YOUR GROUPWARE?! THIS IS WHAT YOU'RE RUNNING?!
WELL HECK—I THINK THIS COULD BE YOUR PROBLEM!"

In this part . . .

Welcome to the wild-n-wooly world of Web publishing. We're really glad to have you here! In this part, you get started with Netscape Communicator's own Web development tools — Composer and Navigator — and HTML (the language Web browsers use to display Web pages).

Chapter 1 introduces you to Netscape Communicator, shows you how to start up Communicator, provides an overview of Composer and Navigator, and then shows you how to move between the two programs.

Chapter 2 shows you the process of creating and publishing Web pages and includes some basic information about creating files, opening existing files, saving files, and viewing files. These are the essentials, folks, so don't miss this chapter!

Chapter 3 tells you how Web pages are created and a bit about HTML (the language that creates Web pages). You see that knowing even just a little bit about HTML can help your Web page authoring in big ways.

So, get your computer warmed up, pour a fresh cup of coffee, and put on your thinkin' cap.

Chapter 1

'Tis a Great Creation . . .

● ●

In This Chapter

▶ Taking a glance at Communicator

▶ Meeting Composer and Navigator

▶ Switching between Composer and Navigator

● ●

*'T*was a mid-summer month and all through the office
All the creatures were stirring, especially our bosses.

Our desks were all mounding with work to be done
With no hope that these piles would ever be fun.

With us at our keyboards and our ears to the phone
We had just settled down without a fuss or a moan.

Our colleagues were nestled all snug at their desks
Or more like trapped under the mid-year mess.

When within our computers there arose such a clatter
Everyone gathered to see what was the matter.

Out of their chairs they flew like a flash
Climbed over our desks and knocked over the trash!

When what to our wondering eyes did we see
"It's Netscape Communicator!" someone yelled with glee.

More rapid than turtles this software did run
Offering really cool features never before done.

"Look at those layers and JavaScript and style sheets and frames . . .
And those Wizards and Templates and toolbars and names."

"A package that e-mails, and designs, and browses
Pretty soon people will have this at all of their houses!"

"And look," said a coworker, "You can create these great Web sites"
With these fantastic new features that are sure to delight!"

"And hark!" said a coworker, "I'm already hooked.
I'll have to go out and get us a book!"

And off to the bookstore he hurridly flew
To buy a ...*For Dummies* book that he knew.

He returned to the office with a game plan charted
"Come on everybody, let's get started. . . ."

It's a Bird . . . It's a Plane . . . No! It's Netscape Communicator!

It's faster than a speeding bullet (well, maybe not a speeding bullet, but it is pretty lickity split)! It's able to leap tall buildings in a single bound (can you imagine the visual on that?)! It's Netscape Communicator! More powerful than its predecessors! More exciting than its competition! It's heeeeeeeeere!

Netscape Communicator (we'll just call it Communicator from here on out) is a big Internet toolbox that includes several different tools that, taken together, provide you with a full spectrum of Internet capabilities. You may already be familiar with the Netscape browser, Navigator, which is now part of the Communicator suite. Netscape took the old Navigator Gold Web page editor, tossed it in with Navigator proper, and gave it some handy friends — ones that round out Internet functions. Using the Communicator suite of tools, you can send and receive e-mail, read and post to newsgroups, hold audio conferences, and of course, create and view totally excellent Web pages. What's more, Communicator runs on several operating systems, including Windows, Macintosh, and various flavors of UNIX.

Note to Rip Van Winkle: The Internet is a world-wide collection of computers linked together into either the world's greatest information resource or the world's greatest time sink, depending on your perspective. The World Wide Web (or just Web) is a key part of the Internet, as are newsgroups and file archives (FTP sites).

To create Web pages with Communicator, you use two of its tools (which we call *team members*): Composer and Navigator. Composer is the team member in charge of letting you create, edit, and save your Web pages. Navigator is in charge of letting you view (or browse, or navigate, we suppose) your Web pages. Together, these tools provide you with all the capabilities you need to design, edit, save, and view your Web pages. (The other team members are benched for the duration of this book. You might check out *Netscape Communicator For Dummies Quick Reference* by Viraf Mohta, published by IDG Books Worldwide, to find out more about Communicator's other team members.)

The rest of this chapter tells you how to start Communicator, tells you a bit more about Composer and Navigator, and shows you how to move between Composer and Navigator. If you need a little extra assistance with using your computer or operating system, we recommend checking out the following books, all published by IDG Books Worldwide, Inc.

- ✔ MacOS users may want to look into *Macs For Dummies*, 5th Edition, by David Pogue.

- ✔ Windows 3.1*x* or Windows 95 users might check out *Windows 3.11 For Dummies,* 3rd Edition, or *Windows 95 For Dummies*, 2nd Edition, both by Andy Rathbone.

- ✔ UNIX users may want to seek out *UNIX For Dummies,* 3rd Edition, by John R. Levine & Margaret Levine Young.

The fun starts *now*.

Revving Up Communicator

Revving up Communicator isn't nearly as hard as revving up that old junker in the garage. For one thing, Communicator isn't rusty. For another, you don't have to call AAA to help you get it started. What you need to do, though, is make sure you have Communicator installed. If you see a Netscape Communicator icon or program group on your desktop, Communicator is installed. If, however, you just can't find it anywhere and don't have a note taped to your computer from your local computer geek saying, "I installed Communicator for you — enjoy!", haul out the box or use an (older and obviously inferior) Web browser to download the latest evaluation version of Communicator from http://home.netscape.com. The installation process differs slightly for each platform but is thoroughly explained on the Netscape Web pages. On the other hand, a couple of doughnuts and a Jolt cola, and you can get your nearest computer geek to do it for you. It's your call, but hurry up! We're ready to get started!

To start up the software, just double-click the icon labeled Netscape Communicator. (Yes, you can start it in other ways, but none of them is worth the trouble right now.) Exactly where you find that icon depends on the operating system you're using.

- ✔ If you're a Windows 95 or MacOS user, you find the Communicator icon sitting right on your desktop for your double-clicking ease.

- ✔ If you use Windows 3.1*x*, you need to look in the Netscape Communicator program group in the Program Manager.

However, just to confuse the issue for all users, Netscape installs a whole slew of icons — one for each team member. You might have a pile of visible icons; you might have a Navigator icon but no Communicator icon; you might even have a Composer icon right at hand. No problem; you'll always have a Navigator icon, which you can just double-click to rev up the program. You can get to all team members from any other one, so the specific starting place isn't that critical.

When you fire up Communicator, you notice that Navigator (the Web browser) is the part that actually opens. Assuming that no one has been monkeying with your Netscape preferences, Communicator takes the liberty of initially connecting to the Netscape home page. Heck, if you have a dial-up Internet connection, Communicator often goes so far as to start your dial-up connection. However, if you don't have an Internet connection or, if for some reason, Communicator can't make a connection, it flashes an "unable to connect" dialog box (see Figure 1-1). No biggie for the time being. Just click OK to dismiss the dialog box.

Figure 1-1:
This dialog box notes that the DNS server could not be found (probably because of no Internet connection).

By the way, if you're a multiple browser kind of person and Navigator notices that it is not your *default browser* (the one that opens up when you double-click an HTML document icon), it gets jealous and asks whether you want to go steady. (Actually, it flashes up a dialog box and asks whether you want to make Navigator your default browser. In the event you say no, it asks whether it can keep asking you. Pathetic, isn't it?)

You can do what you want to do here — if you'd prefer to continue using another browser, you're welcome to do so. Furthermore, you can use Composer to develop Web pages and continue to use another browser to view your pages. Our recommendation, though, is to use Navigator unless you really like another browser much, much better.

You'll find scads more information about Navigator later in this chapter.

See Chapter 5 for the specifics about Communicator preferences; for example, if you don't want to see the Netscape home page every time (or the silly dialog box that pops up if it can't connect), you can check out how to reset the default home page.

Meeting the Web Team Members

The Web Team is composed of two tools that work together to let you develop, preview, and view Web pages. The primary tool, Composer, is what you use to develop and preview your Web pages. The secondary tool, Navigator, is a browsing tool that lets you view your pages (as well as other people's pages) in their native environment. The following two sections introduce you to these tools and help you become familiar with their features.

Getting acquainted with Composer

Composer is a Web page *editor*, which basically just means that it lets you create and edit — or compose — Web pages and sites. After you open Communicator — and are probably staring at the Navigator screen — you can switch to Composer by going to Communicator⇨Page Composer (or pressing Ctrl+4). You find more information about switching between Composer and Navigator later in this chapter.

Take a look at Figure 1-2, which shows a recent mug shot of the Composer features.

The neat thing about Composer is that you can create and preview your pages using this one talented tool. Composer lets you preview your pages as you're creating them. Gone are the days of using a plain text editor to create a Web page and then toddling over to a browser just to find out what you created.

In this sense, Composer is considered a *WYSIWYG editor* — that is, a What-You-See-Is-What-You-Get editor. The idea behind WYSIWYG is that you can see the page's layout and design as you're creating it. As a WYSIWYG editor, Composer lets you easily experiment with different designs, layouts, fonts, tables, graphics, and the like to achieve the look you want.

As you're developing Web pages, keep in mind that Composer is only *pretty much* WYSIWYG. Perhaps the acronym should read WYSI(pretty much)WYG.

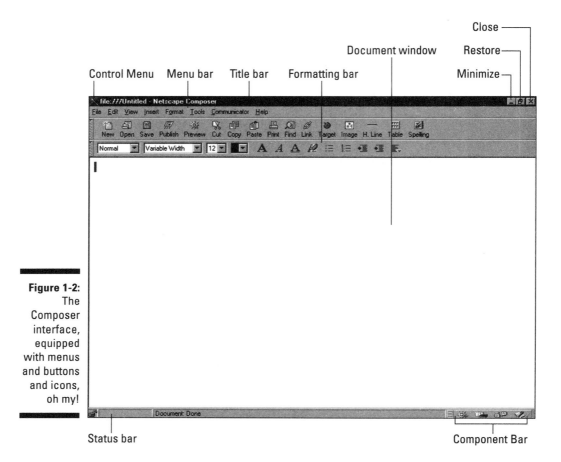

Control Menu   Menu bar   Title bar   Formatting bar   Document window   Close   Restore   Minimize

Figure 1-2:
The
Composer
interface,
equipped
with menus
and buttons
and icons,
oh my!

Status bar   Component Bar

Your pages will vary slightly from Composer to Navigator, as shown in the following two figures. Figure 1-3 shows a page in Composer, and Figure 1-4 shows the same page viewed in Navigator. You'll notice, for example, a couple of little icons in the Composer page that stand in for comments that are hidden in the browser.

Notice that although the Web page appears very similar in Composer and Navigator, the page isn't exactly the same. So use the WYSI(pretty much)WYG feature to help you design your Web pages, but don't rely on the fact that they will appear in all browsers (or even Navigator) exactly as you see them in Composer.

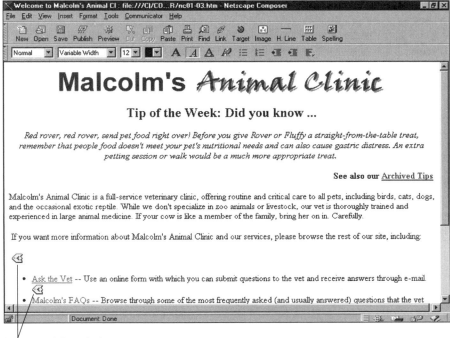

Figure 1-3:
Here's a
Web page
shown in
Composer.

Note special symbols

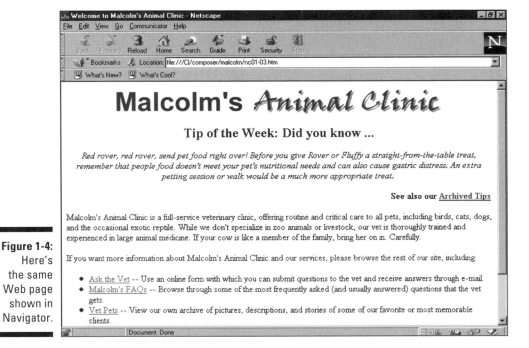

Figure 1-4:
Here's
the same
Web page
shown in
Navigator.

Along with appearing in different ways in different browsers (for example, Netscape Navigator and Microsoft Internet Explorer), Web pages don't look the same on different platforms (for example, Windows, Macintosh, and UNIX). In other words, the pages won't look the same on everyone else's computer as they do on yours. Throughout this book, you can find tips and tricks to help you make your Web pages look as good as possible on *anyone's* computer. Using these tips, you can develop solid Web pages, but remember that you have no guarantee what a page will look like on each and every computer and browser. What's more, the fancier your pages, the more likely they won't be the same on all browsers. That's just the way HTML works. (HTML is further described in Chapter 3, by the way.)

Getting acquainted with Navigator

Though you use Composer primarily to create your Web masterpieces, you also need Navigator, a helper team member in the Web page development process. Navigator is a Web *browser* that you use to view Web pages after you've created them. Navigator allows you to open Web pages saved on your computer, open Web pages located "out there" on the Internet, and easily view pages you've been working on in Composer.

Take a look at Figure 1-5, which shows you Navigator's main features.

If Composer pretty much shows you what your Web pages look like, you're probably wondering right about now why you need to view your pages in Navigator at all. Good question, and we're glad to clarify the matter. Here are some really good reasons you're sure to find most interesting:

✔ Navigator is a browser; therefore, it can show you what your pages look like after they're "out there" for the whole world to see. Viewing pages in Navigator is kind of like getting dressed in the morning and then looking at yourself in the mirror. You may be putting on a familiar, well-worn outfit, but you want to make sure that it all looks right before stepping outside. Just as looking in the mirror points out that your fly is down or that your shirt is on inside-out, using Netscape to view your pages helps ensure that your pages are ready for the world to see.

✔ Navigator shows you all the fancy page elements, even ones like forms and special codes (which generally show up as little *placeholder* icons in Composer). For example, when you're working on forms (see Chapter 14) and JavaScript (see Chapter 15), you'll see these little yellow icons instead of the actual form or script tags until you flip over to Navigator. Without a doubt, you should take a peek at all the page elements in Navigator to make sure that they're what you expect.

✔ Navigator provides you with a closer approximation than Composer does of what your readers will see. Viewing your pages in Navigator gives you a pretty good idea of what your readers will see.

✔ Navigator displays some of the latest and greatest Web formatting. That is, it shows you formatting that this book covers, including frames, JavaScript, applets, and some other cool effects. These latest and greatest effects are discussed in Parts IV and V.

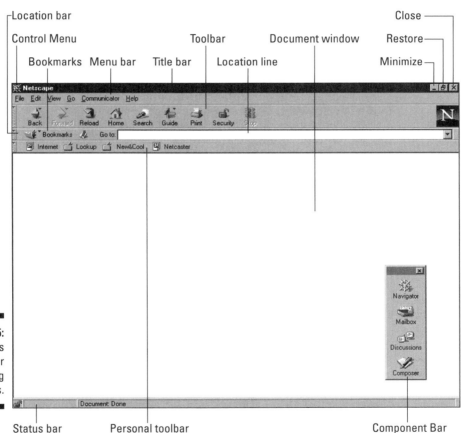

Figure 1-5:
Navigator is your tool for viewing Web pages.

Switching between Composer and Navigator

Before you can wander off and start developing and viewing Web pages, you need to first work out how you want to switch between Composer and Navigator. Otherwise, you could get stuck in one or the other, which of course, would be worse then getting stuck on the potty without potty paper. The developers at Netscape were smart enough to provide you with more than one way to switch back and forth, including the Component Bar and the ol' menu bar standbys.

Say hello to the Component Bar

Heeeeeelllllllo, Component Bar! The Component Bar is a floating button bar that lets you switch between and among Communicator's tools (see Figure 1-6). To switch back and forth between Composer and Navigator, just click the appropriate buttons on the Component Bar.

Click and drag to move.
Right-click for options.

Click to close.

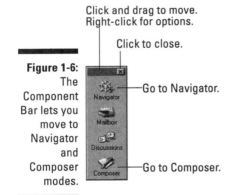

Figure 1-6: The Component Bar lets you move to Navigator and Composer modes.

Go to Navigator.

Go to Composer.

The Component Bar, though handy for switching between Composer and Navigator, can easily get in your way on-screen. That's why the developers added a few extra Component Bar features to help you scoot it out of your way when necessary. (Actually, it may be out of the way when you open Composer, but you may need to move it out of the way after you've worked with it.) At the top of the Component Bar is the title bar, which you can right-click to access a pop-up menu. In this pop-up menu, you can choose from the following:

✔ Choose to keep the Component Bar Always on Top — which means that the Component Bar will be obstructing your view even if you're in a completely different program — for example, Microsoft Word, Excel, or whatever.

✔ Choose to show the Component Bar either Horizontally or Vertically on your screen.

✔ Choose to hide the descriptive text, which actually makes the Component Bar a bit smaller.

✔ <u>M</u>ove or <u>C</u>lose the Component Bar.

⊠ The Close button is at the upper-right corner of the Component Bar. This button is what actually scoots the Component Bar down to the lower-right corner of your screen. The technical term for this is *docking* the Taskbar, which just means that the Taskbar hangs on to the bottom of your screen so that it doesn't get in your way. After you dock the Component Bar, it shows up in the lower-right corner of your Communicator windows, as shown in Figure 1-7.

Figure 1-7:
The docked   Lines
Component
peeks out
from the
bottom of
the window.

To *undock* the Component Bar, double-click the horizontal lines at the left end of the icons, and the Component Bar reappears in its original form.

As with other Windows applications, you can use the title bar (the bar at the top) to manually scoot the Component Bar to somewhere else on the screen. All you do is click (and hold) the title Bar and then draaaaaaag the Component Bar wherever you want it to be.

You can still use the docked bar to switch between icons. Just click on the icon of choice, and enjoy! (If you find that the icons in the docked Component Bar are a little small to discern, just hover the mouse pointer over them and watch the tooltip appear to explain the option. Cool, huh?)

Say hello to some ol' standbys

Heeeeeelllllllo, ol' standbys! If you're not into using the Component Bar to switch among your programs, you can always use these more traditional approaches:

- ✔ To switch to Navigator, select Communicator⇨Navigator or File⇨Browse Page (or press Ctrl+1).

- ✔ To switch to Composer, select Communicator⇨Page Composer or File⇨Edit Page (or press Ctrl+4).

After you open a file in Composer (to edit it) and Navigator (to view it), you can also use any of the normal conventions from your platform to switch back and forth. For example, all Windows users can press Alt+Tab to switch among the open programs, including Composer and Navigator. Windows 95 users can also click the appropriate icons from the Taskbar. MacOS users can choose from the program menu at the upper-right corner of the desktop.

Whew! If you're comfortable with all this opening and closing and switching, check out Chapter 2 to get some real work done. (We're calling it work just in case your boss is watching.)

Chapter 2

Conquering Commonly Cantankerous Conundrums: Getting a Grip on Basic Tasks

. . . .

In This Chapter

▶ Getting a feel for the Web page development process

▶ Creating new Web pages in Composer

▶ Opening existing Web pages in Composer

▶ Saving Web pages in Composer

▶ Viewing Web pages in Navigator

▶ Reloading Web pages in Navigator

. . . .

*R*emember when you were a kid, and your parents made you go through that silly bedtime routine — get into your jammies, brush your teeth, say goodnight, and go to bed? Like, you might have been wondering, "What's the use of having good breath if I'm just going to bed?" Or possibly, "Why do I have to get into my jammies if I'm just going to get into real clothes again in the morning?" And then, what's worse is that you had to go through this stinkin' routine *every* night.

We're happy to inform you that you're about to embark on another routine of sorts — the process of developing Web pages. But you don't have to worry about having good breath, and, no, you don't have to worry about getting into your jammies. However, you will have to take this process and make it part of your Web development regime.

This chapter outlines the basic steps for creating a Web page — getting a Web page started, saving the page, and viewing it in Navigator. Within the steps, you'll also find some handy information about saving Web pages and opening them in Navigator. You'll get the hang of this process very quickly, we promise, because you'll end up doing it over and over and over again. But don't worry, we won't be inspecting your teeth or spot-checking for jammies.

By the way, the process outlined in this chapter should apply to most of the pages that you develop. If you're looking for specific, detailed steps about creating great Web sites — as opposed to pages — check out Chapter 17. And you'll find some tips for creating great Web sites in Chapter 18.

Getting a Web Page Going in Composer

The first step in Web page development is none other than opening a Web page — either a new one or an existing one — on your screen in Composer. What is a Web page, you ask? A *Web page* is a document that appears to the reader as a single entity that includes things like text, graphics, links, Java applets, JavaScript, and style sheets. Actually, as you'll see shortly, a Web page includes text and references to graphics and other cool stuff.

The next two sections tell you how to start a new Web page and open an existing Web page. If you need a refresher on Composer parts, skip back to Chapter 1, which has descriptions and figures that identify the various parts.

Creating a blank — gasp! — Web page

Creating a new Web page is pretty easy — much easier than staring at the blank page after it's opened. Nonetheless, you have to do it sometime, which might as well be now. You can open a new page in Composer by using one of two methods:

  ✔ Select File⇨New⇨Blank Page.
  ✔ Press Ctrl+Shift+N.

A blank Composer page appears. If you already have a page (or more) open, the new page opens on top.

Opening existing Web pages in Composer

Opening an existing Web page in Composer is similar to opening any other file, except that you have a choice of opening a page that's saved on your computer or opening a page that's out on the Web.

Opening a local Web page

A *local* Web page is a page that's saved on your computer — as opposed to a page on the Internet. Most pages that you develop are stored locally until you're mostly finished (they don't have to be perfect before you publish them), at which time you publish them on a Web server. (Don't worry about any of this server stuff yet; that's all covered in detail in Chapter 5.)

To open a Web page saved on your local computer, use the following quick steps (have Composer open first):

1. **Select File⇨Open Page (or press Ctrl+O).**

   The Open Page dialog box appears, as shown in Figure 2-1.

Figure 2-1:
The Open Page dialog box lets you choose a page to open.

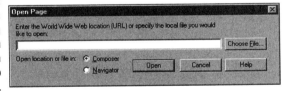

2. **Click Choose File, and use the resulting Open dialog box to browse through your computer to the local file.**

   The Open button on the toolbar takes you to this point, without stopping at Step 1. In other words, if you click the Open button, you don't get the chance to choose whether to browse through your computer before seeing the Open dialog box.

3. **Click once on the filename, and then click Open.**

4. **Make sure you specify to open the file in Composer by clicking the Composer option.**

5. **Click Open to open the file.**

Now that wasn't so bad, was it?

Opening a Web page that's "out there"

To open a Web page that's already on the Web — technically, either on the Internet or on your corporate intranet — use these easy steps:

1. Select File⇨Open Page (or press Ctrl+O).

The Open Page dialog box appears, as shown in Figure 2-2.

Figure 2-2:
The Open
Page dialog
box lets you
include Web
addresses.

2. Enter the Web address in the text box provided.

A Web address is basically just a long-winded filename for a file that's out on the Web. The address should include the protocol indicator (the `http://` part), the host name (`www.xmission.com`), and the folder and filenames (`/~ejray/malcolm/main.html`). You might have something like this:

```
http://www.xmission.com/~ejray/malcolm/main.html
```

3. Make sure you specify to open the file in Composer by clicking the Composer option.

4. Click Open to open the file.

Now you have a Web page open on your screen, and you can even make changes to it. But before you can save changes, you need to save the Web page on your local computer. The next section describes how to save Web pages to your computer by using Composer.

Here are two additional notes about opening files:

> ✔ An address of a file out on the Web is technically called a *URL* (pronounced *you-are-ell*). URLs (Uniform Resource Locators) identify files and their locations on the Web, and you use them all the time when you're creating links and including files. See Chapter 8 for the whole scoop; it's important and fascinating reading, to be sure. In the meantime, we'll try to use only the more generic "Web address" term.

✔ Even if you open a file from the Web and make changes to it, your changes won't reappear on the Web until you upload your files to the server, and you need special permission to do that. You can find out more on this server stuff in Chapter 5.

Save — Oh, Save — Your Web Pages

The second step in Web development is saving your Web pages in Composer. When you see instructions in this book that say something like "save your page," you just save your page on your computer using Composer.

Saving your Web pages in Composer is essential for several reasons. First, you must save your Web pages in order for Navigator (or any other browser) to open and display them. Just because you have a page open in Composer does not mean that Navigator can display it. That would be like asking Navigator to read Composer's mind, and we all know that mind reading is an unreasonable expectation.

Second, you should save your work — frequently — in case Composer takes a nose dive, and your computer crashes. If you don't save your work fairly often, you run the risk of losing all the hard work you've done since you last saved your file. How often should you save? Ummm. That depends. If you're willing to risk losing 20 minutes worth of work, save every 20 minutes. If you're willing to lose only five minutes worth of work, save every five minutes or so. Remember, Murphy is watching you and will show his ugly head at the most-inconvenient times.

Containing all those hard-to-keep-track-of files

When you're working on Web pages and sites, you can make your life much easier by remembering to save *all* the files associated with the Web page or site in one folder. Think of a *folder* as one big container for all the stuff you want to put in your Web pages and sites. This folder should hold all Web page files, all graphics files, all style sheets, all Java applets — everything you want to include. So, if you haven't already, you might want to go ahead and set up a separate folder that will contain files related to your Web site. And if you're developing more than one Web site, create a folder for each site.

By the way, Composer also thinks that it's a good idea to keep everything together in a folder, so when adding a graphic or something, don't be surprised when Composer offers to copy it into the folder for you.

If you need more information about setting up folders, you might refer to *Windows 3.11 For Dummies,* 3rd Edition, or *Windows 95 For Dummies,* 2nd Edition, both by Andy Rathbone; *Macs For Dummies,* 5th Edition, by David Pogue; or *UNIX For Dummies,* 3rd Edition, by John R. Levine & Margaret Levine Young, all published by IDG Books Worldwide.

A name by any other name is not the same

And what should your Web page filenames look like? They should pretty much look like the filenames you ordinarily see and use, for example:

```
main.html
home.htm
cul8erOK.html
```

Or even possibly:

```
MyNewHomePage.html
Ode_To_Joy.htm
```

To be on the safe side, include only letters, numbers, periods (.), hyphens (-), dollar signs ($), plus (+) signs, and underscores (_) in the filename. Also, if your Web server is Windows 3.1*x*-based (highly unlikely), limit the filename to eight characters, and use the .htm extension.

Check with your server administrator and ask what operating system the server uses and about the filename restrictions. If the server is UNIX-based (which is likely), you'll be able to use long filenames, but they can't have spaces in them. If the server is Mac- or Windows NT-based, you might be able to use long names with spaces, just as you do on your own Mac or Windows 95 computer. If either you or your server is restricted to Windows 3.1*x*, you'll be stuck with the plain, old, boring, but fully functional .htm extension and an eight-character filename.

The step-by-steps of saving

So you're sold on saving your Web pages, and you want to make sure you have the process down? Great! Saving files in Composer is actually almost identical to saving files in other applications on your computer.

The following steps show you how to save files, starting with an open page (or a new document) in Composer.

Choose folder.

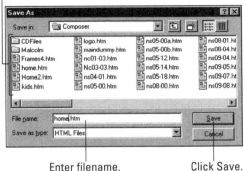

Figure 2-3: Composer's Save As dialog box lets you save files on your computer.

Enter filename.   Click Save.

1. **Select File➪Save As, or click the Save button on the toolbar.**

   The Save As dialog box appears, looking something like the dialog box shown in Figure 2-3.

2. **Choose the folder that you want to save your work in.**

3. **Type a filename in the File name text box.**

   For example, type home.htm.

4. **Click Save when you're done.**

   If you start with an existing HTML document, Composer suggests that you save it with the same name (by filling in the File name text box for you). As long as you're sure you want to keep your changes and obliterate the original document, go with it. Otherwise, use a different name. Generally, Composer warns you before you wipe out an old file with a new one by using Save As.

That's all there is to it.

After you name the file and save it for the first time, you can select File⇨Save, press Crtl+S, or click the Save button. Composer then replaces the previous copy, saving all the changes you've made since your last save.

Peeking at Your Pages in Navigator

The third step (after creating and saving) in Web development is taking a look at your pages in Navigator. If you're looking for flexibility, you've come to the right place because you can open your files in Navigator all sorts of ways. However, we show you a selection of our favorites in the following sections.

If you need a quickie refresher on Navigator parts, check out Chapter 1.

Viewing a page you're working on

If you've been working on a Web page in Composer, you can easily open that page in Navigator. You don't have to mess with toggling over to Navigator, with fumbling for files, or with location lines or bookmarks.

To open a page you're working on, save the page and then click the Preview icon located in the Button Bar. A Navigator screen opens, with the Composer page you've been working on staring at you.

Opening a file in Navigator

To open and view a file in Navigator, you follow a process remarkably similar to (some might say almost identical to) the process of opening a file in Composer. To open and view a file in Navigator, follow these quick steps, which will work for opening local files or files from the Web:

1. **Select File⇨Open Page (or press Ctrl+O).**

   The Open Page dialog box appears, as shown in Figure 2-4.

Figure 2-4:
The Open Page dialog box lets you open files.

Open Page
Enter the World Wide Web location (URL) or specify the local file you would like to open:
C:\COMPOSER\MALCOLM\main.html   Choose File...
Open location or file in: ○ Composer
⦿ Navigator   [Open] [Cancel] [Help]

2. **Enter the Web address or local filename in the text box provided.**

   You enter a Web address in the text box to open files already published on the Web. Be sure to get the capitalization right — many Web servers require precise capitalization.

   If you're opening a local file and are not sure what the local filename is, click Choose File, and select the filename by browsing through the resulting Open dialog box.

3. **Make sure you specify to open the file in Navigator by clicking the Navigator option.**

4. **Click Open to open the file.**

5. **Marvel at the open Web page.**

   Oooooh! Aaaaahhh! (***Hint:*** It's like watching fireworks.)

Using the Location line

The *Location line,* at the top of your Navigator window, is the easiest place to enter a Web address for a file you want to open. You can also enter the address for a local file, but that's often more of a pain than it's worth — easier to just open local files with the dialog box.

To open a page using the Location line, do the following:

1. **Click in the Location line to place the cursor.**

2. **Type the Web address.**

   Keep in mind that many Web addresses are case-sensitive addresses. For example, if you enter **HTML** (in all uppercase letters) when the original address called for lowercase letters, the address you enter won't work. When in doubt, first try all lowercase letters.

3. **Press Enter.**

That's it!

Opening by using Bookmarks

Navigator's *Bookmarks* feature gives you an alternative way to access Web pages — and it's easy! The Bookmark is very similar to a bookmark you might use in the latest Tom Clancy novel you're reading, assuming that you can tear yourself away from it long enough to even need a bookmark. Just as you use a bookmark to mark a place in a book, you use bookmarks in Navigator to mark Web pages you want to return to.

Using the Bookmarks feature when developing Web pages can be a huge time-saver because they can help you quickly bring up pages you've been working on in Composer. Say that you've been working on several new Web pages and you want to view them in Navigator. Normally, you'd have to go to Navigator, select File⇨Open Page, and then root around in directories until you find the page(s) you want to open. If you bookmark a page (or all the pages), all you do is go to Navigator, click the Bookmarks icon, and select the page from the resulting menu.

Another, more general advantage to using bookmarks is that you don't have to keep track of a bazillion little scraps of paper that you use to jot down Web addresses — you know, those scraps you find in your chair, under piles on your desk, and even under the bed, consorting with dust bunnies. The point is that you can never find those important addresses when you want them. Using bookmarks, you can let Navigator keep track of all those pages and addresses for you.

To set a bookmark, use these quick steps:

1. **Open a Web page you want to bookmark.**

   Yes, the first time, you have to go through that whole opening process outlined above.

2. **Click the Bookmarks icon.**

3. **From the resulting pop-up menu, select Add Bookmark, as shown in Figure 2-5.**

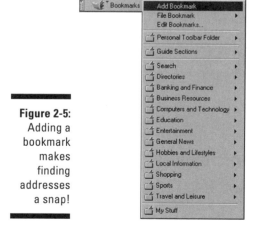

Figure 2-5:
Adding a
bookmark
makes
finding
addresses
a snap!

TaDaaaaa! Now all you do is click the Bookmark icon and select the bookmarked page from the pop-up menu, as shown in Figure 2-6.

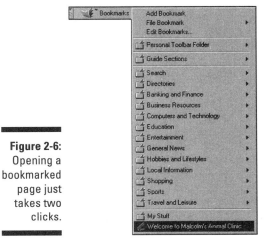

Figure 2-6:
Opening a
bookmarked
page just
takes two
clicks.

Bookmarks are incredibly customizable. If you like that sort of thing, you'll be interested in the following steps, which show you how to make bookmarks do your bidding:

1. **Click the Bookmark icon, and choose Edit Bookmarks from the pop-up menu.**

   In the Bookmarks window (see Figure 2-7), you can add, delete, and rename bookmarks and insert new subfolders and categories.

2. **Right-click in the window, and choose an option from the pop-up menu.**

3. **Close the Bookmark window by clicking the Close button in the title bar or choosing File⇨Close (or pressing Ctrl+W).**

Reloading Web pages in Navigator

Reloading a file just means updating a file that's already open in Navigator in order to reflect changes you've made in Composer. As you get on a roll developing Web pages, you're likely to create a Web page, test it in Navigator, go back to Composer and make changes, test it again in Navigator, and then go back to Composer. You get the idea. Navigator makes it easy to retest and retest and retest your pages by letting you reload them instead of having to reopen the files every time you want to test them.

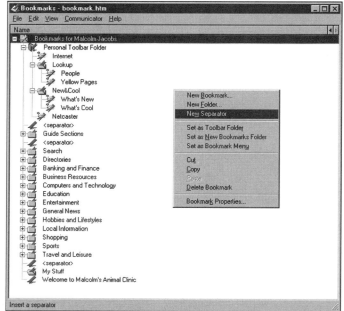

Figure 2-7:
The
Bookmarks
window
helps
you set
bookmark
options.

To reload a Web page, all you do is click the Reload button. Your screen flickers and twitches for a second or two, and then the reloaded Web page appears on your screen. Like magic. Sort of.

After you've made a change in Composer and then reloaded in Navigator, you may find yourself swearing at the computer and getting extremely frustrated because none of your changes took effect. That's the first sign that you forgot to save your file in Composer before you reloaded in Navigator. Just go back to Composer, save, and then reload again in Navigator. Of course, if you use the Preview button to head back to Navigator from Composer, you'll be prompted to save anyway — it all depends on the path you take.

However, at times, you will make and save changes and they still won't show up in Navigator. Often, in those cases, if you exit completely out of all your Communicator windows and restart Navigator, your changes will magically appear. It's not a bug; it's a feature.

Peeking in as many windows as possible

Just as your Web pages vary slightly when viewed in Composer and Navigator, they also vary slightly when viewed in different browsers (like Internet Explorer, Lynx, and Mosaic), on different computers, and across different platforms (like PCs, Macs, and UNIX). Your pages will have all the same elements, such as text, graphics, lists, and headings, but the elements may not appear the same.

For example, suppose that you include a heading in your Web page. Navigator might display this heading using 16-point Arial Bold font, but Internet Explorer might display the same heading by default using 14-point Times New Roman Bold. Both browsers display the heading as larger and more bold than regular text, but the specific fonts and sizes vary.

Yes, as you might have heard, newer Web browsers support specifying font names in addition to identifying text as a heading. However, you have little assurance that your readers will have the font you specify or that they'll even be using a browser that supports different fonts.

Likewise, your Web pages can vary from computer to computer, depending on your readers'

monitors, resolutions, and general settings. For example, if a reader's monitor has high resolution, the monitor can show more of a Web page on the screen with less scrolling. Conversely, if a reader's monitor has low resolution or if the browser isn't occupying the whole screen, the reader will likely see fewer items per screen.

Finally, you can expect that your pages viewed in, say, Navigator on a PC will look slightly different than they will when viewed in Navigator on a Macintosh. These differences are generally not too noticeable, but you should be aware that they occur.

To overcome these differences, your best bet is to view your Web pages in as many browsers on as many computers using as many different platforms as you can. You may decide that your pages look pretty good in all these cases (we show you some good ways to ensure this throughout the book), but you may also spot some problems you should fix. Better to find them in the testing stage than to have someone like your boss point them out to you, right?

Chapter 3

Where Do Web Pages Come From?

*A*h, yes, a very good question, indeed — where do Web pages come from? They don't live in your computer. They don't lurk under your bed. They're not delivered by the mail person. You can't call up and have them delivered with your pizza. They don't eat anything (except disk space, maybe). Hmmm.

This chapter answers the big question: Just where the heck *do* Web pages come from, anyway? You'll find out how some funny-looking code works to create Web pages, and you'll see how knowing a bit about this code can come in handy. Then you'll see just what this code looks like and discover that it's not nearly as ugly as it first looks.

Finding out about this code — which, by the way, is called *HTML* — is important for a couple reasons. First, HTML is the language that browsers "read" so that they can display page elements. This language is sort of like a script that tells browsers exactly which elements to include and where to place them. Second, HTML is the code that Composer creates every time you add stuff to your Web pages by clicking buttons, using menu options, or keyboard commands. Although you view the effects in Composer, a lot of gobbledygook code is actually being added behind the scenes. Third, as you'll see in this chapter, Composer can't add every effect for you, and knowing a bit about HTML can help you add the effects you want.

By the way, if you want to know more about HTML, take a gander at *HTML For Dummies Quick Reference,* 2nd Edition, by yours truly, published by IDG Books Worldwide.

A Highly Untechnical Explanation about HTML

Web pages are created from a language called *HyperText Markup Language* (aka, *HTML*). HTML is what tells browsers (for example, Netscape Navigator and Microsoft Internet Explorer) what to do with the text, graphics, and other bells and whistles you include in your Web pages.

Using HTML is kind of like telling your spouse (or significant other, or nearly anyone else for that matter) how to arrange the furniture in your living room: "Honey, I'd like to put the couch under the window . . . and the TV in the corner . . . and the Degas painting over the fireplace . . . and while you're at it, I'd like the walls painted mauve with a wallpaper border on top. . . . Honey? . . . Honey! . . . Is that you trapped under the couch!?" In this same sense, HTML more or less tells browsers that you'd like that cool photo displayed on the right and the headings and text on the left, the background color to be mauve, and so on; and the browser obediently does what it's told. (Wow, now why can't we all have browsers for pets . . . or spouses?)

But what's perplexing about HTML is that not all browsers (or computers) follow the directions exactly same way. For example, if you tell your spouse to put the recliner over on the left wall, he or she might cram it up right against the wall, but your friend's spouse might put the recliner close to the wall and leave some room in between. The same goes for HTML and browsers. Just because you specify in HTML that the awesome photo of bungee-jumping should be put on the left side of the screen does not mean the photo will appear in the same spot from browser to browser. One browser might cram it along the left border; another might more appropriately place it close to the left border.

No, not the stork!

Although blaming the stork would be easier, HTML was actually created in the early 1980s at CERN, a physics laboratory in Switzerland. HTML was designed as a quick and easy way for researchers to make information available via the computer to other researchers. Just check out some of these original considerations. HTML was meant to

✔ Be platform-independent so that people working on different computer systems could access the information.

✔ Specify the role that different pieces of the document performed, not what the pieces looked like. Appearance was the role of the reader's browser.

✔ Be based on public standards so that it would always work and be viewable on any browser.

However, those original design characteristics have been more or less overwhelmed by the sheer marketing force of one-upmanship.

Different companies, particularly Netscape and Microsoft, keep "extending" HTML to add unique capabilities or to make Web pages more aesthetically appealing. Then developers include the extensions from other companies and add yet more on their own. Anarchic? Yes.

At this point, many of the HTML extensions proposed by both Netscape and Microsoft have been codified into the HTML standard, but more extensions are on the way. If you want to check out the actual HTML specifications, look at the World Wide Web Consortium pages at `http://www.w3.org/`.

HTML: Long-winded geek stuff, or just a naked Web page?

HyperText Markup Language is pretty long-winded but not nearly as confusing as it sounds. The *HyperText* part of HTML is what allows you to jump from Web page to Web page or even to specific places within a Web page. The *Markup* part indicates that HTML is a code of sorts. And the *Language* part is probably just thrown in for grins. So what does all this mean? HTML is code you apply in a text editor (for example, SimpleText or Notepad) that tells browsers how to display your pages and lets you (and your readers) jump from page to page in the Web site.

Netscape Composer performs the same function as a plain editor, but hides all the HTML codes from you so that you see only a pretty screen with formatted text.

You enter HTML into a document, called (guess what?) an *HTML document*. You can think of an HTML document as being a naked Web page — the Web page is all there, but it doesn't wear all its fancy coverings. Eeeeek! Eeeeek! A naked document! (The really gross thought is that all these naked HTML documents hang out together in your Web page folder . . . a clothing optional folder, that is.)

Anyhoo, each HTML document is a single file and can contain lots of references — or pointers — to other files that you add, such as graphics files, Java applets, video files, and so on. For example, your HTML document might contain text, headings, and — oh, throw in a bulleted list or two. These are all common elements of an HTML document. However, if you include graphics, or, say, sounds, these do not appear in the HTML document itself. Instead, the HTML document contains pointers to these elements.

Pointers are little snippets of HTML that summon images, sounds, or other cool stuff. For example, a Web site with ten pages might very well have 20 to 50 different files associated with it. That's why you should keep all your documents for a particular Web site in one particular folder. (Check out Chapter 2, the section called "Save — Oh, Save — Your Web Pages," for more information about keeping files in one folder.)

Why HTML Is Important

Composer is a great tool for developing Web pages, but it can't do everything for you. At some point in your Web page composing career, you'll want a little more flexibility than Composer provides, and knowing a bit about HTML can help. For example, you may want to add frames or extensive JavaScript scripts, which aren't actually within the scope of what Composer lets you do. But using HTML, you can easily add these effects.

Also, if you know a bit about HTML, you can use it to see how other people created their Web pages, borrow code from other pages to experiment with, and even borrow code and tweak it to meet your own needs. The following sections show you how to do these things.

Taking a look at other people's HTML

Imagine that you're out surfing the Web . . . er, that is, doing some research. Yeah, research! That's it. Anyway, you're out on the Web, and you find a Web site that's absolutely stellar. Wonderful! It does all the things you want your site to do. How'd they do that, you ask? Well, if you're so inclined, here's how to look at other people's HTML code to see how they used it in their pages:

1. **In Navigator, browse around until you find a cool Web page.**

   Take your time; this is a great surfing excuse. If you'd rather follow along with the example, just type `http://www.xmission.com`.

2. **Choose View⇨Page Source (or press Ctrl+U).**

   Voilà! Figures 3-1 and 3-2 show, respectively, the Web page of Xmission (our Internet Service Provider) and the HTML source used to create it.

Believe it or not, you can actually decipher what the code means, too. For example, look at the browser page, and note the words in the title bar (the example page title is Xmission Internet Access) of your browser. Then look in the source code for those words. The funky code around them (`<TITLE>` and `</TITLE>`) is what places the words in the title bar. Pretty cool, huh? It takes a little time and effort, but you can pretty much identify the code that makes everything happen. Check out "What HTML Looks Like," later in this chapter.

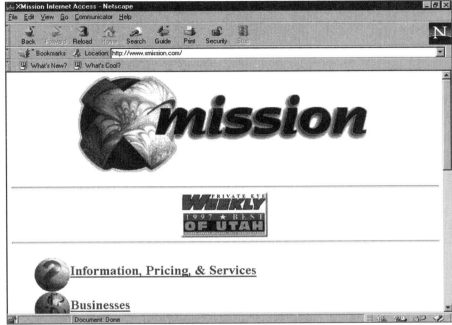

Figure 3-1:
In the Web browser, you see text, images, and cool formatting, all created with HTML.

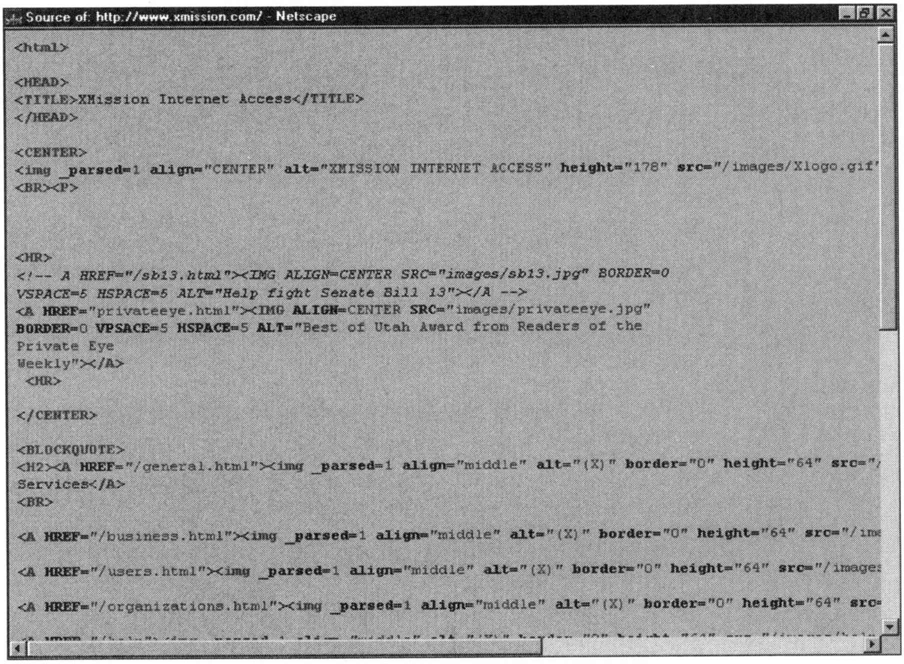

Figure 3-2:
You can see how the page was developed just by looking at the code. For example, the title on the third line of text produces the same text in the browser title bar in the previous figure.

You may be still asking, "So what?" And to a certain extent, you're right. Composer does generally take care of doing all that stuff for you. But if you're not quite sure how to achieve the effect you want in Composer (and sometimes HTML code is a little finicky), you can just snag that example and learn from it. The following section tells you how.

Borrowing code from other pages

Borrowing code is sort of like Monkey-See-Monkey-Do. You see an effect in someone else's Web page that you'd like to place in your own page. Borrowing code is a great way to practice creating effects. You can look at the code, see how it's done, and apply it to your document.

Web pages are just like pages published in a book. Someone out there created them and has the rights to them. Before you grab your surfboard and start surfing the Web for great ideas, beware! Information on the Web falls into two categories: stuff that you can borrow *just to learn from* (which is most of it) and stuff that explicitly states that you can use it as your own. If it's not explicitly marked as available for public use, then assume that it's not.

Note that you can still borrow and learn from any Web pages, even though they're not available for public use. Just make sure that you don't copy them and then use them exactly as they appear on the existing Web pages!

Borrowing HTML code

The following jiffy steps show you how to borrow code:

1. **Browse to the Web page that contains code you want to borrow.**

2. **Select** <u>V</u>iew⇨Page So<u>u</u>rce.

3. **Use the mouse to select the text, graphics, or items you're interested in, and then press Ctrl+C to copy.**

   If you want, click the upper-right corner of the Source window to close it.

4. **Open your own Web page in Composer, and then select** <u>E</u>dit⇨<u>H</u>TML **Source.**

   Note: If you need to start Composer, select <u>C</u>ommunicator⇨<u>P</u>age Composer (or press Ctrl+4).

   The first time you select <u>E</u>dit⇨<u>H</u>TML, you'll probably receive a Choose HTML Editor Application dialog box (see Figure 3-3). Navigator just verifies which editor you want to use.

Figure 3-3:
Browse
through
your
computer,
and find the
program to
use for
editing
HTML code.
In this
example,
we choose
Notepad
on a
Windows 95
computer.

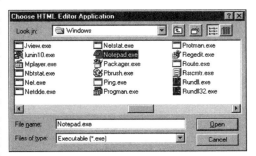

If you're a MacOS person, select TeachText or SimpleText; if you're a Windows nut, use Notepad (not Wordpad) from your Windows folder; and if you're a UNIX-type, choose vi or pico.

Note: You can also use the text-editing program of your choice; you're not limited to Composer.

5. **Click to place the cursor where you want the code, and then select Edit⇨Paste (or press Ctrl+V).**

6. **Save the HTML document, and close the editor.**

Composer will probably prompt you to reload the page. If so, then do so. Even if it doesn't prompt, you can view your page in Navigator or edit it in Composer again.

Are you wondering whether you can write HTML code by hand in a text editor? Well, yes, you can. As a matter of fact, many people do. However, we've found that it's generally easier to let Composer provide a great big head start; then you just need to tweak the existing code.

Just another tidbit about borrowing code: We're kind of fussy about the general concepts of borrowing code. Learning from what other people did (standing on the shoulders of giants) is one thing, but stealing other people's hard work wholesale is quite another. Be careful . . . and nice.

What HTML Looks Like

An HTML document, until you figure out how to read one, looks like a huge train wreck. You see big stuff, little stuff, and pointy things strewn everywhere (but no screaming or panic). Basically, HTML documents are composed of tags and attributes, as pointed out in Figure 3-4.

This section provides some background information that can be helpful throughout this book. Don't think for a minute that we expect you to jump up and start hand-coding HTML. Just put on your thinking cap and absorb. It won't work through your pillow, though.

All about tags

Tags are the HTML codes that determine what each page element is and, to some extent, what the page elements look like. Tags also provide references to additional information. Check these out one at a time.

- ✔ Tags identify the *logical* parts of the page — paragraph, heading, list, footer, and so on. For example, if you want text to appear as a heading, you tag it as a heading; if you want text to appear in a numbered list, you tag it as a numbered list.

- ✔ Tags identify to some extent what the physical parts of Web pages look like in a browser. For example, you can include tags to make text appear in *italics* or in **bold**. You can even specify what fonts you want to use, but whether these embellishments show up depends on your readers' browsers.

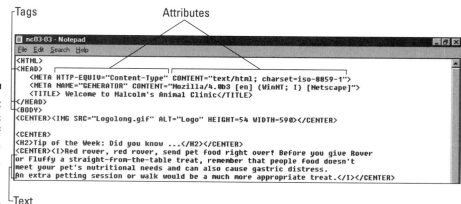

Tags

Attributes

Figure 3-4:
This
sample of
HTML code
shows text,
tags, and
attributes.

Text

> ✔ Tags identify pointers to other information, such as links to other pages, graphics, applets, or style sheets. These pointers don't actually appear in the HTML document, but including the tags tells the browser where to look for the linked information, graphics, and so on.

When entering tags, keep three ideas in mind. First, you enter all tags by using a pair of pointy dealies (< >), called *angle brackets*. So, for example, you'd use the angle brackets around a tag, like <THIS>.

Second, most tags come in pairs, with an *opening tag* (<TAG>) and a *closing tag* (</TAG>). Notice that the closing tag uses a forward slash (/), which is what identifies the tag as a closing tag. Sample tags might look like this: <TAG>some text goes here</TAG>.

Third, tags are commonly *nested* within each other — that is, you put one set of tags inside another set of tags. Suppose that you want to mark text as a heading and make that heading appear in italics. In that case, all you do is nest one set of tags within the other, like the following code, which nests the italic tag inside a first-level (hence the 1) heading (hence the H) tag:

```
<H1><I>Your Heading Goes Here</I></H1>
```

Notice that the tag closest to the text on the left is also the one closest to the text on the right. This characteristic is called the LIFO (Last In First Out) principle. If you start writing HTML by hand, make sure that the first tag you open (<H1> in the preceding example) is the last one you close (</H1> in the example), the second tag you open (<I> in example) is the next to last one you close (<I> in example), and so on.

The essentials of attributes

Attributes are a part of HTML tags that identify additional information. For example, you might use the <BODY>...</BODY> tags to indicate that all the information between them should be included in the document body. You can add an attribute to specify that the document body should include, say, an aqua background.

Attributes always appear in an opening tag. So to add that lovely background color attribute to the <BODY> tags, you enter the following:

```
<BODY BGCOLOR="AQUA">some text goes here</BODY>
```

Here are some totally titillating tidbits about tags and attributes:

✔ You can enter tags and attributes just about anywhere in an HTML document. Adding spaces, tabs, or entire lines does not affect how the resulting Web page appears in Navigator (or other browsers). For example

```
<BODY BGCOLOR="AQUA">some text goes here</BODY>
```

and

```
<BODY
BGCOLOR="AQUA">
some text goes here
</BODY>
```

will look the same in Navigator.

✔ You probably want to get in the habit of typing your tags and attributes using all UPPERCASE letters. This way, particularly when your HTML document gets cluttered with lots of information, you'll be able to easily spot the tags and attributes amidst the sea of text.

✔ We recommend entering both the opening tag and the closing tag at the same time so that you don't forget the closing tag.

Even blank Web pages have tags

Technically speaking, even blank Web pages contain some HTML. Behind the scenes, whenever you tell Composer that you want to create a new page, Composer fills in all kinds of document *structure tags* for you. These structure tags are necessary so that the Web browsers (the software, not people) know what's going on.

The current HTML standards require that documents have, at the very least, *doctype* (which tells the browser the HTML version) and title elements, which look like this:

```
<!DOCTYPE HTML PUBLIC "-//W3C//
   DTD HTML 3.2 FINAL//EN">

<TITLE>Title goes here</TITLE>
```

Generally, it's clearer and easier to also include <HTML> and <HEAD> and <BODY> tags, like this:

```
<!DOCTYPE HTML PUBLIC "-//W3C//
   DTD HTML 3.2 FINAL//EN">
<HTML>
<HEAD>
<TITLE>Title goes here</TITLE>
</HEAD>
<BODY>
</BODY>
</HTML>
```

All of the actual text in the Web page goes between the <BODY> and </BODY> tags.

Again, if you're letting Composer take care of the work for you, you don't have to worry about placing the body text in the right place, except in the context of not accidentally deleting the tags. However, if you get a wild hair to go and manually code your whole Web site because you can, remember to include these structure tags.

Part II
Creating Awesome Web Pages

In this part . . .

Welcome to Part II! In Chapter 4, you see the elements to include in every Web site — a must for anyone planning on publishing Web sites (you are planning to, aren't you?). In Chapter 5, you see just how lazy you can be and still develop great Web sites. Then in Chapter 6, you move on to the thrilling excitement of using formatting options. Finally, in Chapter 7, you get *seated* in Composer's table features.

Chapter 4

What Every Guy and Gal Ought to Know . . . before Getting Started

*Y*ou don't walk outside in the winter without your coat, right? You don't go on long car rides without visiting the rest room first, right? You don't leave the house without zipping your fly, right? Likewise, you shouldn't go any further in this book without reading this chapter.

This chapter presents the essentials of good Web sites. Every Web site you create — as well as every page within your sites — should address the very basics of reader needs, theme, timeliness, and snazziness. Anything less, and you might as well work for the Jones' Web team. What's more, addressing these basics can help set your Web sites apart from other peoples'. Just because these essentials are good to address doesn't mean everyone does — do it, and be better!

The following sections tell you about addressing reader needs, establishing theme, being timely, and making your Web site snazzy. These are the essentials, guys and gals, so saddle up and come on!

Addressing Reader Needs

Readers refers to the people who access, read, and use your Web sites. And you're probably not surprised to hear, readers are needy people. Not needy like a clingy date. Not needy like a cat whining for food. Rather, needy in terms of the specific information they require.

Think of it this way. Most readers visit your site for a reason: They're looking for information. And what kind of information they're looking for depends on who they are and what they'll do with the information. You can categorize your readers into these different types (or perhaps combine them):

- Decision-making types
- Techie types
- Casual types

The following three sections tell you more than you ever wanted to know about these readers. From these descriptions, you should be able to determine what category (or categories) your readers fall into. Then you can use this information to establish content, design, and effects you want to use.

You should make finding out who your readers are part of your Web site development process. Refer to the steps in Chapter 20 for handy information on creating a terrific Web site.

Decision-making types

Decision-making types read because they need to make a decision — whether to purchase something, choose a service, hire a contractor, reschedule shipping dates, give raises (yeah, right), or clear the calendar and go play golf (more likely). They want bottom-line information, such as how much something costs, when it can be delivered, or possibly how it can make them look good.

These decision-making types are finicky readers, though, because they don't want to get bogged down with fluffy details. For example, they may want to know how a product can benefit their company, but they don't want to know all the fluff about how the product works, how long it takes to manufacture, or the details about how your company struggled for 17 years perfecting it. Or they may want to know about when a product will be delivered, but they don't want the gory details about how you rearranged 18 employees' schedules to deliver it on time.

How to address their needs in your Web site? Good question, and you can consider several answers:

- **Make the bottom line information the most apparent information on the Web page or site.** In doing so, you allow these busy people to find the information they need quickly without having to wade through information they don't want.

✔ **Include fluffy details about your product, service, or staff *only* on secondary or tertiary pages — and only if you have to.** That way, these folks can choose to read that information, but they won't be forced to wade through it.

✔ **Use images to convey concepts or to make your pages more interesting.** These folks don't want to wade through boring text; in fact, they'll quickly move on to a more exciting site and probably won't return to yours if you present the information in an uninteresting manner. Adding images not only helps you provide information more efficiently, but it also keeps decision makers interested in the content you provide.

See Chapter 10 for more information about images.

✔ **Use tables to make interesting layouts.** For example, you can make side headings (headings that appear to the left of paragraphs, rather than above them), juxtapose text and images, or create multicolumn text — all of which makes your pages more visually appealing to the "I ain't gonna read it if it ain't pretty" decision makers.

See Chapter 7 for more information about tables.

Techie types

Techie types look for one of two types of information: How-to information that they can use to troubleshoot or fix something, and information that teaches them something new — something beyond their existing knowledge or expertise.

In either of these cases, techies do want the gory details — the more the better. First, if they're troubleshooting or fixing something, they need all the information possible to help them determine what is wrong and how to fix it. Second, if they're reading to learn something new, they'll need details that they can use to build on existing knowledge and master new knowledge. When in doubt, more detail is better.

Techies, like decision makers, want to see images in Web pages; however, they want them for a different reason. Instead of wanting images that make a page look more appealing, techies want images that describe processes, show parts, or explain configurations. These images don't have to be pretty, but they do have to include enough information for techies to work from.

Here are a few ideas on how to meet techies' needs:

✔ **Start with an overview.** Either a text description or a diagram that announces what they need to know before diving into the information and that forecasts the information or process they'll use. Overviews give them a launching point and announce information they'll need before they get started.

✔ **Use numbered lists when describing processes or procedures.**
Following a list of steps is much easier than following several sentences crammed into a paragraph. Make each step clear and concise, and make it doing-oriented by starting each step with a verb. (*Do* this; *make* that; *place* the other.)

See Chapter 6 for more information about making lists.

✔ **Follow procedures with a diagram or image of what the results should look like.** In doing so, you help them know (a) that they've completed the steps and (b) that they've completed them successfully.

See Chapter 10 for more information about including images.

✔ **Provide reference materials on secondary or tertiary pages that point them to other sources for information.** Remember that these folks seek to expand what they know, and a few hints for more information might be appreciated.

Casual types

Casual types refers to the casual Web surfer — you know, people who just skip from site to site following links that interest them. These folks read because they're interested, not necessarily because they have to make a decision or fix something.

Keep in mind that these casual types probably lead a double life. They casually Web surf when they're decompressing from a long week, nursing that third cup of coffee, or killing a few minutes before a meeting. The other life may have them as decision makers, techies, or other types that you may have an interest in impressing.

The key point is that they visit your site because they want to, not because they seek information — immediately, anyway. They may not be seeking information at the moment, but they may be casually looking for information they can use when they have their decision-making or techie hats on. Therefore, you have to make your site as appealing to them as possible because the content itself isn't likely to be enough to keep them glued to your site. Casual surfers are, looking at it another way, potential customers, clients, or patrons.

Here are some ideas on how to keep these folks glued to your site:

✔ **Make your site spiffy by using colors, images, and cool formatting.** Even though all these special effects are great, don't spiff up your site too much with them because they can slow download time. If you make casual users wait too long to see the snazzy effects, they'll quickly lose interest and visit someone else's page.

✔ **Provide easy-to-use navigation.** Although good navigation is essential in any site, it's particularly important to encourage these readers to visit multiple pages in your site and return again and again.

Chapter 11 tells all about navigation, the different types, and the different locations.

✔ **Change information frequently.** Casual users won't return to your site if you always have the same hum-drum information. Giving them new material with each visit helps ensure that they return again. The "This of the Day," "That of the Week," or "Whosis of the Month" techniques are good, but you must remember to keep the information updated. If it's a joke of the day that you provide, you need to make sure that your original and creative "Man from Nantucket" limerick endures one and only one day.

The section "Making Web Sites Timely" later in this chapter tells more about changing Web site content.

✔ **Use formatting options such as headings and bulleted lists to provide at-a-glance reading.** Rest assured that casual Web surfers aren't going to take the time to slog through paragraphs of text. You can easily summarize your main points (and make them easy to spot) by frequently using headings and bulleted lists.

Check out Chapter 6 to see how to create headings and lists, and check out Chapter 18 for more information about how headings and bulleted lists can make a Web page more reader-friendly.

Establishing Web Site Theme

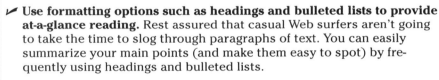

Web site theme refers to the colors, formatting, background, and images that work together to make your Web pages one cohesive unit. Think of individual Web pages as being part of a family. Each family member has certain traits that look similar to other members and help identify him or her as part of the family. For example, your brothers and sisters may have similar facial features, bone structure, or hair and eye coloring. These traits, when all of you are standing together at the family reunion, stand out as being similar. You can easily see the similarities between and among your siblings just by comparing these features.

Likewise, all of your Web pages should have similar characteristics that help identify them as being part of a group of pages — or, more precisely, part of a cohesive Web site. Just as you and your siblings may have similar features and coloring, your Web pages should be structured similarly. They should use the same background and, perhaps, use similar images, buttons, or icons to help the pages be part of a site.

Giving Web pages common threads has several advantages, both for you and your readers:

✔ Readers can easily identify that they're still on the same site.

✔ Readers will focus on the content because they won't always be looking for what's going to pop up on the next screen.

✔ You can remind readers on every page that they're visiting the Fleabags-Are-We site, which is very important if you're selling or promoting a product or service.

✔ You can create theme images, buttons, or icons only one time and reuse them from page to page, which makes the pages look consistent and cuts your work and your readers' download time.

For more information about colors and formatting, see Chapter 5. Or for more information about including images, wander over to Chapter 10.

Making Web Sites Timely

Timely refers to keeping information up-to-date. Fresh. Recent. Not old. Not moldy. Interesting to the readers. Unlike much of the stuff on the Web. You'd be surprised how often untimeliness shows its ugly head in your Web pages. Here are a few examples of things to consider to keep your Web site timely:

✔ **The date last modified:** Specifies the last time the Web page (or site) was updated and indicates to your readers whether the information is current. Particularly hot topics, such as medical research or current events, become outdated quickly. Many people looking for timely information will find no value in an article dated even as recently as December 1996.

✔ **The collar size, tie width, and bell-bottom circumference of clothing shown in photos:** Heck, these days, big collars, skinny ties, and enormous bell bottoms could mean either ultra '70s or '90s. In either case, including photos of leisure suits is a definite no-no. Seriously, find some kids — your own or someone else's — and ask to see the pictures in some of their school books. They'll snicker and show you the really-dated pictures. Make sure that the pictures in your Web site don't evoke the same reaction.

✔ **The cutting-edgeness of equipment or facilities shown in photographs:** If your company produces technologically-advanced equipment, be sure marketing photos reflect the leading technologies, not square wheels.

- ✓ **References to date-specific events:** This includes elections, Olympics, play-off games, lunar eclipses, Elvis sightings, comets, seasons, and so on. Mentioning these is okay; however, be sure the Web site doesn't reference the "current" election between Bush and Clinton or "yesterday's" Olympic coverage.

- ✓ **Old logos or corporate colors:** Every once in a while companies refresh their image by updating logos and colors. Make sure that these are updated on Web pages.

- ✓ **Cooler Web effects (lack of use):** Come on, folks. Even the most stuffed-shirt-type readers don't want to access a text-only-on-gray-background Web page time after time. So much more is available, and — if you're using Composer — easy to include.

- ✓ **Information that never changes:** Okay, some information doesn't need to change. A company's mission statement and logos (assuming they're updated as company needs change), contact information, corporate address, and the founder's picture are all considered *static information*, which generally stays the same over time. However, other information, such as announcements, introductory descriptions, and eye-catching effects should be dynamic, which means that you change them frequently to give your readers new information each time they visit your site. Figure 4-1 shows some examples of static and dynamic information. Even static information should get a face-lift from time to time.

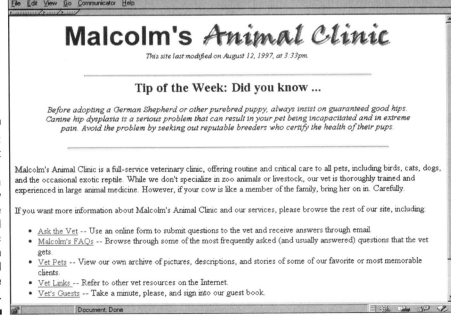

Figure 4-1: Note that static information generally stays the same, and dynamic information should change frequently.

Making Web Sites Snazzy

Snazzy? Didn't that term go out with the '60s? Well, maybe, but it still applies to Web pages. *Snazzy* refers to a couple of different things. First, it refers to the enhancements you add, such as images, imagemaps, applets, JavaScript, and forms, that transform hum-drum pages into ones that are more exciting and visually pleasing. Second, snazzy refers to the overall page presentation — that is, how all the page elements appear as a whole. For example, you can include the most-awesome applets, the coolest of buttons, and the greatest photo of your cat; however, none of these elements can enhance your Web page unless they all work in unison.

So, snazziness, at least as it applies to Web pages, is a two-parter; it's bifold; it's bifurcated (hee hee, we always wanted to use that word). But nonetheless, snazzy means that you not only have to include cool enhancements, but you also have to incorporate them in ways that help to achieve an effective page presentation.

Illustrations throughout this book give you some ideas, but the best way to get a real grasp on snazziness is to go out and surf the Web. Hit all the sites you can find, particularly those run by competitors, suppliers, clients, and any other sites that might tie into your needs. Then head back out and look for fun sites — from TV shows to the latest marketing extravaganza. Pretty soon, you'll know snazziness when you see it.

Chapter 5

There's More than One Way to Be Lazy

. . . .

. . . .

*I*n addition to being a slick program that takes most of the work out of developing Web pages, Composer (and Communicator in general) offers a whole variety of neat ways to make your life easier. Heck, with all Composer's nifty features, you can pretty much sit around dunkin' your doughnuts while Composer does the work for you.

This chapter takes a run through useful or neat ways to let the computer work while you relax. In particular, you'll see how to use the Composer Wizard, templates, and spell checker and how to publish your site and set preferences.

Using the Composer Wizard

Netscape provides a page Wizard that helps you quickly and easily develop Web pages. A *Wizard*, in this case, is actually a clever set of Netscape Web pages that asks you questions, lets you fill in information, lets you choose formatting and colors, and — like magic — creates the Web page for you. The Wizard is great for newbie Web page authors; you just fill in the information, and the Wizard spits out the Web page. And for experienced Web page authors, the Wizard provides a great starting page that you can add to and modify as you want.

Before you start, make sure that you're connected to the Internet and that you have Communicator open.

1. **In Communicator (either Composer or Navigator), go to File⊅New⊅Page from Wizard.**

   You now see a new Netscape window, like the one in Figure 5-1.

2. **Read through the instructions in the upper-right frame, scroll down, and click Start.**

   The upper-left frame fills in with step-by-step instructions, and the content of the right frame has a preview of your new (under serious construction) Web page.

3. **Work your way through the instructions by clicking on the high-lighted links and following the instructions that appear in the bottom frame.**

   For example, the first link lets you give your page a title, so select that. You see the bottom frame fill in with a blank for you to complete, as shown in Figure 5-2.

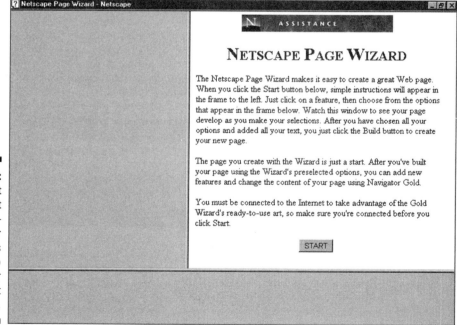

Figure 5-1:
Click Start
in the right
frame —
other
instructions
and help
will appear
in the left
frame.

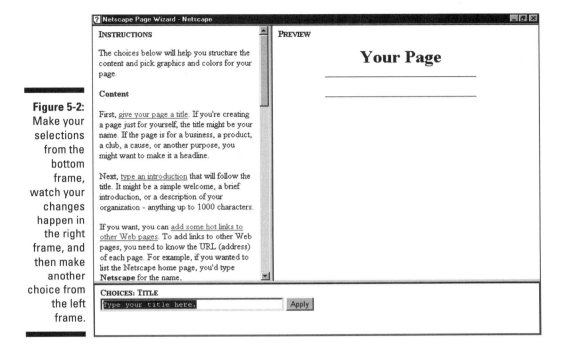

Figure 5-2:
Make your
selections
from the
bottom
frame,
watch your
changes
happen in
the right
frame, and
then make
another
choice from
the left
frame.

4. Complete the blank, and then click Apply.

You see the new title (heading, actually) appear over in the upper-right frame.

5. Continue working your way through the upper-left frame, choosing any elements you want to address and disregarding the other ones.

For each item you choose at the left, you get a menu, choices, or a blank to fill in at the bottom of the frame, and then you see the results at the upper-right. In this example, we tried a little of everything — like visiting a smorgasbord. See Figure 5-3 for the final result.

If you decide you want to change a choice you made, just click that link again from the upper-left, and make a new selection. The new selection replaces the old one.

Keep in mind that if you feel hemmed in by the 1000 character limits imposed by the Wizard, you can be as lengthy as you want later. You'll just have to wait until after you're in the Composer editor, rather than working through the Wizard.

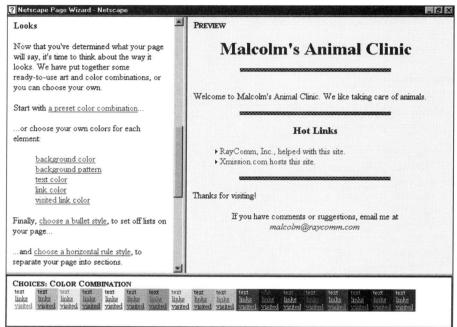

Figure 5-3:
The page isn't too bad, for no longer than it took to do, right?

6. **After you finish, scroll all the way to the bottom of the upper-left frame and select Build, as shown in Figure 5-4.**

   You can also Start Over and erase everything you've done, but it's probably easier to fix things you don't like than it is to start over.

   Your page appears in a new Navigator window. All that you have to do is choose File⇨Edit Page to bring up the page in Composer and then File⇨Save As to save it on your local hard drive.

   When you save the document like this — by editing and then saving — all of the images and associated files are saved with the document on your local hard drive so that you can continue developing your document.

Here are some tips to help improve your relationship with the Wizard:

✔ Make sure that you close any help windows before you start with the Wizard, and after you start the Wizard, check to make sure that the window has the standard menu items — File, Edit, View, and so on. If the Wizard starts in a kiosk-type window (without all of the menu options), you won't have a way to save your document at the end of the process and will have to throw it away and start over. Sigh. Been there, done that.

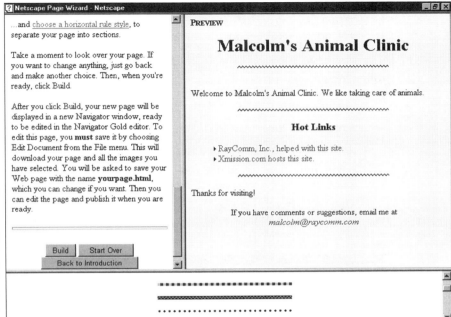

Figure 5-4:
Click Build
from the left
frame to
start the
process of
saving the
file locally.

✔ You might notice that your spiffy new page gains a "This page created with Netscape Navigator Gold" or with Netscape Communicator message when you save it. We probably shouldn't tell you this, but you can just delete that message from your Composer window. Just select the message, and press Delete.

✔ On your hard drive in the same folder as your new document, you can find the images for all the fancy buttons and bullets you selected. You can include those in other documents just as you include other images.

✔ If you think that little Wizard process is pretty cool, you might also try out the Netscape PowerStart application. Head for http://personal. netscape.com/custom/index.html and enjoy. Oh, it's for building a personal most-often-used links page so that you'll have your favorites all together in one place. Have fun!

Using Composer's Templates

A *template* is a master HTML document of sorts that you can use as a starting point to create Web pages. Generally, these templates contain most of the formatting and layout you want, and all you have to do is fill in the blanks with information. Creating pages from templates isn't nearly as interactive or exciting as using the Wizard, but in a lot of ways, the process is much more useful because you have more control over the results.

To create a new document from a template from the Netscape site, use the following procedure:

1. **In Communicator, go to File⇨New⇨Page from Template.**

   You see the New Page from Template dialog box.

2. **Select Netscape Templates to reveal the mother lode of templates.**

   If you have an existing document that you'd like to use as a template, you can go to Choose File and then select the file you want to use.

   After selecting Netscape Templates, you find yourself at the Netscape site, as shown in Figure 5-5.

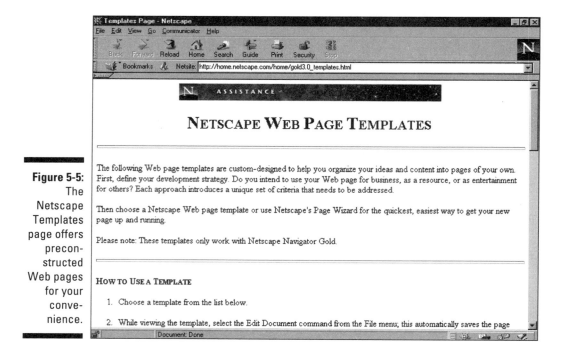

Figure 5-5: The Netscape Templates page offers preconstructed Web pages for your convenience.

3. Scroll through the page, and check out the templates that seem fairly close to meeting your needs. At press time, the list included:

- **Personal/Family**

  My Home Page

  Résumé

  McNab Family

- **Company/Small Business**

  Flower and Garden Supplies

  Home Sale Announcement

- **Department**

  Human Resources

  Job Listings

  Department Overview

- **Product/Service**

  Product Data Sheet

  Catering Service

- **Special Interest Group**

  Travel Club

  Windsurfing Club

- **Interesting and Fun**

  My First JavaScript

  My Calculator

4. Click on each of the links, and check out the templates.

They all come with graphics, formatting colors, and everything else you need to give you a running start on Web page development. For an example, look at Figure 5-6.

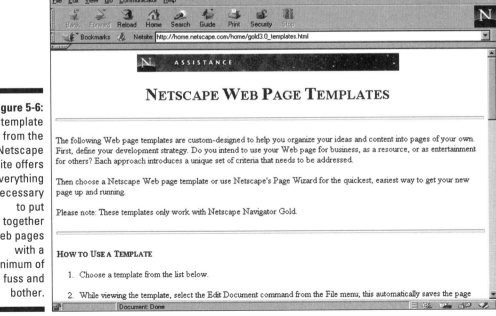

Figure 5-6: A template from the Netscape site offers everything necessary to put together Web pages with a minimum of fuss and bother.

When you find a template or two that you like, you can take the template for your own use (thanks, Netscape!). How? Read on!

5. **Choose File⇨Edit Page to bring up the page in Composer, and then File⇨Save As to save it on your local hard drive.**

When you save the document like this — by editing and then saving — all of the images and associated files are saved with the document on your local hard drive so that you can then proceed to develop your document.

Here's more from the newsroom about Netscape templates:

✔ There's nothing particularly special or exciting about a template. Any HTML document can be a template, and if you think about it, nearly any document should be your template. Say that you've created a wonderful page. You say to yourself, "Self, you know, all of my pages should look just like this." No problem. Just save the document somewhere safe. When you want to create a new document, go to File⇨New⇨Page from Template, click Choose File, and browse right to your favorite. You get a new blank untitled document with all of the content and formatting, without the danger of accidentally saving the new creation over the existing masterpiece.

✔ If you like the last tip, you'll love this one. You can use templates to ensure (nearly) foolproof formatting. Create a page that you like, but instead of putting real content in it, just type phrases like "Fill in today's date here," "Add joke here," or "Complete list of award winners here on Fridays, otherwise delete." Then you delegate and tell your delegee to go to File⇨New⇨Page from Template, click Choose File, and browse right to the template. In the template, the delegee just follows your instructions to have a fine-looking page.

✔ At press time, there was a link near the bottom of the Templates page to the Netscape Gold Rush Tool Box (although the name may change to something more in keeping with the Netscape Communicator/Composer motif). Check out that link for a whole collection of clip art and other pointers for making cool Web pages.

✔ Keep in mind that templates downloaded to your computer can still be used as templates; just click Choose File from the New Page from Template dialog box and browse to the templates you've downloaded — and save a trip to the Netscape site.

Using the Spell Checker

Even if U lik kreatif speling, ewe wil find that most readers just can't handle it. What's more, if you do on occasion, either accidentally or purposefully, engage in creative spelling, your audience is likely to decide that you're careless, clueless, or just plain inattentive to detail. Regardless of which of the options it is, they don't bode well for you or the reception of your Web page. With this in mind, you'll be glad to know that Netscape Composer comes equipped with a flashy little spell checker.

To check your spelling in Netscape Composer, use the following steps:

1. **Go to File⇨Open Page, click the Open button, or press Ctrl+O.**

   The Open Page dialog box appears, as usual.

2. **Click Choose File to browse to the file, select the file, and click Open.**

   You can also type the filename if you happen to know it.

   When you're done, you should have the filename and path in the file text field.

3. **Verify that the radio button beside Composer (as in, Open location or file in) is selected, and then choose Open.**

4. **Click the Spelling icon or go to Tools⇨Check Spelling to bring up the Check Spelling dialog box.**

   As soon as Composer finds a word that you misspelled (or just a word that it doesn't recognize), you get the chance to figure out what to do with it, as shown in Figure 5-7.

Figure 5-7: The Check Spelling dialog box gives you a good selection of options for dealing with those spelling problems.

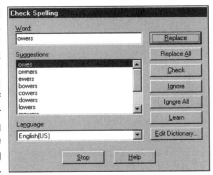

The Check Spelling dialog box — chock-full of options — includes the following key components:

- The _Word_ field is where the allegedly misspelled word appears, as well as where you type the correction, if necessary.

- _Suggestions_ gives you Composer's best guesses about the word you intended to spell correctly. If your spelling attempt was too far off base, you might not get any suggestions at all.

- _Language_ lets you choose, within the constraints of the Communicator version you have, what language's dictionary should be used for the spell checking. For example, if you're working on a _colourful_ and _humour_-filled page, you'll _recognise_ the need to choose an English (UK) dictionary rather than the default English (US) dictionary. Of course, some spelling problems can't be corrected just by picking a new dictionary, which is why more buttons remain at your disposal.

- _Replace_ puts the _W_ord in the place of the highlighted word in your document. Generally, if you've chosen carefully, this will fix the spelling error.

- _Replace All_ acts just as _R_eplace does, but corrects all words that are misspelled exactly the same way. If you've been living in Germany too long and type _ich_ every time you mean _I,_ just click Replace _A_ll the first time Composer asks, and it'll fix every one of those _ich-es_ throughout the document. What's more, Composer is smart enough to fix the _ich-es_ and leave the whiches alone.

Unlike many spell checkers in word processing programs, Composer doesn't just whip through and make all the changes at once when you choose Replace All. It handles the words as it gets to them.

- _Check_ heads back to the dictionary to look up the current word in the _W_ord field. Hypothetically (because we're sure that you're a great speller), say that you messed up a word so badly that Composer can't even guess what you meant and you get the dreaded (no suggestions) message. Sigh. Well, you can try to get closer and click _C_heck to tell Composer to work harder and come up with suggestions.

- _Ignore_ and _Ign_o_re All_ skips over the current word and all occurrences of the current word, respectively. Use this when you have some oddball misspelling that's a proper name or rare jargon.

- _Learn_ adds the word — spelled as is — to Composer's dictionary. Be sure that you spell the word correctly before you click _L_earn. After Composer has _learned_ a word, Composer doesn't flag that word as misspelled in any other document. Use _L_earn for jargon in your field or other common words — to you — that Composer just doesn't know.

5. After you finish checking the spelling, click Stop or Done.

The Check Spelling dialog box vanishes forthwith (spelled correctly, we might note), and you're zoomed back to Composer. Sure beats using a paper dictionary, doesn't it?

Here are some crib notes about spell checking:

- If you arrived at the Check Spelling dialog box in error or just want to be prepared with a way to return to your document, never fear. Click <u>S</u>top to dismiss the dialog box and return to the regularly scheduled program.

- To add words directly, type them in the <u>N</u>ew Word field, and then click <u>A</u>dd. To remove words, click to select the words in the Words window, and then click Re<u>m</u>ove. To replace a word within the dictionary, type the new word in the <u>N</u>ew Word field, click to select the word to replace, and click <u>R</u>eplace. When you finish editing your personal dictionary, click OK to return to the Check Spelling dialog box.

- If you've been keeping up with all of the "interesting" spelling errors and suggested spellings in some commercial software programs, you might wonder whether Composer suffers the same plight. Unfortunately for the rumormongers, we couldn't come up with anything interesting.

- Although the <u>E</u>dit Dictionary option sounds like you can go right in and edit Webster's to your own satisfaction (and possibly justify kreatif spelling), that's not actually the case. You can edit only the words you've added.

- Regardless of where your cursor is when you start spell checking, Composer heads back to the top of the document to start over.

Publishing Your Site

When you're developing Web pages, you're probably saving them all on your hard drive and testing them as you go, which is as it should be when you're working on the pages. However, a time will come, and probably sooner rather than later, when you will want the rest of the world to see the fruits of your labors. This section explains what "publishing your site" means to you and how to go about it.

What's the deal with publishing?

When you finish (for the time being) developing your Web pages — and think they're pretty spiffy as well — you're ready to move on to the next level. When that time comes, you have a few choices, only one of which is really worthwhile:

✔ Publish your pages to a Web server so that people in your company or on the Internet can type an address like `http://www.xmission.com/coolstuff/yourpage.html` into their Web browsers and see your page magically appear before their very eyes.

✔ Keep the pages as a nice little secret between you and your computer.

✔ Invite everyone in the company or that you'd ever want to see your pages into your office and show them what you've done. Serve coffee and doughnuts while you're at it.

So, you'd like to know more about this first option? We thought so.

Publishing to a Web server means, in normal language, to copy all of the HTML documents and associated files to a computer that will then send them out on request to anyone who wants them. The *server* (or *host computer*) is on the Internet or on an intranet and has an address something like `http://www.xmission.com/`. You'll have a special folder on this computer, so your pages are located at an address like `http://www.xmission.com/~yourid/yourpage.html` or `http://www.intranet.xmission.com/research/homepage.htm`.

How do you go about finding a server to host your pages? That depends.

If you have Internet access, ask your current service provider about publishing your pages (or just check out their help pages for information). Most Internet Service Providers (ISPs) provide Web hosting services within the normal service agreement. In addition to hours of Net surfing and e-mail, you also can generally put up to about 5MB worth of Web site on the ISP's server, depending on the specific ISP. (5MB is a *lot* of Web site, by the way.)

If you're developing your Web pages in a work context, either for an Internet site or for the corporate intranet, a procedure is probably in place to put your Web pages out there. Check with your help desk or Information Services department for the specifics. If you don't yet have Internet access, check out the ISP software, called AT&T WorldNet Service, on the CD that comes with this book.

Publishing with Composer

Now that the background information is out of the way, we can get down to the bare essentials of Web publishing with Composer. First, you have to collect a little information from your corporate computer gurus or from your ISP so that you know exactly what information to put in the blanks.

Check with the powers-that-be (henceforth referred to as the server administrator or your personal demigod) and obtain the following information. Write it down here so that you don't forget it (except the password, of course).

Basic Info

- My user name on the Web server

  _____

- My HTTP address (if you publish files to an HTTP location)

  _____

- My FTP address (if you publish files to an FTP location)

  _____

- The Web address (URL) where I'll find my pages

- My password (don't write it down, just remember it)

Questions

- Do I have to put the files in a specific folder or name them anything special? Is there a special process I have to follow to publish pages?

  _____

  _____

- What else should I know?

  _____

  _____

By the very nature of the Internet, each one of the thousands of servers is slightly different, so we can't give you the one answer to the procedure. The rest of this section walks you through the most typical scenario, and with this information and anything else that your personal demigod provides, you should be set.

Our server administrator told us that we're publishing our pages with FTP, not HTTP (which is fairly typical), that the FTP address is `ftp://ftp.xmission.com/public_html/`, that the browse-to address is `http://www.xmission.com/~ejray/`, and that we can use any filenames we want to use. Armed with this information, onward into the Abyss!

FTP (File Transfer Protocol) is the traditional "language" used by computers on the Internet to send files to other computers. _HTTP (Hypertext Transfer Protocol)_ is used to get Web pages but is rarely used to send files.

If you have some experience with Web development or the closely-related joys of FTP and UNIX-ish commands, you'll really appreciate the fact that Composer will upload your pages and associated files with the click of a button. If this whole thing is new to you, just trust us. You can use the Composer-upload-with-a-click approach or descend into the dark ages and do it the hard way. If you prefer the hard way, you're on your own.

To publish your pages with Composer, use these easy steps:

1. Finish your Web pages.

You can go back and publish your pages again and again, so they don't have to be completely finished, final, and never to be changed again. However, they should be presentable, spelling-error- and typo-free, and approved by whoever is in a position to approve your work (boss, spouse, kids, cats, whomever — or whatever).

2. With the HTML document open in Composer, go to File⇨Publish.

You see the rather intimidating Publish dialog box, as shown in Figure 5-8.

Figure 5-8:
The Publish dialog box is the starting place to getting your hard work recognized.

Publish: C:\COMPOSER\ns05-12.htm

Page Title: ives from Malcolm's Animal Clinic   e.g.: "My Web Page"

HTML Filename: ns05-12.htm   e.g.: "mypage.htm"

HTTP or FTP Location to publish to:
ftp://ftp.xmission.com/./public_html/malcolm/

User name: ejray   Use Default Location

Password: _____   ☐ Save password

Other files to include
◉ Files associated with this page   ○ All files in page's folder

Select None   file:///C/COMPOSER/feedback.gif
Select All   file:///C/COMPOSER/homepage.gif
file:///C/COMPOSER/links.gif
file:///C/COMPOSER/LOGOLONG.GIF
file:///C/COMPOSER/return.gif

OK   Cancel   Help

3. Verify or change the information that appears in the Page Title field.

The *Title,* in HTML lingo, is what most readers will see up in the title bar of their browsers when viewing your site. The title is also usually the name used when your readers bookmark your pages. The title doesn't appear anywhere within the body of the document.

4. Verify that the HTML Filename is the filename (and contents, of course) that you want to have on the Web server.

Unless you have a real reason to specify a different filename, you should just accept the suggestion that Composer makes (which is the same as the current filename on your local computer).

Possible reasons to use other filenames would be if your ISP or company requires that your filenames follow a specific naming convention. Or if the main file in the folder should be called something specific like `index.html` or `homepage.htm`, you might make the adjustment here. See the sidebar "What's in a name" later in this chapter for details.

If you've set your publishing preferences and are uploading to the default server, just click Use Default Location and skip down to Step 9. See "Setting Preferences" later in this chapter for the specifics.

5. **Verify that the HTTP or FTP Location to publish to is the address your server administrator provided, including any folder names necessary.**

   If you're publishing to an HTTP location, you should be able to put in the address your administrator gives you and have everything work just right. However, if you're publishing to an FTP location, you may have to tweak the instructions a little, as discussed here.

   The server administrator probably has the Web server set to use FTP to receive files and HTTP to send and maybe receive files. You don't need to worry about how the files get from the FTP server to the HTTP server — either way it's automatic or nothing at all happens . . . and it's someone else's headache.

   The server administrator told us that the FTP server name is `ftp://ftp.xmission.com/` and that we should put the file in the `public_html/malcolm/` folder. Because of the way Composer talks to FTP servers, we added a period (.) between the server name and folder name, yielding

   ```
   ftp://ftp.xmission.com/./public_html/malcolm/
   ```

   Keep in mind that this is just an example — the information you provide will be different and dictated by your ISP.

   If you've tried this process with and without the period and you're just not having any luck and are getting an error message, verify that the user name and password are correct, and then contact your server administrator for help, if needed. It's likely to be a server configuration or an ISP-specific setting issue.

6. **In the User name field, put the user name that you use to log onto your ISP.**

   Capitalization often counts, so you'll probably type it in all lowercase.

7. **In the Password field, type your password.**

   Again, it's case-sensitive, so be sure to use the correct capitalization.

8. **If you want Composer to remember your password, put a checkmark in the Save password checkbox.**

   You may want to wait until you've worked out the publishing process before you tell Composer to save your password. It'll be easier to debug typos and other problems if you type everything as you upload.

   The advantages of saving the password are the conveniences of hassle-free Web publishing. For example, you don't have to enter the stinkin' password every time you publish or republish pages. The disadvantage is that anyone sitting at your computer can upload Web pages to your site. What's the matter with that, you ask? If they want to do my work for me, that's great! However, they could upload *any* pages, images, or files to your Web site. At the worst, a little prank with some readily-available-on-the-Net images could be humiliating or career limiting. That said, if you are using Composer at home and you're the only one who uses it to upload files, sure — why not!

9. **In the Other files to include part of the dialog box, put a checkmark to upload either the Files associated with the page you're uploading, or to upload All files in the page's folder.**

   The whole Other files to include bit is the most useful, handy, impressive, and can't-believe-I-ever-lived-without-it part of the publishing setup. As you may already know (depending on the route you took to this chapter), Web pages include HTML documents and associated files like images and sounds. Remembering each of the associated files and uploading them all at once is a bit of a hassle, unless you let Composer do the work for you.

   At the least, upload the associated files. If you've been religiously keeping all of your documents and images and sounds and stuff together in one folder (like we mention throughout other chapters), you can upload the whole mess at once. That's the easiest course of action.

   Or in the field next to the Select None and Select All buttons, you can individually select or deselect files to upload. Click Select None to upload only the file that you came here to upload, and click Select All to (obviously) upload them all. If you want to pick and choose, use Ctrl+click to select or deselect files individually.

 We like to upload the whole mess of files each time we make any major changes. Then if we have made trivial changes or "improvements" to some of the pages, we can be sure that the newest pages are all up on the server.

10. **When you finish and you're sure everything is right, click OK (or click Cancel if you're having second thoughts).**

    With much flashing and excitement (if you look closely), Composer uploads your files for you.

 If you're an old hand at the Internet and recall the necessity to set binary or ASCII flags when you were using traditional command line FTP, you'll probably also remember that FTP protocol required you to specify what kind of file you were uploading before you uploaded. You'll be pleased to know that Composer takes care of all that for you. You say Publish, and Composer does it.

As it uploads the files, Composer checks to make sure that all of the links look like they'll work. If it finds problems, Composer warns you. If you know that the files are all there and will work fine, click OK. Otherwise, click Cancel, and double-check your files before you try again.

You may also be warned with the Security Information dialog box. This box was designed to keep readers from accidentally sending their credit cards over the Internet, but the dialog box tends to just startle and confuse in this context. Heck, you're making your Web pages public anyway; what do you care if someone snoops as you upload them. Consider unchecking Show This Alert Next Time and just remember to be careful when sending personal information or credit card information over the Net. When you're done, click Continue.

If you forget your password (likely, if you didn't tell Composer to remember your password and you are uploading for the second or later time), Composer will come back and remind you about it, as in Figure 5-9. Just type your password and continue.

Figure 5-9:
If you forget to enter your password, Composer gently reminds you to put it in.

As Composer uploads the page, you see the Publishing Page dialog box as each file gets uploaded. This is just a feel-good status report, like when someone you love calls to tell you that everything is fine.

Finally, Composer tells you how many files it published successfully. Just click OK. Pretty cool, huh?

Here are some other notes about publishing your documents:

- ✔ After you publish your files, head over to Netscape Navigator and browse through them. Make sure that they all look OK, in particular that all of the graphics and other files loaded properly. Try all of the links and verify that they work. Murphy's law is in full force when publishing your pages, and you just can't be too careful. Even if you've uploaded the same folder of files 50 times and found everything fine, the first time you forget to find out if they all work, they won't.

✔ After you successfully publish your files at least once, consider going into the Composer Preferences dialog box and setting the publishing preferences so that publishing will be a little faster and easier the next time.

✔ Remember that every file you publish is, at least potentially, available to everyone on the Internet or on your intranet. Even if you don't have links to the file (or don't think you have links to it), people could find it, or an Internet searching program (like the ones associated with AltaVista or HotBot) could track it down. The last thing you want is for your employer to search out your name through AltaVista and find a Web page (that you thought wasn't publicly available, although it is on the server) with the heading "Great Ways to Goof Off at Work without Getting Caught." If it's on the server, anyone — including parents, kids, and employers — may see it.

✔ If you want to make sure that your pages are found by everyone — say, if you're launching your new Web-based business — you'll want to announce the site. For no cost at all, you can go to individual directories and search engines (such as `http://www.yahoo.com` or `http://www.altavista.digital.com/`), look for the Add URL link, and fill out the brief form. Or you can use a site submission service like Submit It at `http://www.submit-it.com/`, with a few submissions for free and even more for a small fee.

✔ If you choose to submit your site to search engines and directories, make *sure* that your pages are done, complete, finished, attractive, spell-checked, typo-free, functional, all links working, with a functional address, and ready for prime time. It's that old saw about getting only one chance to make a first impression, and boy is it ever true.

Setting Preferences

Composer offers you a ton of ways in which to customize, tune, and tweak the program into doing the grunt work for you. Although we could go through and laboriously discuss each and every option available, that wouldn't help you much in terms of knowing what you should tweak and what to leave alone. (Besides which, our lawyer warned us about potential legal exposure if we write the exhaustive version and you drop the book on your toe.) Therefore, the following sections cruise through the preferences and touch on the ones you'll really need.

You can't hurt anything by fiddling with your Composer or Communicator preferences, so don't hesitate to just dive in and experiment.

To bring up the Preferences dialog box, which is where you go to set and adjust these settings, go to Edit⇨Preferences. You see something like the dialog box shown in Figure 5-10.

What's in a name?

What's in a name? A rose by any other name would smell as sweet. . . .

Lovely sentiment, but to a Web server, there is actually something in a name. You see, in addition to just serving up pages by name when readers request them (Server, could I have http://www.xmission.com/~ejray/malcolm/freebies.html? That is, could I have the freebies.html document from the malcolm folder from the ~ejray folder from the www.xmission.com server? Sure, here you go.), servers also have their own agenda for which files to send out.

If you type a URL from a TV ad or one that your friend gives you, you'll probably enter something like http://www.dummies.com/ and not specify a filename. You may think, based on your experience testing documents locally, that you'll just get to see the list of documents in the folder — you didn't specify a filename, after all. But no, the server spits back a real page. How'd it do that?

If a reader indicates just a server name or just a server and folder name, the Web server looks around for the default file and sends that back. You get the whole file listing only if no default file is available *and* if the server is configured to let readers browse around that.

The default file, in addition to being a convenience for readers because they don't have to type as much, is also an advantage for you. If you provide a default file, your readers can't browse through your site and can't readily access pages that you don't directly link to.

Taking Malcolm's Animal Clinic as an example, suppose that a page is under construction but up on the server so that the developers can get feedback from select people (who all have the address). If no default file is provided, any reader can come and find that page. If a default file is provided, readers are forced into the site as planned and don't ever see the test stuff unless there's a link to it.

Good thinking? We thought so.

Ask your server administrator what the default filename is for the Web server. It's probably one of these choices: index.html, index.htm, homepage.htm, default.htm, or default.html.

You should either name your main page by the default filename or upload your main page both under its real name and the default filename. That way, you have a file with the right name, and your links back to main.html or whatever still work. Try it!

Each of the main categories at the left (Appearance, Navigator, Mail & Groups, Composer, Offline, and Advanced) has subcategories. If you can't see the subcategory listing (as it appears in Figure 5-10), double-click on the little + signs beside each of the main categories.

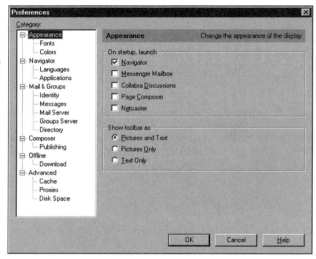

Figure 5-10:
The
Preferences
dialog box
is the
central
clearing-
house for
customi-
zation
options of
all sorts.

When you click on a category or subcategory at the left, the possible settings, choices, and options appear at the right of the dialog box. You can keep clicking subcategories and making changes, and Communicator will remember all of them. When you click OK, Composer saves all of the changes you made on each of the panels. If you change your mind and click Cancel, Composer discards them all.

The following sections describe the preference options.

Appearance

Appearance gives you the option of choosing which program(s) start when you double-click the Communicator icon. The default setting is just Naviga- tor, which is a good, safe choice. If you use Messenger to read mail or if you are actually using Composer to develop HTML documents nearly every time you start Communicator, you might put a check beside each element that should start. Remember, though, the more you start, the longer it will take to start the program.

Also on the Appearance panel are options to show the toolbar as Pictures and Text, Pictures Only, and Text Only. These options are pretty self-evident. The only thing to add here is that you might consider Text Only to give you more editing space on your desktop — Text Only buttons are smaller than the other two varieties.

The *Fonts* and *Colors* subcategories under Appearance aren't necessarily anything you want to change, but they do offer your readers some options you should be aware of. Looking first at the Fonts panel, readers can set the

<u>V</u>ariable Width Font and <u>F</u>ixed Width Font typefaces and sizes. Additionally, readers can specify that all documents should be formatted with the readers' own default font settings or with a couple of variants on using the document-specified fonts.

So what, you say? To each his own, you say? The point to be made here is that you, the author, *cannot* control what your readers see. You can try, but if you have a reader who likes using Technical 16 point for body text and Letter Gothic for monospace formatted text, that reader will see your page in those fonts. Period. Just to get an idea of what this might do to the document appearance, check out Figure 5-11, which shows a page using (fairly exotic) reader-modified settings.

The Colors panel, another subcategory of Appearance, offers the same basic problem, but in the context of document colors. If a reader really wants to see all documents in black text on a white background (because it's easier to read that way), that is how the document will appear. You can attempt to prescribe colors, but the reader can always overrule you.

If you're working on a Web page and find yourself worrying about getting the design and layout "just so," you might want to monkey with these settings to find out how badly it screws up your carefully formatted page. Then relax, lay off the coffee, concentrate on providing content first, and force yourself to worry less about that which you can't really control: layout and design.

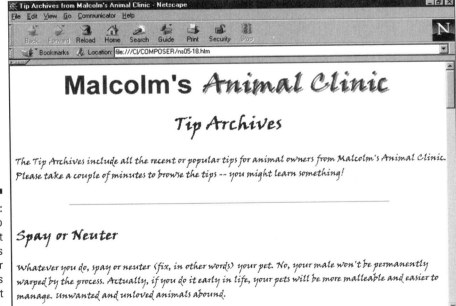

Figure 5-11: You have no idea what settings your readers might choose.

Navigator

Navigator preference settings, shown in Figure 5-12, don't offer much that you need. The only suggestion here is to set the Home page Location to your own home page or to a local file with the links you most commonly use. The Netscape home page isn't a very practical choice because it has few links you're likely to use daily and tends to be slow because of the high traffic.

If you want to set your own home page location, type the address of the page you want to use and browse through your local drive for a file, or use Navigator to browse to the page you want, come back to this panel of this dialog box, and click Use Current Page.

Figure 5-12:
Setting
a new,
personal
home page
and other
Navigator
options can
make your
browsing
more
efficient.

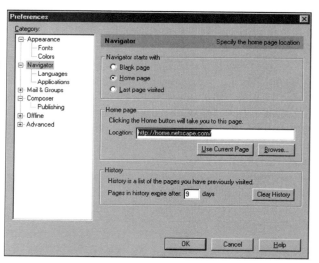

Mail & Groups

Mail & Groups is useful for tuning the settings for reading mail and newsgroups and for sending mail, but that information was probably correctly set the first time you used Communicator. If not, browse through the settings — they're all either self-explanatory (like your name) or probably require input from your system administrator (for example, your mail server address). Either way, we can't be of much help here.

Composer

Composer. Aha! Now we're at the real heart of the matter, as shown in Figure 5-13. Author <u>N</u>ame is pretty obvious, huh? If it's not set correctly, don't worry — your name just won't be listed in Composer's memory as the person who wrote the document. Big deal.

Figure 5-13:
Setting external editors and autosave information are the most useful options on the Composer panel.

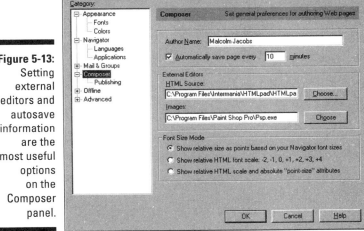

A seriously big deal is the <u>A</u>utomatically save page every <blank> <u>m</u>inutes. Without a doubt, put a checkmark next to this option. It's the only thing that will save your bacon when your computer crashes, the cat bumps the outlet and knocks the plug out, or your next door neighbor accidentally miswires his garage and shorts out the neighborhood. How frequently should the page be automatically saved? It depends on how much work you're willing to lose. If you're willing to lose 30 minutes of work, set it to 30 minutes. If only 15, set to 15. Personally, we have it set to about 5 minutes.

The External Editors settings let you specify external text editors and image editors. Sometimes Composer just isn't the right tool for the job — obviously, if you're editing graphics, it's not the right tool. Also, when you're adding JavaScript to a page or working on frames, you really need to use a text editor or supplemental, code-based HTML editor. By setting your preference in this dialog box, you can summon the "correct" editor directly from Composer and work much more efficiently.

Particularly when you're using JavaScript, having an HTML editor set up will help tremendously. Composer isn't the ideal tool for JavaScript development, unless you're using another editor for the fancy stuff.

If you want to specify which HTML editor Composer should summon, use these jiffy-quick steps:

1. **Click the Choose button next to HTML Source.**
2. **Browse through your computer to select a text editor or a code-based HTML editor.**
3. **Click Open.**

We generally recommend a plain text editor like Notepad, SimpleText, or pico, but also sometimes you can use a "light" HTML editor like BBEdit or HTMLPad (both of which are on the CD that comes with this book).

To specify which image-editing program Composer should summon, use these steps:

1. **Click the Choose button next to Images.**
2. **Choose an image editor.**
3. **Click Open.**

We recommend Paint Shop Pro if you're a Windows type or Graphic Converter if you're on a Mac (again, both are on the CD).

To find your programs, browse to the desktop or top level of your computer, and then look for the icons that represent the program you want to choose.

Finally, you have three choices for "Font Size Mode." Because there's no easy way to relate a specific font size from the world of paper documentation to online use, you can choose either the traditional use, the HTML font scale use (which is handy if you spend any time editing plain HTML code), or a combo choice.

The one subcategory under Composer is *Publishing*. The Links and images choices at the top of the panel (see Figure 5-14) let you tell Composer to make your life easier. For example, by automatically adjusting all local (on the same computer as the page) links, Composer tries to keep your links functional even as you move pages to the server computer. Also, keeping images with the pages makes it easier to maintain and upload your Web pages because the images stay right there with everything else, so you don't have to go track them down to get the page uploaded properly. You could do all of this stuff yourself, but there's no reason to.

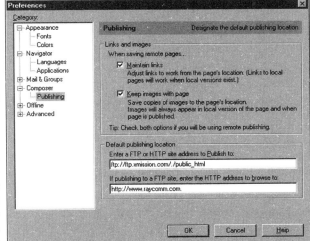

Figure 5-14:
Setting
publishing
options
can make
Composer's
publishing
feature
invaluable.

The bottom of the panel — Default publishing location — specifies where you will usually be uploading your documents to and what address you will enter in a browser to view those documents. Setting this option makes it easier to publish your documents. We recommend ironing the bugs out of your publishing process first and then transferring the Publish to information and the Browse to information from the Publish dialog box to these fields when everything works fine.

Even if you will be using multiple locations to publish your documents, if you set the most common one for your default location, you'll be able to save yourself some typing time and wear and tear on the fingers.

Offline

The *Offline* category doesn't offer much that will help you — the Offline/Online work environment tends to be more confusing and frustrating than anything else from our perspective. We leave O̲nline work mode set, even if we're not working online.

Advanced

Advanced lets you control some of the features that primarily affect Navigator. To use all of the goodies in this book, you need to make sure that at least Automatically load i̲mages, Enable J̲ava, Enable JavaScr̲ipt, and Enable style sheets are selected. Autoinstall will allow Communicator to automatically download and install software updates over the Internet — your call on this one. Send e-mail address as anonymous FTP password is often required to get information from FTP file archives on the Internet, but you can choose to check it or not, depending on whether you want your e-mail address sent over the Net for that purpose. We usually just check it.

The cookies choices don't provide for an afternoon snack. *Cookies* are used by fairly sophisticated Web sites to track information about you. When you visit the site, cookies put information about your preferences at that site on *your* computer, and then check out that cookie each time you return to the site. Additionally, the cookies can be sent back to the server that placed them, or they can be sent to other servers on the Internet. Whether cookies are worth their weight in privacy loss is your call, but we usually either Disable cookies or choose Warn me. Unless most of your Web surfing is on commercial and reputable sites or within an intranet, Accept all cookies isn't a good option.

When you're completely through setting your preferences — at least for now — click OK. Click Cancel to throw away your changes and revert to the way things were when you opened the Preferences dialog box.

Chapter 6

Applying Common Formatting

- -

In This Chapter

▶ Taking the grand tour of formatting options

▶ Applying paragraph formatting

▶ Applying character-level formatting

▶ Applying some page-level formatting

- -

*T*his chapter gives you an overview of the formatting options Composer offers and shows you how to effectively apply and use formatting. After all, you have so many different things you can do but only so much space to work with. You need to make the most of what you have. (Is that profound, or what!? Better go write that down. . . .)

The Formatting Options Grand Tour

A great way to figure out all that Composer enables you to do is to take the formatting options grand tour. Right this way, please. No pushing, no shoving, no talking, and . . . hey . . . no making faces at us!

Composer lets you do all sorts of cool formatting, all of which breaks down into two types:

- ✔ **Paragraph-level formatting:** Includes choices for headings, paragraphs, lists, and alignment

- ✔ **Character-level formatting:** Includes choices for individual letters, such as colors, fonts, italics, boldface, and so on.

To get an overview of these formatting options, take a look at the Character Properties dialog box, accessed by doing one of the following in Composer:

- ✔ Select Format⇨Character Properties.
- ✔ Right-click on a word or object, and then select Character Properties or Paragraph/List Properties from the resulting pop-up menu.

  Click once on a word or object, and press Alt+Enter.

The Character Properties dialog box contains three tabs: Character, Link, and Paragraph. For text and paragraph formatting purposes, you use the Character and Paragraph tabs.

The Character tab, shown as selected in Figure 6-1, provides you with formatting options for fonts, colors, sizes, and styles. To use these options, click the appropriate down-arrow and choose from the resulting drop-down list, or place a check mark in checkboxes and then click OK.

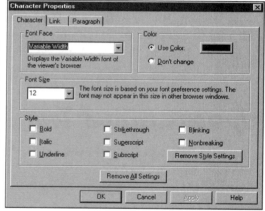

Figure 6-1:
The Character Properties dialog box includes scads of character formatting options.

The Paragraph tab, shown as selected in Figure 6-2, provides you with the formatting options for paragraphs, lists, and alignment. To use these options, click the appropriate down-arrow and choose from the resulting drop-down list, or click the radio buttons to select alignment options and then Click OK.

The Character Properties dialog box is the central clearinghouse for formatting options. Generally speaking, if it ain't here, it ain't available. A word of caution about formatting in particular and HTML in general: Applying specific formatting — typefaces, indents, colors, and so on — is a little chancy. The formatting options visible to your readers depend greatly on the Web browsers they are using and how their computers are configured.

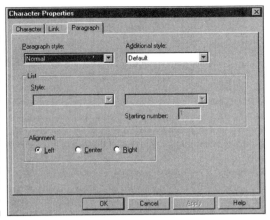

Figure 6-2:
The
Character
Properties
dialog box
also
includes
scads of
paragraph
formatting
options.

For example, specifying (or requiring) precise formatting is sort of like going to a fast food restaurant and ordering a super-combo-value meal (or whatever they're called these days). Each super-combo-value meal comes with certain food items, a sandwich, a potato, a soda, and maybe a mystery sauce. If you order super-combo-value meal #27 at one restaurant, you may get a cold fish sandwich, greasy fries, watered-down soda, and mayonnaise. On the other hand, if you order the super-combo-value meal #27 at another restaurant, you may get a cheeseburger, potato cake, milk shake, and barbecue sauce. Nonetheless, you order meal #27, and you get the included foods, all within one package. If you're satisfied with a sandwich, potato product, drink, and optional sauce, you're fine. However, if it's really important to you to have a Giant O'Burger, Huge-ie Fries, and a brand-name cola, you might be disappointed.

HTML formats are sort of like a super-combo-value meal; they include general characteristics of size (bigger or smaller) and optionally — depending on the browser — information about font type, a particular font size, and perhaps an emphasis such as bold or italic. Specifics may or may not happen, depending on the browser and computer. Generalities should be fine.

Applying Paragraph Formatting

Using paragraph formats, you can apply various formats to a large chunk of information. For example, you can make a line of text into a heading, create a regular paragraph, create lists, change alignment, and indent stuff. The following section shows you how to include paragraph formatting in your Web pages.

Creating headings

Headings play sort of a Howard Cosell role in a Web page — they announce the topics and information contained in the page. "This is Howard Cosell speaking to you from the 'I Can't Get Rid Of My Elmo' Web Site. Yes, ladies and gentlemen, today's page has just the information you're looking for — information about the dropping Elmo stock prices, recent Elmo sightings at garage sales, and even a 'Stop That Awful Giggling, Elmo' prize drawing! And the crowd goes wild! Now for an instant replay, just hit that Reload button, folks!"

Actually, headings aren't usually as wordy as Howard Cosell, but if you develop them right, they can be just as informative. The purpose of headings is to announce the topic(s) provided in the Web page. A good heading is *informative* — that is, it summarizes in a few words what the information is about. Each time the topic changes, you include a new heading.

Figure 6-3 shows three very informative headings.

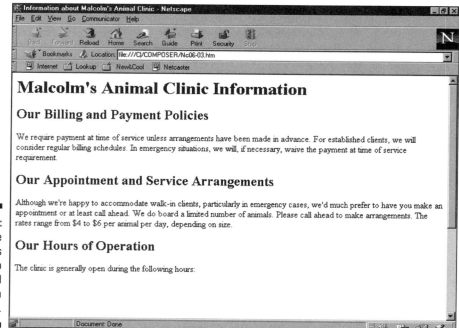

Figure 6-3:
Informative headings help readers find information quickly.

Web page headings come in six levels, each easily created in Composer:

1. **Select the word or words you use as a heading.**

2. **Go to Format⟹Heading.**

3. **Choose a heading level from the resulting pop-up menu, shown in Figure 6-4.**

   What do these numbers mean? The numbers represent heading levels: 1 stands for a first-level heading, which is the largest and most bold; 2 stands for a second-level heading, which is somewhat smaller and less bold; 3 stands for a third-level heading, and so on, through 6.

4. **Stand in awe of the heading you just created.**

Figure 6-4: Choose a number — any number — come on, give it a shot!

You can also create headings using the paragraph formatting drop-down list. Just select the text you want to use as a heading, click the drop-down arrow, and then choose the heading level you want.

Creating paragraphs

Paragraphs have taken on a whole new identity! They are no longer limited to something you write under great duress for your class report, employee evaluations, or bad-news business letters. They're no longer dictated into a microphone, only to be transcribed into a document that nobody reads. And, best of all, they're no longer hard to compose and make "look right" on the page.

Composer offers you six different paragraph formats that you can use as a pretty reliable way of presenting information. These paragraph formats give you preformatted ways of presenting information, varying from a standard line-by-line format to an address format to a dictionary definition-type format. Figure 6-5 shows you three common paragraph formats: Normal, Block Quote, and Formatted.

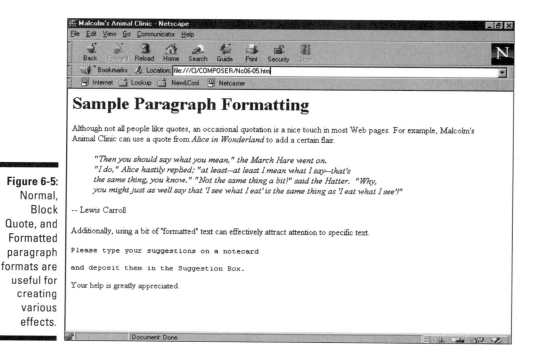

Figure 6-5:
Normal,
Block
Quote, and
Formatted
paragraph
formats are
useful for
creating
various
effects.

For the most part, you use the Normal paragraph format, which is the default for text that you enter in Composer. To apply one of the other paragraph formats, use these quick steps:

1. **Select the text you want to format.**

2. **Go to Format⇨Paragraph.**

3. **Choose a paragraph format from the resulting pop-up menu, shown in Figure 6-6.**

   • **Normal:** Provides default paragraph text that is used for body text in a Web page.

   • **Address:** Creates italicized text that is used for providing contact information.

   • **Formatted:** Gives you a monospace font (like this) that's good for showing programming code and the like.

   • **Block Quote:** Indents text from both margins just as you once did with extended quotes in English class.

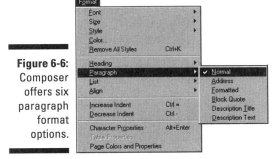

Figure 6-6:
Composer
offers six
paragraph
format
options.

- **Description Title:** Provides a format used for a term preceding a definition — as in a glossary term. Used in description lists.

- **Description Text:** Provides the format for a term definition — used immediately after the description title. Used in description lists.

4. Take a look at your newly-formatted paragraph!

You can also apply most of these formats (in addition to several others) using the paragraph formatting drop-down list. All you do is select the text you want to format, click the drop-down arrow, and then choose the paragraph format you want. For some reason, only five of these paragraph formats are available from the drop-down menu (the Block Quote format is missing). However, as a stand-in, you get List Item. Pretty mysterious changes going on, if you ask us.

Creating lists

A *list* is just a way of formatting information into a single column, easy-to-read format. Using lists, you can provide your readers with procedural information as well as information that might otherwise be buried in a paragraph. Figure 6-7 shows instructions formatted as a paragraph and as a numbered list. We bet you find the list easier to read, too.

Creating lists using Composer is a cinch. Here's how:

1. Type list items on separate lines.

2. Select all list items.

3. Go to Format⇨List

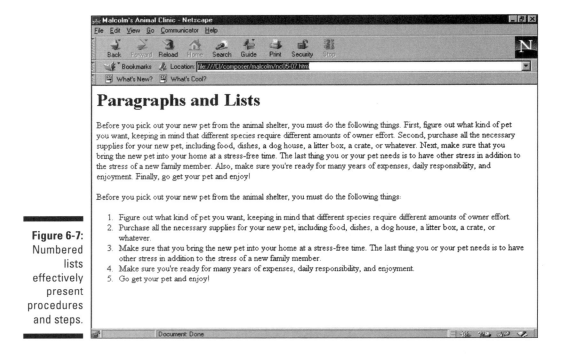

Figure 6-7:
Numbered
lists
effectively
present
procedures
and steps.

4. Choose a list type from the resulting pop-up menu, shown in Figure 6-8.

- **None:** Use to remove list formatting.

- **Bulleted:** Use to provide a nonsequential list with bullets preceding each item.

- **Numbered:** Use to provide a sequential list with numbers preceding each item. (Actually, you get numbers in a browser, but only # symbols in Composer.)

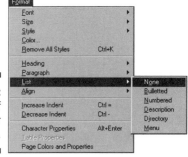

Figure 6-8:
A listing of
Composer
lists.

- **Description:** Use to provide a multilevel list with terms and their descriptions, as in a glossary. Use in conjunction with description title and description text paragraph.

  - *Note:* There are two other list types, Directory and Menu, but you'll likely have little use for them.

5. Take a look at the really cool list!

You can create bulleted and numbered lists using the Bulleted list and Numbered list buttons on the Toolbar. Just type your list items, select all items, and click the appropriate list button.

A numbered list will show up in Composer with # in place of the real numbers. Don't worry — the numbers will appear in the browser without problems.

Modifying lists

If you're feeling really creative, you can tweak the list formatting to provide different bullet types or different numbering schemes. After you apply the list formatting of your choice, use these nifty steps:

1. **Go to the Character Properties dialog box (go to Format⇨Character Properties, press Alt+Enter, or right-click within the list), and choose Paragraph/List Properties.**

2. **Select the Paragraph tab, if necessary, as shown in Figure 6-9.**

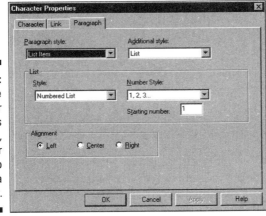

Figure 6-9: The Character Properties dialog box, ready for you to format a list.

3. Select List Style from the list (ahem) of available choices.

- None
- Bulleted
- Numbered
- Description
- Directory (rarely used, very similar to Bullet)
- Menu (rarely used, very similar to Bullet)

4. If you selected a bulleted list, choose the Bullet Style.

- **Automatic:** Creates solid circle, square, and open circle, depending on the level of information. For example, a first-level list will have a solid circle, whereas sublists will use a square.
- **Solid Circle (default):** Often called disk.
- **Open Circle:** Creates an unfilled circle.
- **Solid Square:** Creates a filled square.

5. If you selected a numbered list, choose the Number Style.

- **Automatic (default):** Creates a list with Arabic numerals.
- **1, 2, 3...:** Creates a list with Arabic numerals. (Yes, this option is just like the default, but it's useful when changing list numbers back to Arabic numerals from a different format choice.)
- **I, II, III...:** Creates a list with uppercase Roman numerals.
- **i, ii, iii...:** Creates a list with lowercase Roman numerals.
- **A, B, C...:** Creates a list with capital letters.
- **a, b, c...:** Creates a list with lowercase letters.

6. If you selected a numbered list, you can also choose the Starting number for the sequence.

Regardless of the number style, you must enter the Starting number as a number. For example, if you're starting with an E, you use 5 in the starting number field.

7. Finally, choose the Alignment for the list.

Center and Right both look pretty dorky with lists. We strongly recommend leaving Left as the choice.

Read on for a couple of list tips:

✔ Both <u>M</u>enu and D<u>i</u>rectory are rarely used in HTML documents. Also, they don't offer the breadth of choices that regular bulleted lists do. We recommend sticking with regular bulleted lists.

✔ You can create a multilevel bulleted list — bullets within bullets. Start by applying the bullet format to the whole set of items. Highlight and indent (with the Indent button on the Formatting toolbar) the bullets destined for the second level and then, if you want, use the steps in this section to change the bullet style for the secondary list.

Changing alignment

Alignment refers to where paragraphs, headings, tables, graphics, and so on appear on a page. By default, browsers display these elements using left-alignment, meaning that they appear along the left side of the page. However, you can also specify that these elements appear in the center or along the right side of the page.

Having this flexibility to use center and right alignment allows you to be a little more creative in designing your Web pages. Take a look at Figure 6-10, which shows elements that are left-, center-, and right-aligned.

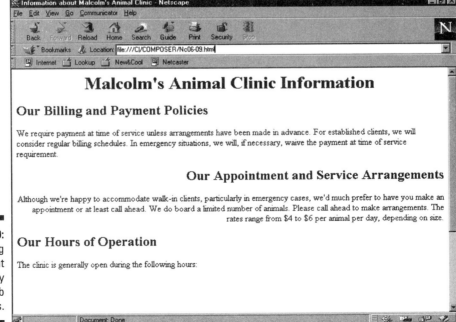

Figure 6-10: Changing alignment adds variety to your Web pages.

Here's the procedure for applying left-, center-, and right-alignment:

1. **Select the text or element.**

2. **Go to Format➪Align, or click the Align button from the right end of the Formatting toolbar.**

3. **Choose either Left, Center, or Right from the resulting pop-up menu.**

   You have text choices if you choose the menu options or graphical choices if you click the Align button.

4. **Take a look at the new alignment.**

You can also use the keyboard shortcuts of Ctrl+L (left), Ctrl+R (right), or Ctrl+E (center). Just select the item you want to realign, and then press the key combination of your choice.

Indenting stuff

As though all these cool paragraph formatting options aren't enough, you can also *indent* sections of text — that is, move text away from the left margin. Indenting text is handy for setting off or drawing attention. Figure 6-11 shows how indenting a paragraph draws attention to it.

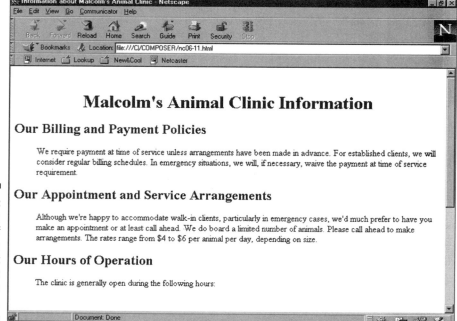

Figure 6-11: Indenting text sets off information so that it stands out on the page.

To indent text (move to the right):

1. **Select the text you want to indent.**

 2. **Go to Format⇨Increase Indent and click the Indent button from the Formatting toolbar, or press Ctrl+=.**

3. **Repeat Step 2 until you've indented the text as much as you want.**

   You can *scoot* text all the way over to the right side, if you want.

To decrease the indent (move back to the left):

1. **Select the text.**

 2. **Go to Format⇨Decrease Indent and click the Decrease Indent button from the Formatting toolbar, or press Ctrl+-.**

3. **Repeat Step 2 until you decrease the indent as much as you want.**

Here are a couple more notes about indenting text:

✔ You can't decrease the indent of text that hasn't been indented. That is, you can't move text beyond the left margin.

✔ You can also indent images — just select the image and follow the steps in this section. See Chapter 10 for more information about images.

Applying Character Formatting

In addition to using paragraph formatting features, you can also use *character formatting*, which applies formatting to individual letters and words. In particular, you can add different kinds of emphasis and change font styles, sizes, and colors. The following sections show you how to apply these formatting options.

Some mighty interesting information

The HTML tags that Netscape uses to indent text are, strictly speaking, not designed to signify indented text — that is, these tags are not officially part of the "correct" HTML code. It's like using a kitchen knife to pry open a peanut butter jar. A lot of times, it works just fine, but once in a while, you come across a jar that you can't open with the peanut butter knife.

Indent tags are similar. They work just fine in most browsers; however, they don't work at all in others.

Actually no HTML tag lets you indent text, unless you're using Style Sheets, which allow you to indent text properly for the browsers that support them (only the newest browsers do).

Emphasizing text

You can change the appearance, significance, and emphasis of text to better communicate the importance (or unimportance) of information. By adding emphases to only a few words here and there, you call attention to words that you want your readers to notice.

The point is to emphasize, not overemphasize. To avoid overemphasizing, keep the following in mind:

- ✔ Use only one or two kinds of emphasis in your pages — to keep the text from becoming a **real** *eye* <u>sore</u>.

- ✔ Use emphases sparingly — on words that really do need to stand out; otherwise nothing stands out.

We can't `<blink>overemphasize</blink>` these points enough.

To apply emphases to text, try these steps:

1. Select the word or words you want to emphasize.

2. Go to Format⇨Style.

3. Choose a style from the resulting pop-up menu, shown in Figure 6-12.

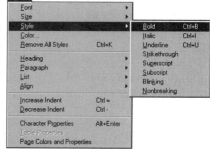

Figure 6-12: Composer's eight style choices, screaming "pick me, pick me!"

- • **Bold:** Makes the text appear in **boldface**. You can also use Ctrl+B.

- • **Italic:** Makes the text appear in *italics*. You can also use Ctrl+I.

- • **Underline:** Makes the text appear <u>underlined</u>. You can also use Ctrl+U.

- • **Strikethrough:** Makes the text show up like ~~this~~.

- **Superscript:** Makes the text superscript, for example, ^{2}.

- **Subscript:** Makes the text subscript, for example, $_2$.

- **Blinking:** Makes the text blink (flash on and off, which by the way, only does so in Navigator, not Composer).

- **Nonbreaking:** Prevents line breaks within text.

You can also apply and remove four of the more common emphases by using the button bar:

✔ Click the **Bold** button to apply bold emphasis.

✔ Click the *Italics* button to apply italic emphasis.

✔ Click the <u>Underline</u> button to apply underline emphasis.

✔ Click the Clear all styles button to remove all of the emphases (or select Format⇨Remove all Styles or press Ctrl+K).

Changing fonts

By default, Composer and Navigator display text using an oldie-but-goodie font called Times New Roman for body text and Arial for heading text on Windows and using similar fonts called Times and Helvetica on Macintosh and UNIX. These fonts, though easy to read, are pretty standard and — well — pretty boring.

Using Composer, you can change the typeface to almost anything you want, but keep in mind that fonts that are available depend on your readers' computers and browsers. Your readers must have the particular fonts installed on their computers *and* use a browser that supports those fonts. If you include a fancy font and your readers don't have the font installed or don't have a browser that supports it, they'll see the closest approximation available or the default font.

So, if you're designing only for yourself, you can use any font on your system. If you're designing for a broader audience, however, fonts are optional and not central to your design. Depending on what you know about your readers' systems, configurations, browser options, and willingness and ability to go download new fonts so that your pages will look good, you can broaden your choices. Table 6-1 lists fonts available in Navigator and Windows as well as those available for download through Microsoft.

Table 6-1	Fonts Available in Navigator and by Download from Microsoft	
For Navigator (version 4.0 or newer)	*Standard on Windows (Mac users can download these from the Microsoft Web site:* `http://www.microsoft.com`*)*	*Available for Windows & Mac (download from* `http://www.microsoft.com`*)*
serif	Arial	Trebuchet MS
sans-serif	Times New Roman	Georgia
cursive	Courier New	Verdana
monospace		Comic Sans MS
fantasy		Impact
		Arial Black

Figure 6-13 shows you what a couple of fonts (Comic Sans MS for headings and Trebuchet MS for text) look like.

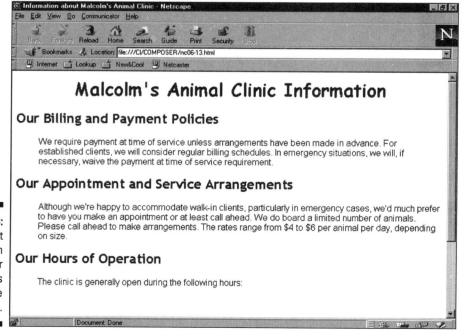

Figure 6-13: Different fonts can make your documents more interesting.

If you decide to change fonts, use this quick process:

1. **Select the text you want to change.**

2. **Go to Format⇨Font.**

3. **Choose a new font from the resulting pop-up menu, or select Other for a broader selection.**

   If you want, you can also just select a typeface from the Font drop-down list on the Formatting toolbar.

   Variable Width and Fixed Width indicate only that the characters in a typeface take up varying amounts of space (like in this book) or the same amount of space (like on a typewriter . . . remember those?). These options don't specify anything about the face beyond those characteristics, so to speak.

4. **If you select Other, you see a Font dialog box, like the one in Figure 6-14.**

5. **Select the Font, Font style, and Size from the dialog box.**

   The Script menu allows you to select other character sets — for example, for Greek letters. The Script menu is only available for some fonts.

6. **Click OK when you finish.**

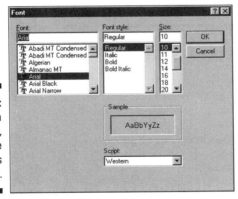

Figure 6-14:
Choose a
font, style,
and size
from this
dialog box.

Changing font size

Changing font size is a cinch. As with the rest of this stuff, it's not precise — even if you choose 18-point text in Composer, the HTML code will just specify to make the text somewhat larger than normal. Just follow these quick steps:

1. **Select the text you want to change.**

2. **Go to Format⇨Size.**

3. **Choose a new font size from the resulting pop-up menu, shown in Figure 6-15.**

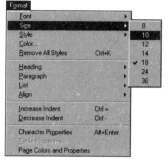

Figure 6-15: Choose a font size from this pop-up menu.

4. **Ooooo and ahhhhh very loudly.**

You can also use the Font Size drop-down list to change font sizes. Just select the text, click the Font Size down-arrow, and then choose a size from the drop-down list.

And the runner-up is . . .

If you don't want to leave font substitution to chance, you can specify first, second, and additional choices. You must do all of this in the HTML source code, so go to Edit⇨HTML Source. For example, say that you want to use Gill Sans if it's available, Arial as a second choice (good for Windows), and Helvetica (a good safe Macintosh and UNIX choice) as a third choice. Just find the line of code that looks like

```
<FONT FACE="Arial">Your text
    here</FONT>.
```

Add your other choices to the FACE= attribute in your preferred order. In this example, you might have:

```
<FONT FACE="Gill Sans, Arial,
    Helvetica">Your text here
        </FONT>.
```

Save your document and start calling friends with different computers to have them try it out. However, there's nothing wrong with just letting the computer take care of it.

Changing font color

While Web surfing, you may notice several different text colors in Web pages — one color for regular text, another color for links, another color for visited links, and (if you look closely) yet another color for the link as you're clicking on it. All these different colors help readers see the difference between regular text and link text, and they also help readers see the difference between links they've visited and ones they haven't. (If you or your readers are using Microsoft Internet Explorer 4.0 for your Web surfing, you'll notice that hypertext links do not appear in different colors. Sigh.)

For more information about links, check out Chapter 8.

One thing to keep in mind before you get too carried away changing text color is that any text color you choose — whether it be for regular text or link text or whatever — needs to contrast adequately with the background colors, patterns, or images you use. In Web pages, it's highly important that the text show up against any background you use; otherwise, readers will not be able to see the text, and, more important, they will not take the time to try to read it.

To change text colors throughout the whole document, just take a quick trip to the Page Properties dialog box, accessed by going to Format⇨Page Colors and Properties and clicking the Colors and Background tab. The Page Properties dialog box is shown in Figure 6-16.

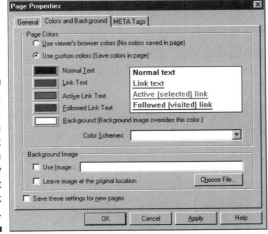

Figure 6-16:
The Page Properties dialog box lets you easily change text and link colors.

Just follow these quick steps:

1. **Access the Page Properties dialog box (go to Format⇨Page Colors and Properties).**

2. **Click the Colors and Background tab if it's not already on top.**

3. **Verify that Use custom colors is selected so that your selections will show up in the document.**

4. **Select a color scheme from the Color Schemes drop-down menu, shown in Figure 6-17.**

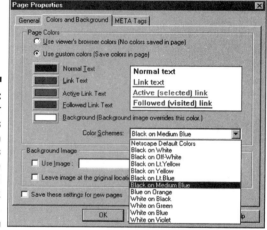

Figure 6-17: The Color Schemes drop-down menu lets you choose prematched text and link colors.

5. **If you want to manually specify the colors, select the type of text you want to change by clicking one of the following buttons:**

   • **Normal Text:** Changes the color of regular body text.

   • **Link Text:** Changes the color of links that have not been visited.

   • **Active Link Text:** Changes the color of links as they're being clicked on.

   • **Followed Link Text:** Changes the color of links that have been visited.

   • **Background:** Changes the color of the document background that have been visited.

   After clicking one of these buttons, the color dialog box appears, as shown in Figure 6-18.

Figure 6-18:
The color
dialog box
lets you
choose
great text
and link
colors.

If you don't see a color you like, click <u>O</u>ther and create a shade of your own. Just click the Color Finder tool (crosshairs) and drag it around in the color window. And you can even adjust color depth by using the Depth spectrum at the right of the dialog box. Just click (and hold) the little triangle and move it up or down. Click <u>A</u>dd to Custom Colors to add your color to the <u>C</u>ustom colors palette. Click OK to close the Color dialog box.

6. **Click OK.**

7. **Select other types of text you want to recolor by clicking on the appropriate button, selecting a color in the Color dialog box, and clicking OK.**

   You can also change the background color while you're at it, just to make sure that the text and background colors contrast adequately.

   If you've created a number of custom colors, you might choose Save these settings for <u>n</u>ew pages.

8. **Click OK in the Page Properties dialog box when you're done, or just click <u>A</u>pply to see your settings take effect and leave the dialog box open for more tweaking.**

9. **Say "Zowie!" look at the new colors!**

Here are some bright notes about changing text colors:

✔ Unless you're pretty good with colors, consider using the premanufactured color schemes that coordinate text and link colors. In the Page Properties dialog box (Colors and Background tab), just click the down-arrow under Color <u>S</u>chemes and choose a scheme that you like. The color scheme sample shows up in the text window. Click OK when you're done.

✔ You can easily add spot color to text in your Web pages by selecting the word or words, going to F<u>o</u>rmat⇨<u>C</u>olor, and choosing a color from the color dialog box.

✔ You can use the Color drop-down menu on the Button Bar or the Character Properties dialog box (go to Format⇨Character Properties or press Alt+Enter) to apply some of the more common colors to text. These options are actually pretty handy for applying colors because you see not only the color but also the color name.

✔ You can reapply default colors by selecting text and going to Format⇨Default Color.

Don't be a *dithering* idiot

What's dithering? Simply put, *dithering* is what happens when the computer is told to display more colors than it can — the colors end up looking splotchy or spotty.

If your computer is set to display millions of colors (not unlikely), you can easily choose a color that will not display properly on other people's computers. For example, if someone's computer is set to 256 colors, any color that falls between #257 and "millions" will not display properly. The computer set to 256 colors tries to combine and blend those 256 colors for an approximate version of the real color. (Think of trying to make a gourmet meal but starting with only pepper, salt, sage, and Cajun spice blend. Your creative substitution still will not capture the nuances of French sauces, right?)

How to avoid being a dithering idiot? Try one of these ways:

✔ Set your computer to 256 colors — at least while you're choosing colors. By choosing from a 256-color palette, you can help ensure that a wider portion of your readers' browsers can display the colors properly.

✔ Use the Netscape standard colors rather than the color finder to specify spectacular colors that aren't good on all browsers.

✔ Specify colors by using RGB (red, green, blue) numbers. You can enter specific RGB numbers using the Colors dialog box but be sure to use combinations of only these numbers: 0, 51, 102, 153, 204, and 255. For example, 51 parts of red, 204 parts of blue, and 0 parts of green. Or whatever. Using these numbers helps ensure that your colors will display properly.

For more information about RGB numbers, check out Chapter 10.

Chapter 7

Including Tables and Other Cool Stuff

● ●

In This Chapter

▶ Creating tables

▶ Formatting tables to make them look *mmm-mmm* good

▶ Making horizontal lines

▶ Making nonbreaking spaces

● ●

*I*ncluding tables and other cool stuff probably isn't an ideal title. Heck, if you haven't already read the chapter, you might not even know that tables are cool stuff. However, take our word for it. They are. This chapter could also be subtitled "Layout and Design for HTML Documents 101," but it's not. Read on to see just how tables aren't just for breakfast anymore.

Including Tables

"Yes, hello. I'd like to reserve a table for 56, please. Yes, 56. That's right. The party name? Ummm. We're the Cells. Uh-huh, that's right, C-E-L-L-S, and we'd all like to sit at the same table."

A *table* is just a grid of rows and columns — kind of like the tic-tac-toe grid you drew as a kid, or, okay, maybe at recent staff meetings. These rows and columns intersect to form *cells*, which are the places where you include information. Not only can you control how the overall table appears, but you can also control how individual rows, columns, and cells appear.

Take a look at Figure 7-1, which shows a simple table in the fictitious Malcolm's Animal Clinic Web site.

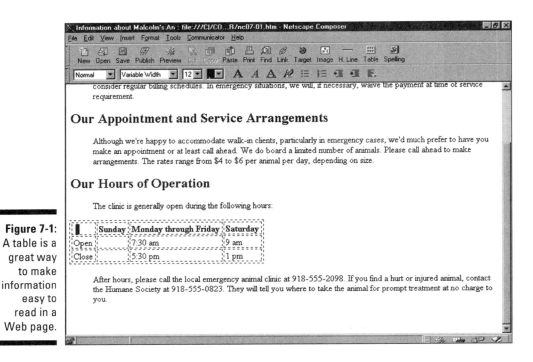

Figure 7-1:
A table is a
great way
to make
information
easy to
read in a
Web page.

Tables are useful in Web pages in several ways:

- ✔ **Tables can help readers find complex or detailed information quickly.** If you want to list schedules, prices, or output of two variables, you can create a table that readers can easily scan for the information.

- ✔ **Tables can replace long lists.** If you have lots of information that looks good in a list, try putting that information in a table to create a two- or three-column list.

- ✔ **Tables can help you design with text.** You can create *side headings*, which are headings that appear next to the related text, rather than above it.

- ✔ **Tables can help you combine graphics and text into cool layouts.** You can place a graphic next to a related paragraph of text so that readers can get the full effect in one screen. (Yes, you can accomplish the same thing with alignment tags, but you have more control when you use a table.)

Creating a basic table

Composer makes it hugely easy for you to include tables in your Web pages. All you have to do is use the New Table Properties dialog box, accessed by doing the following:

1. **Go to Insert⇨Table, and choose Table from the resulting pop-up menu.**

2. **Click the Insert Table button.**

   The New Table Properties dialog box appears, as shown in Figure 7-2.

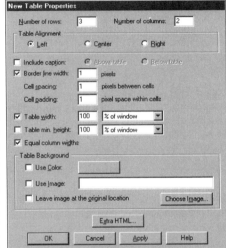

Figure 7-2:
The New
Table
Properties
dialog box
will get your
cells seated
properly.

To create a basic table, all you do is specify the Number of rows and the Number of columns you want. Just use these steps:

1. **Go to the New Table Properties dialog box by following the preceding two steps or by clicking the Insert Table button.**

2. **Specify how many rows you want in the Number of rows text field.**

3. **Specify how many columns you want in the Number of columns text field.**

   Yes, there are a bazillion more options, and we'll cover all of them in the context of formatting your table. For now, we'll stick to the basics.

4. **Click OK.**

   TaDaaaaaa!

Here are some additional notes to sit at the table and think about:

- ✔ **You're not stuck with the table you create.** You can easily modify it by adding or deleting rows and columns. For example, if you want to add a row to the table, click in the row above where you want to insert the row, right-click your mouse, and then choose Insert⇨Row from the resulting pop-up menu. Or you can add a column by clicking in the column to the left of where you want to insert a new one, right-click your mouse, and then choose Insert⇨Column from the resulting pop-up menu. To delete a row or column, just select the row or column, right-click your mouse, and then choose Delete⇨Row or Delete⇨Column.

  If you're a Mac user, just click and hold your mouse where the instructions say to right-click.

- ✔ **You can also insert or delete individual cells.** To insert a cell, click in the cell to the left of where you want to insert one, right-click your mouse, and then choose Insert⇨Cell. To delete a cell, click in the cell you want to delete, right-click your mouse, and then choose Delete⇨Cell.

- ✔ **Inserting or deleting larger portions of the table is equally straightforward.** To delete rows, columns, or the whole table, right-click, choose Delete, and then choose Table, Row, Column, or Cell. Likewise, to insert en masse, right-click, choose Insert, and then choose Table, Row, Column, or Cell.

- ✔ **If you're feeling really creative, you can insert tables inside tables.** Just click in the cell in which you want to insert a new table, access the New Table Properties dialog box, and click the Insert Table button, or right-click in the existing table and choose Insert⇨Table.

That there table looks mighty fine

If you use tables for more than just presenting dry and boring tabular information (or even if you just want to jazz up that dry tabular information), you might be interested in knowing that you can change how tables look. For example, you can make the borders thicker or make them disappear completely. You can add space between *and* within cells. And you can even determine how wide the table is and where it appears on the page. And add colors and backgrounds. And more. Whew! Pretty neat, huh?

To make tables look *gooder* (or even more gooder), you use the Table Properties dialog box, accessed by clicking in an existing table, right-clicking your mouse (click and hold for you Mac-types), and choosing Table Properties from the resulting pop-up menu (or click in the table and go to Format⇨ Table Properties). The Table Properties dialog box is shown in Figure 7-3.

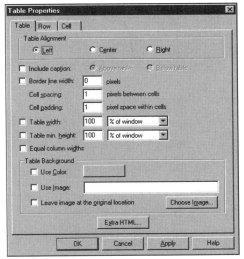

Figure 7-3:
The Table
Properties
dialog box's
Table tab
lets you
spiff up
your tables.

Notice that the Table Properties dialog box contains three tabs:

- ✔ **Table tab:** Lets you specify how the table looks as a whole, including borders, cell spacing and padding, table width and height, color, captions, and alignment.

- ✔ **Row tab:** Lets you specify text alignment and row color.

- ✔ **Cell tab:** Provides formatting options for individual cells, including cell span, alignment, width, and height.

As you set your tables, keep in mind that you can choose to apply formatting to the entire table, a single row, or only a single cell. The next several sections show you how to tweak your tables to make them look spiffy.

Don't confuse the New Table Properties dialog box with the Table Properties dialog box. You use the New Table Properties dialog box for developing new tables, and you use the Table Properties dialog box for modifying existing tables. You can specify cool formatting using either of these two dialog boxes.

Placing a table in that just-right spot

Figuring out just where to place a table in a Web page is much easier than placing your kitchen table (particularly if you're doing the lifting, eh?). By default, Composer places tables using left alignment, but you can easily change this alignment to either center or right. Figure 7-4 shows a fairly narrow table neatly moved to the center of the screen for your viewing enjoyment.

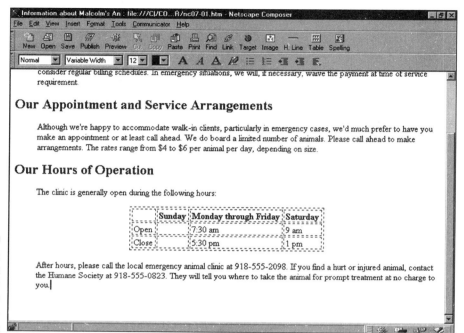

Figure 7-4:
A table
schooched
over to the
center.

1. **Click somewhere in the existing table.**

   You can change table alignment as you're creating a new table, too, using the New Table Properties dialog box.

2. **Go to the New Table Properties dialog box (right-click in the existing table, and choose T̲able Properties from the pop-up menu).**

   Make sure that the Table tab is on top. (Is that like putting a table top on your tab? Hmmm.)

3. **Under Table alignment, choose either C̲enter or R̲ight.**

   If you've already changed the alignment to C̲enter or R̲ight and you want to change it back to the default setting, just choose L̲eft.

4. **Click OK.**

Here are some extra legs to support your tables:

✔ If your table is set to a width of 100% of the window size, you won't see table alignment options take effect. See the next section to put your fat old table on a diet down to 50% of its former self.

✔ If you like the alignment options on the Table tab, you'll love the alignment options on the Row and Cell tabs. On the Row tab, you can set the horizontal alignment for all the cells in the row to Left, Center, or Right to shuffle the text around. You get the same options on the Cell tab to move the text within that cell.

✔ You can align the contents of your table rows and cells vertically as well. On the Row tab, you can choose to have the contents of the cells in the row aligned to the Top, Center, Bottom, or Baselines. On the Cell tab, you get the same choices, but just for that cell. By the way, the *baseline* is the bottom line of a letter — the letters in the word *letters* sit on the baseline, while *j g q* and *p* all hang below the baseline. No, for all practical purposes, there's very little difference between bottom and baseline.

✔ As you experiment with alignment options, remember to click Apply to force your changes to take effect while leaving the dialog box open.

Making tables wiiiiiide, skinny, short, or tall

If you create a table using default settings, Composer creates a table that spans the entire width of the computer screen and has a predetermined minimum height. Is this good or bad, you ask? Well, it's mostly good because these default settings guarantee that the entire table appears within the borders of the monitor. If a reader has a particularly small screen or low monitor resolution, the columns appear more squished than they do on a bigger screen or high resolution. The point is that the whole table appears on the screen.

But using this default setting can also be bad, particularly if your table has many columns or has a lot of information squished into the cells. For example, if a reader has a small monitor or a low resolution, the information might be squished so badly that it's impossible to read, not to mention being an eyesore.

Given the possibility that you might not want squished information, Composer allows you to specify the width of the table, as follows:

1. **Right-click within your table, and choose Table Properties or Format⇨Table Properties.**

2. **Make sure that the Table tab is on top, as in Figure 7-5.**

3. **If you want to set the minimum width of your table, put a check in the Table width checkbox.**

4. **Under Table width, specify the width in a percentage of the window width (default is 100% or all the way across) or in pixels.**

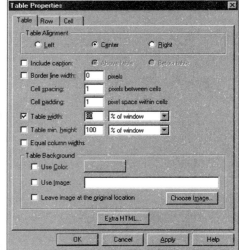

Figure 7-5:
The Table
Properties
dialog box's
Table tab
offers table
sizing
options.

Bear in mind, many readers will have screens that show only 640 pixels across, minus the scroll bars, and so on, yielding only about 600 pixels as a functional maximum. Of course, if you know that your readers will have mongo-big monitors at a high resolution, go wild.

In general, it's better to use percentages to ensure that your readers will see more or less what you want them to see.

5. If you want to set the minimum height for the table, put a check in the Table min. height checkbox.

In our opinion, you're not likely to want to specify a minimum height for your table. Because readers are used to scrolling up and down, just let the height fluctuate according to the content of the cells.

6. If necessary, set the minimum height for the table in terms of pixels or percentage of the available vertical space in the window.

7. Click Apply (to stay in the dialog box and keep tweaking) or OK (to apply and close the dialog box) and proceed.

That's it! Figure 7-6 shows the resulting table.

Here is another leg to stand on about table and size: If you choose to use tables as a layout tool, rather than just to present tabular information, you might set the width to 100% and the height to 100% to make sure (as sure as possible) that your layout works for all browsers.

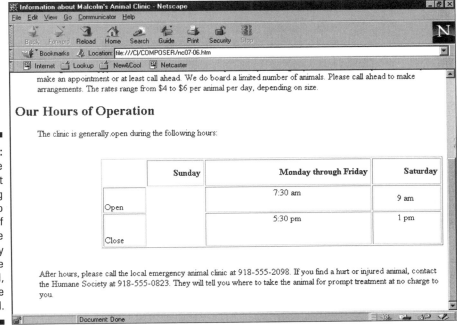

Figure 7-6:
Table
alignment
and sizing
taken to
extremes. If
this table
were any
more
aligned,
it'd be
maligned.

Captions that say, "Ehhhh, what's up, doc?"

A table *caption* is a quip of information that summarizes information within a table. Using captions with your tables is a way to help you announce what information the table includes and lets your readers decide at-a-glance if the table contains the information they need. No reason to make your readers wade through a table of information if they don't need to, right?

Composer lets you easily include table captions either above or below a table. Just use these steps:

1. **Click your mouse in the table in which you want to add a caption.**

   You can add captions to tables as you're creating them, too, using the New Table Properties dialog box.

2. **Right-click your mouse (or if you're a Mac user, just click and hold), and choose T̲able Properties from the resulting pop-up menu.**

3. **Make sure that the Table tab is on top.**

4. **Click your mouse in the checkbox next to I̲nclude caption.**

5. **Specify whether you want the caption to appear a̲bove or b̲elow the table.**

6. Click OK.

You see a dotted caption box above or below the table, depending on where you selected the caption to appear, as shown in Figure 7-7.

7. Click in the dotted caption box.

8. Type a table caption.

9. Click outside the caption box when you're done.

Here are a few captivating thoughts about captions:

- ✓ Composer displays all captions in dotted boxes to help you distinguish caption text from other text on the page. When you flip over to Navigator to view the page, the dotted boxes go away.

- ✓ Try to make your table captions as informative as possible to help readers get the gist of what's in the table without having to wade through it.

- ✓ Over-zealous captions can say in 1,000 words what a table can say in 10. Make your captions informative, but don't babble on and on. And on. Don't say the same thing again and again. Don't repeat yourself either.

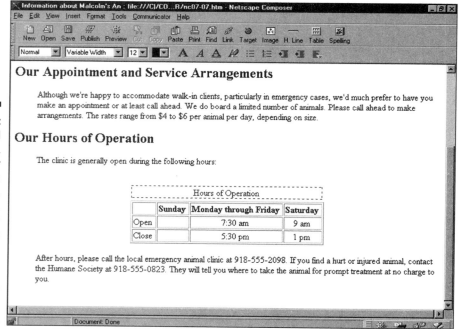

Figure 7-7:
The dotted caption box, ready for you to type "Ehhhh, what's up, Doc?," or perhaps something more prosaic like "Hours of Operation."

Teetering on the border

Table *borders* serve a couple of purposes. First, they act as a visual container for the information within them. Each piece of information is nestled within its own little pod. Second, they serve as a divider between rows and columns so that the information is (usually) more readable. (We say usually because borders in particularly large tables can often overshadow the information. In these cases, you might try removing all borders and see how that looks.)

Table borders in Navigator (as well as many other browsers) are displayed as *embossed* lines — that is, lines that appear to be raised slightly from the rest of the page. For special effects, you can increase the width of the outside table border, like this:

1. **Click somewhere in the existing table.**

   You can change the border width as you're creating a new table, too, using the New Table Properties dialog box.

2. **Go to the Table Properties dialog box (right-click in the existing table, and choose Table Properties from the pop-up menu).**

   Make sure that the Table tab is on top.

3. **Type a number (higher than 1, which is the default) in the Border line width text field.**

   The higher the number, the wider the border. Entering the number 0 removes the border.

4. **Click OK.**

   Isn't that cool? Figure 7-8 shows some sample borders.

Making room at the table

A great way to improve table readability and appearance is to increase cell spacing and cell padding. *Cell spacing* refers to the amount of space between individual cells. Think of cell spacing as adding an empty seat between people when they're sitting at the dinner table. By adding an empty seat or two, your guests can have plenty of room and don't have to bump elbows or play footsie (if they don't want to, that is). By increasing cell spacing, you provide more room between cells, which makes information easier to read because its not bumping elbows, knees, and footsies.

Cell padding refers to the amount of space between text in a cell and the surrounding cell border. Think of cell padding as spreading individual place settings so that each person gets a little more room. By adding extra room on the table, you can put the turkey, stuffing, deviled eggs, potatoes,

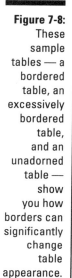

Figure 7-8:
These sample tables — a bordered table, an excessively bordered table, and an unadorned table — show you how borders can significantly change table appearance.

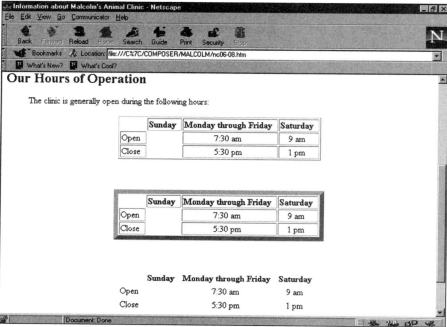

cranberries, Aunt Martha's Waldorf salad, gravy, and pumpkin pie on the table — with plenty of room for each dish. By increasing cell padding, you provide more room within cells, which also makes information easier to read because it's not all mooshed together.

Check out Figures 7-9 and 7-10, which show a crowded table and a table with ample room.

To increase cell spacing or cell padding, follow these steps:

1. **Click somewhere in the existing table.**

   You can change cell spacing and cell padding as you're creating a new table, too, using the New Table Properties dialog box.

2. **Go to the Table Properties dialog box (right-click in the existing table, and choose Table Properties from the pop-up menu).**

   Make sure that the Table tab is on top.

3. **Type a number (higher than 1, which is the default) in the Cell spacing or Cell padding text fields.**

   The higher the number, the more space you get.

4. **Click OK.**

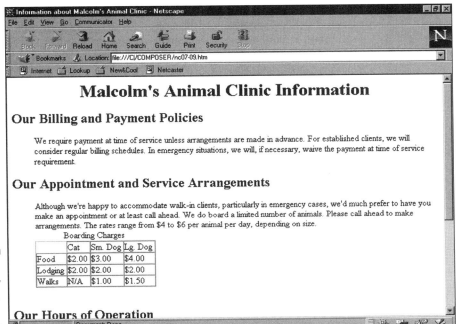

Figure 7-9:
A pretty
crowded
table!

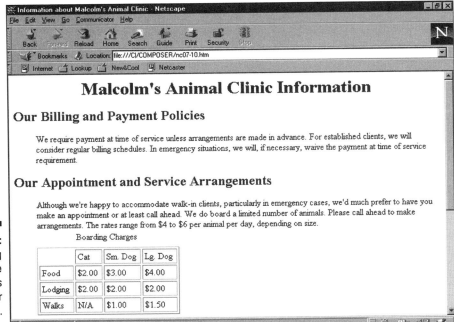

Figure 7-10:
Adding
room at the
table makes
it easier
to read.

Here's a note left on the table: You can increase cell spacing and cell padding even if you've removed the borders. The result is that you have increased blank space between the cells.

Adding a splash of color to tables

Adding color to your tables is a great way to make them stand out from the rest of the page. You can add color to the entire table, just like putting a colored tablecloth on your kitchen table. Or you can add color to individual rows and cells, sort of like putting placemats on the kitchen table. Unlike tablecloths and placemats, coloring tables won't help you keep spaghetti sauce or mustard off your Web page tables.

Figure 7-11 shows a table that has a few colored rows, intended to help readers more easily read the information. (Of course, you have to assume that the colored rows are really spectacular because you can see only shades of gray. Trust us; the color is marvelous.)

To add color to entire tables or to individual rows or cells, just use these steps:

1. Select the table, row, or cell you want to color.

You can add color to tables as you're creating them, too, using the New Table Properties dialog box.

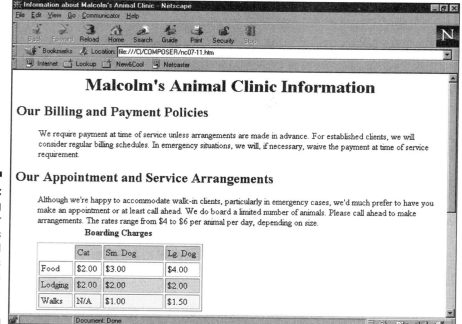

Figure 7-11: Adding color for emphasis looks cool and helps readers see the information.

2. **Right-click your mouse (if you're a Mac user, just click and hold), and choose Table Properties from the resulting pop-up menu.**

3. **Select the appropriate tab, either Table, Row, or Cell, depending on what you want to color.**

4. **Put a check beside Use Color in the appropriate background section (Table, Row, or Cell).**

5. **Choose a color from the offerings, or click Other Colors and choose a custom color from the Color dialog box, shown in Figure 7-12.**

   If you don't see a color you like, create a shade of your own. Just click the Color Finder tool and drag it around in the color window. And, you can even adjust color depth by using the Depth spectrum at the right of the dialog box. Just click (and hold) the little triangle and move it up or down. Click Add to Custom Colors to add your color to the Custom colors palette.

6. **Click OK.**

   Voilà!

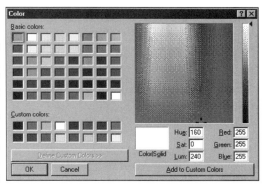

Here are a few table scraps for you to munch on:

✔ As with most formatting options, don't go overboard!

✔ A nice touch for many tables is to shade alternate rows lightly and choose no borders. Depending on the colors you choose, you can either pleasingly highlight information for ease of reading or remind everyone of that old green bar computer paper. (Did we just date ourselves?)

Adding background images to tables

In addition to the glory of choosing a background color for your table, you can (alternatively, actually) choose a background image. As with most of these options, you can set them at the table, row, or cell level.

1. **Click within the table, row, or cell you want to add a background graphic to.**

2. **To access the Table Properties dialog box, right-click your mouse (if you're a Mac user, just click and hold), and choose T̲able Properties from the resulting pop-up menu.**

   You can also go to F̲ormat⇨T̲able Properties to access the Table Properties dialog box.

3. **Click the appropriate tab — Table, Row, or Cell.**

4. **Click Choose I̲mage, and click on the appropriate image from the Choose Image File dialog box, as shown in Figure 7-13.**

5. **Put a check beside Use I̲mage, as shown in Figure 7-14.**

6. **Click A̲pply or OK, and survey the results.**

Figure 7-13:
The Choose Image File dialog box allows you to browse to the image file you want to use.

Imag-ine what other stuff might be said about background images in tables:

✔ Background images in tables do not necessarily appear in their entirety — if the cell is smaller than the image, you see only part of the image. If the image is essential — that is, not just a background — use the regular procedure outlined in Chapter 10 for inserting an image and put it in a table cell.

✔ Background images are tiled throughout the table, row, or cell. If the background image is 10 x 10 pixels in size and the cell is 100 x 100 pixels, 100 copies of the image appear in the cell.

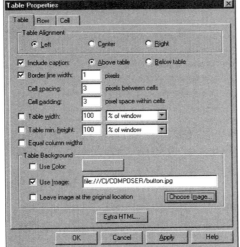

Figure 7-14:
Select Use
Image to
pick a
background
image.

✔ You probably do not want to select Leave image at the original location because it's going to be easier for you to put all the images together in the same folder, as Composer wants to do for you. Additionally, Composer occasionally gets confused and mucks up the path to the original document. Better to just let Composer move it for you. Stand back and watch.

Adjusting cell spans and cell format

Cells, as the smallest chunk of information within a table, also have some additional formatting options. Particularly, text styles and cell spans. Note that text styles are different from and in addition to the regular emphases like boldface and italics.

1. **Click within the cell or cells you want to format.**

2. **Right-click your mouse (if you're a Mac user, just click and hold) and choose Table Properties from the resulting pop-up menu, or go to Format⇨Table Properties.**

3. **Click the Cell tab.**

4. **Under Text style, choose Header style to indicate that the cell or cells are table headers.**

   Table headers are usually formatted to look bolder and more pronounced than the rest of the table, as shown in Figure 7-15.

   If you want the header style to apply to each cell in the row, as in this figure, you must apply the style individually to each cell.

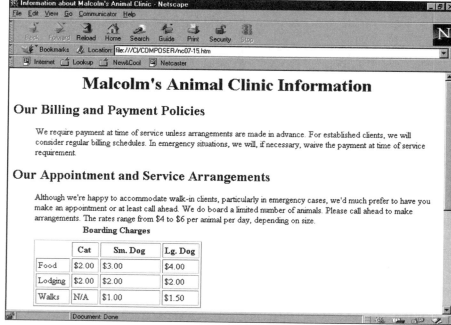

5. Also under Text style, choose Wrap text if the browser should wrap the text to multiple lines to improve the look of the whole table.

If you don't check Wrap text, the browsers will try to keep everything in the cell on one line, which could get pretty long and funny looking. Your table as a whole will look better if you allow the browsers to wrap the text.

6. Under Cell spans, choose the number of rows and (or) columns the cell should cover.

In some cases, you would want a cell to cross over multiple columns or multiple rows — perhaps to include a label for the following text or allow you to center or align text within a complex layout. Just enter the number and try it out.

See Figure 7-16 for examples of cell spanning.

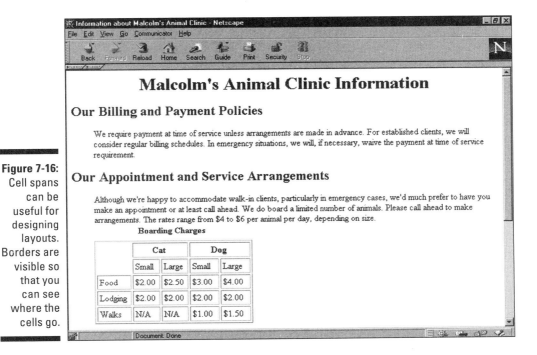

Figure 7-16:
Cell spans
can be
useful for
designing
layouts.
Borders are
visible so
that you
can see
where the
cells go.

Including Horizontal Lines

A *horizontal line* is a — well — horizontal line that you insert into Web pages that can serve as a visual break or as an information break. For example, you can use horizontal lines to set off initial or concluding information on your Web page, as shown in Figure 7-17.

Or you can use horizontal lines to break up long chunks of information, as shown in Figure 7-18.

You can insert horizontal lines into your Web pages using one of these two methods:

- ✔ Go to Insert➪Horizontal Line.
- ✔ Click the Insert Horizontal Line Button.

After you insert a horizontal line, you may decide to make it over by changing its thickness, length, or alignment. All you do is use the Horizontal Line Properties dialog box, shown in Figure 7-19.

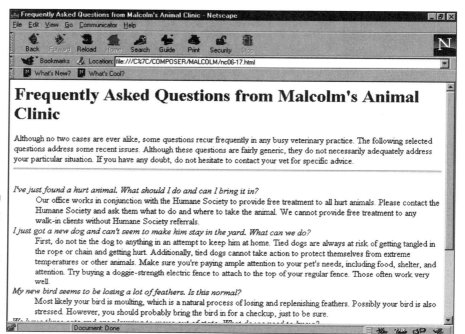

Figure 7-17:
Horizontal
lines can
help set
information
apart from
the rest of
the page.

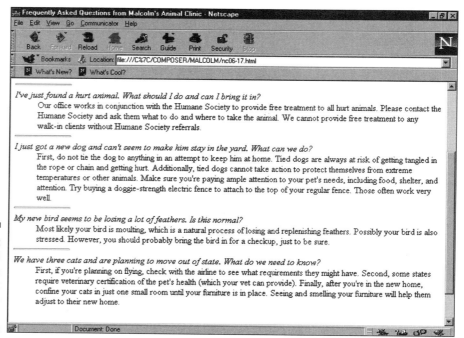

Figure 7-18:
Horizontal
lines can
help break
up seas
of text.

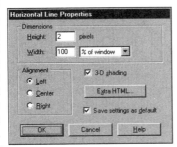

Figure 7-19:
The
Horizontal
Line
Properties
dialog box
lets you
design with
lines.

Even horizontal lines come with extra baggage:

- ✔ Any time you make a change in the Horizontal Line Properties dialog box, Composer updates the screen to reflect your changes.
- ✔ If you want to be able to save your changes as the default setting, just click the Save settings as default option at the bottom of the dialog box.

Changing line height

To change a line's height (thickness), use these quick instructions:

1. **Access the Horizontal Line Properties dialog box (click once on the line, right-click [click and hold if you're a Mac user], and then choose Horizontal Line Properties from the pop-up menu).**

   You can also go to Format⇨Horizontal Line Properties, or you can press Alt+Enter.

2. **Under Dimensions, change the number in the Height text field.**

   The larger the number, the fatter the line.

3. **Click OK.**

   There you go!

Changing line width

To change a line's width (length across the page), use these quick instructions:

1. **Access the Horizontal Line Properties dialog box (click once on the line, right-click [or click and hold if you're a Mac user], and then choose Horizontal Line Properties from the pop-up menu), or go to Format⇨Horizontal Line Properties or press Alt+Enter.**

2. **Under Dimensions, click the down arrow to the right of <u>W</u>idth.**

   A drop-down menu appears, giving you the option to choose the % of window or pixels.

   • The % of window option is the default and lets you specify the line width as a percent of the total window width. The line width will vary from computer to computer, depending on the size and resolution of your readers' monitors.

   • The Pixels option lets you specify an exact line width. The line width will remain the same from computer to computer.

3. **Choose whether you want the line width to be measured as a percentage of the window or in pixels.**

4. **Enter a number in the text field next to <u>W</u>idth.**

   If you choose % of window, the number you enter must be less than or equal to 100. If you choose pixels, the number can be much bigger. Just for reference, most monitors range from 640 to 1280 pixels wide.

5. **Click OK.**

   Wasn't that loads of fun? Adding multiple horizontal rules on top of each other with differing line lengths can yield a pleasing effect — vaguely *pyramidish.*

Changing line alignment

As with other formatting effects, horizontal lines are displayed using left alignment by default. If you're feeling creative or just want to experiment, you can change the alignment to either center or right, depending on what hair is tickling your tush. Before you start, keep in mind that if the line already goes all the way across the screen, you won't see differences in alignment. Here's how to change the alignment:

1. **Access the Horizontal Line Properties dialog box (click once on the line, right-click [or click and hold if you're a Mac user], and then choose Horizontal Line <u>P</u>roperties from the pop-up menu).**

2. **Under Alignment, choose <u>L</u>eft, <u>C</u>enter, or <u>R</u>ight.**

3. **Click OK.**

   You're cooking now!

Giving lines that 3-D effect

The Horizontal Line Properties dialog box offers you yet another fun trick: making your horizontal lines 3-D. Actually, the 3-D effect is a default setting — you have to take special steps not to have 3-D lines.

To change from 3-D to regular and back again, just select the 3-D shading option in the Horizontal Line Properties dialog box (click once on the line, right-click [click and hold if you're a Mac user], and then choose Horizontal Line Properties from the pop-up menu).

Including Nonbreaking Spaces

Just as you can force lines to break where you want them to, you can include spaces called *nonbreaking spaces,* which — guess what — won't break. These spaces are often used to keep terms tied together. For example, you can bet that a certain mongo-huge software corporation in the Northwest uses a nonbreaking space between the word Microsoft and Windows so that the phrase always stays together and doesn't split onto two lines.

To include a nonbreaking space, use these jiffy steps:

1. **Position your cursor where you want the space.**
2. **Press Shift+space, or choose Insert⇨Nonbreaking Space.**

   TaDaaaaa!

Part III
Connecting Your Web Pages and Including Goofy Pictures

The 5th Wave   By Rich Tennant

"Children- it is not necessary to whisper while we're visiting the Vatican Library Web site."

In this part . . .

In this part, you see how to connect your Web pages and include pictures in them. No, these activities aren't like playing connect-the-dots or pin-the-picture-on-the-Web-site; instead, these are essential skills for unifying your Web pages into a coherent site and making your pages look snazzy. Don't worry, just because they're "essential" doesn't mean they're complicated.

Chapters 8 and 9 give you the lowdown on creating links and developing navigation. Chapter 10 shows you how to include images. Then in Chapter 11, you see how to use images as links and clickable images. These chapters are way-cool because they not only show you how to do these tasks, but they also give you guidelines for doing them well.

After working through these chapters, you'll soon have an entire Web site filled with links, navigation menus, and imagemaps — and even pictures of a famous author, I.P. Freely, or your new friend, Ben Dover, or his wife, Ann O'der, or their cat, Hairy Pickles (Hair Pic for short) or. . . .

Chapter 8

Dropping In on Other Web Pages and Sites (Linking to Other Stuff)

*R*emember the panic when Aunt Myrna came for a visit? You know, the panic in trying to find that "lovely" gift so that you could display it on the table during her visit (the one she brought back from the School for the Artistically Impaired; she'll notice if it's not there, you know). Wouldn't it be easier (if somewhat tacky) to just put a big sign on the closet door and say, "Open here, dig to the bottom of the pile on the left, and carefully open the box labeled Rummage Sale. There's that lovely present that we haven't forgotten."

Besides the obvious aesthetic elements, it's just not possible to have *everything* you own in public view at all times. Just as you can't have all of your real possessions out at once, you can't (or shouldn't) have all of your content for the Web visible at once. If you create just one long page with everything from your résumé to your kids' pictures to your vacation activities, you'll end up with an enormous and unusable page.

Fortunately, it's very easy — and not at all tacky — to just hang signs on your Web pages to direct people to other pages and other content. Sign: Kid's Pictures. Sign: Résumé. Your readers select the sign, and there they go! In the technical jargon of the Web, those signs are called *links,* which is what this chapter covers. In particular, you'll see what kinds of links you can make, how to make them, and how to use e-mail links. (And, by the way, a link to "a photo of that ceramic thing from Aunt Stella, taken just before we trashed it" is still considered tacky, even in this brave new world.)

What Is a Link?

A *link* is the connection between two Web pages — or, more precisely, a connection from an HTML document to another document or a graphic or anything else on the Internet. Within a Web page, the links can be just text — probably blue and underlined — or an image that your readers can click. Either way, after your readers select a link, the new page (the linkee page) will replace the current document in their browsers. Figure 8-1 shows what text and image links look like in a Web page.

When you move your cursor over a link, the target URL (that is, the address of the page that appears if you select the link) shows up in the Status bar of the window.

Putting In a Link

Putting in a link is just as easy as doing most other tasks with Composer — you just select the text or graphic you want to be a link, click a button, and then specify where the page should link to. When specifying where the page should link to, you have three options:

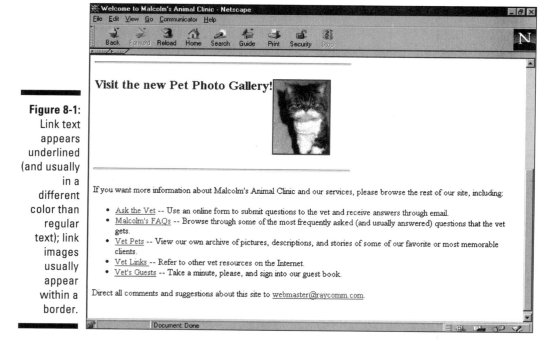

Figure 8-1:
Link text appears underlined (and usually in a different color than regular text); link images usually appear within a border.

  ✔ To another page within the same Web site

  ✔ To a page within a completely different Web site

  ✔ To a specific place within a Web page

Later in this chapter, you see how to include e-mail links, which are special links deserving their own section and instructions.

The procedure for doing all three options is basically the same; the difference is how much information you need to specify so that the browser can make the link. This information, called a *URL (Uniform Resource Locator),* is essentially just an address on the Web.

URLs (pronounced You-R-Ell) are kind of like street addresses. Just as every house has its own address, every Web page also has its own address. Your goal is to specify enough information to the browser so that it can make the leap from one page to another one that you specify.

How much information you provide varies depending on where you're linking to. Think of it this way. If you are giving instructions on how to get to your house to a friend who lives in your town, you're likely to tell her the neighborhood name, street name, and house number. However, if you're telling an out-of-town friend how to drive to your house, you'll probably start by getting her to the city and directing her to the right part of town before giving specific details about neighborhood, street, and house number. You give more information to out-of-town friends because they need more points of reference in order to find your house.

Links work the same way. Generally, if you're linking to a page within the same Web site, the URL will be pretty short because the browser is already in the right area; it just needs specific information to get to the next page. On the other hand, if you're linking to a page on a totally different Web site, the URL will be much longer because the browser has to find the equivalent of the right state, city, area, neighborhood, street, and house. If you don't provide enough information to that out-of-town friend, she won't find your house easily — or perhaps at all. Browsers work the same way; they won't find the linked page without the appropriate level of detail in the URL.

The next three sections show you how to make the different kinds of links: ones within your Web site, to a different Web site, and to a place within a Web page. You'll notice that the instructions are similar; however, each URL requires somewhat different information.

Uncle Earl sometimes doesn't zip his fly!

URLs actually come in two varieties:

- **Absolute:** These are complete URLs, which contain a protocol indicator (like `http://`), a host name (like `www.company.com`), and possibly even folder and filenames (like `foldername.filename.html`). Put together, an absolute URL might look like `http://www.companyname.com/foldername/filename.html` or like `http://www.xmission.com/`.

- **Relative:** These are partial URLs, which can contain just a filename or perhaps everything except the protocol indicator and host name. These are called relative URLs because they are relative to something — a filename can be relative to a folder name or a folder name can be relative to the host.

Use absolute URLs only when you have to — that is, when you're linking to a different location on the Internet or on your intranet. Remember that browsers need all the information you can give them when making a leap from your page to pages outside your site. Even if it's to a Web page at a company down the street, the browser might as well assume that it's halfway around the world.

Relative URLs are generally easier to use for a couple of reasons. First, they require less effort on your part. You have to type only part of a complete URL, which means less typing for your fingers. Second, if you use relative URLs, you don't have to redo the links if, say, you have to move your files to a different server or onto a disk. You only have to make sure that the relationship between the files isn't disturbed. For example, if your Web pages are stored on the `www.xmission.com` server in the `mystuff` folder, you'll have a URL of `http://www.xmission.com/mystuff/` followed by whatever the filenames are. By using relative URLs to just point to the nearby files, everything will still work when you copy the files onto a disk for use in a job interview or when your boss lets you move your site onto the company intranet. If you use absolute URLs and specify the host name throughout, all those links will need to be changed — one by one — if or when you move the files to a different location.

Oh, and about this sidebar heading. Ummm. Catchy, isn't it?

Linking to a page within your own site

Linking to a page within your own site is really easy, particularly because you're using Composer. Heck, it practically does all the work for you. The following steps show you how:

1. **Start with an existing Web page that includes some text or a graphic that you want to link to another page within the site.**

   It also helps to have the second (linkee) page saved somewhere on your computer.

2. Select the text or image.

You can select a single word or several words, your choice; however, you can select only one image at a time.

3. Go to Insert➪Link, or click the Link button (or press Ctrl+Shift+L).

The Character Properties dialog box appears, with the Link tab already selected.

4. Click Choose File.

The Link to File dialog box appears, as shown in Figure 8-2.

Figure 8-2:
The Link to File dialog box lets you scroll to files in your Web site.

5. Click the file that you want the text or graphic to link to.

You may need to select the drive and folder before you can scroll to the particular folder.

Your links will be easier to create, manage, and maintain if you keep all of your HTML documents together in one folder.

6. Click Open.

The Character Properties dialog box returns, but it now includes the filename (URL) in the Link to a page or local file text area.

7. Click OK.

The text or image now appears in the Web page as a link. Remember, text appears underlined (and perhaps a different color), and images usually appear enclosed within a border.

Linking to a page on another Web site

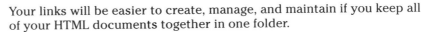

Linking text or images to pages within other Web sites is also fairly easy. Composer does some of the work for you but gets lazy when it comes to specifying the particular URL. So, it's hi ho, hi ho, and off to work you go.

1. **Start with an existing Web page that includes some text or a graphic that you want to link to another page within another site.**

2. **Select the text or image.**

3. **Go to Insert⇨Link, or click the Link button (or press Ctrl+Shift+L).**

   The Character Properties dialog box appears, with the Link tab already selected.

4. **Type the URL of the page you're linking to in the Link to a page location or local file field.**

   Eeek! More technical stuff. Not to worry. Just type `http://`. This is the part of the URL that tells browsers and servers how to communicate. It's called the protocol indicator, in case you're interested.

   To check out the information for the next two bullet points, visit the Web page that you want to link to, and look for the information located in the title bar at the top of the page.

   • Type the particular Web site address — it'll be something like `www.companyname.com` or `www.universityname.edu` or `www.organizationname.org`.

   • Type the exact folder and filename — it'll be something like `foldername/filename.html`.

   Your completed URL should look something like `http://www.raycomm.com/photos/winchester/html`.

5. **Click OK.**

   The text or image now appears in the Web page as a link. Remember, text appears underlined (and perhaps a different color), and images now appear enclosed within a border.

Another way to put the URL into the dialog box is to copy and paste it. Less typing, no chance of typos, and less typing. Ideal solution, right? Just use Navigator to browse to the Web page you want. Click in the Location line at the tjop of the browser. Use the mouse to highlight the whole URL, and then press Ctrl+C to copy it. Back in Composer, click in the Link to a page location or local file field, and then press Ctrl+V to paste it.

Linking to a specific place within a Web page

In addition to being able to link to individual Web pages — either within your site or at another site — you can link to a specific place within a Web page. For example, suppose that you want to include a list of your pets' names in your Web page. Seeing how there's probably scads you could list, you might want to give your readers a way to access names without having to scroll down the entire list. By providing a link to specific places within the Web page, you can let your readers jump right to the names that start with P or U or T or Z — or whatever.

To make these links to specific places (they're called *targets*, by the way), you have to do two things:

- ✔ **You need to specify the target in the receiving end.** For example, you could make a new heading for each letter of the alphabet and specify that each one of those headings should be a target.

- ✔ **You need to make a link to the target.** Continuing with this example, you might just list the letters of the alphabet and link the letters in the list to the letter headings farther down the page. Figure 8-3 shows an example.

Figure 8-3:
Linking each letter in the alphabet to the corresponding letter in the list of names can save your readers loads of time in scrolling to the information.

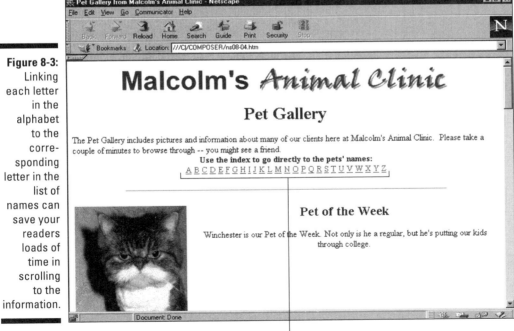

These letters link to the corresponding letters in the list of names.

As you can see, providing readers with targets can save them a lot of time and hassle. You can make targets from almost anything — text, images, applets, whatever. Most commonly, you'll create target links to a heading or major division within a Web page because that's where your readers want to be taken. Because you have to edit pages to insert targets, you'll generally make targets and link to targets in pages within your own Web site. However, you can link to targets outside your Web site, provided that people on the other end have placed targets within their Web pages. You can't make a link to a target that's not there, unless you have magical powers that we don't have.

The following two sections show you how to make and link targets.

Making targets

Remember, targets are the specific places in Web pages that you can make links to. Within the Malcolm site, shown in Figure 8-3, a heading exists for each letter of the alphabet to make it easier to find pet names.

To add targets, use the following process:

1. **Select the target-to-be.**

   Just a word or two is plenty.

2. **Go to Insert➪Target, or click the Target icon to bring up the Target Properties dialog box.**

3. **In the Enter a name for this target field, type a name for the target.**

   If you like the suggested name, of course, you can keep it. The name is what you'll be linking to, so select something intuitive and logical.

4. **Click OK.**

   You see the cool "here's a target in case you'd forgotten!" icon immediately to the left of the target when you are editing the page. However, when you view the document in a browser, the icon won't be there, and no visible indications will show that a target exists.

Here are a few pointed words about targets:

- ✔ If you are developing a table of contents, of sorts, as in this example, it's also a good idea to insert a target at the top of the document so that your readers can select a link and go back to the list of links at the top of the documents.

- ✔ If you think there's any possibility you'd ever want to link to a specific location within a document, put in a target. It only takes a second, requires very little effort, and will be well worth the effort if it's ever used. Going back into existing documents and adding targets later tends to be a real pain.

Making links to targets

If you have a document — yours or someone else's — that has targets in it, you can link to the targets with a quick click of the mouse. This example sets up the links from the letters of the alphabet at the top of the document to each letter's heading/target throughout the rest of the document.

To link to targets, use the following process:

1. **Highlight the text that will be the link.**

   In this case, highlight one of the letters of the alphabet from the list at the top of the page.

2. **Go to Insert⇨Link, or click the Link button (or press Ctrl+Shift+L).**

   The Character Properties dialog box appears, with the Link tab already selected.

3. **In the Character Properties dialog box, select the named target to link to.**

   If you're linking to a target within the same document, as in this example, all of the targets are visible at the bottom of the dialog box. However, you can also link to targets within other documents by selecting Choose File, finding the file, and then selecting Show targets in Selected file.

4. **After you select the target, click OK to close the dialog box and return to Composer.**

If you're interested, these links to juicy tidbits might be helpful:

✔ After you've selected a named target, in the Link to a page location or local file field, you might notice a #, followed by the name of the target. For example, you might see #E if you are linking to a target named E. This convention of using a # to separate the rest of the URL from the target name is standard in HTML, so you can do it manually as well. Say that you need to link to `http://www.xmission.com/~ejray/malcolm/gallery.html`, but you really want to link directly to the W entries in the list. You can just add the # and the W to the end of the URL so that you have something like the following URL:

```
http://www.xmission.com/~ejray/malcolm/gallery.html#W
```

✔ If you know what the target names are, you can use them, regardless of whose pages they're on. If you don't know but you want to know, just browse to the page and go to View⇨Page Source (or press Ctrl+U). Within that mass of HTML code, there may be snippets like `<A NAME= "ABC">Alphabet</A>`. That's a target in its native environment, and you can use that target — ABC — for any links into the document. Just for reference, Figure 8-4 shows a view of a target from the source of the Pet Gallery pages.

Targets

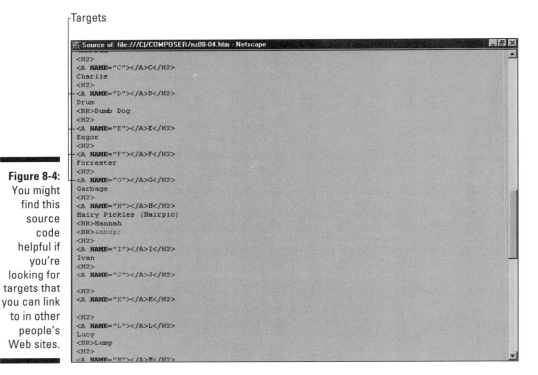

Figure 8-4:
You might
find this
source
code
helpful if
you're
looking for
targets that
you can link
to in other
people's
Web sites.

Making E-Mail Links

One final link to mention is an *e-mail link*, which lets your readers click the link and send a message directly to your e-mail box. Ain't technology great?

Suppose that you include an e-mail link in your Web page, and someone uses it to send you love letters. Here's how the e-mail link will work. First, the reader clicks the e-mail link, which shows up as a regular text link in the Web page. Communicator opens an e-mail window, which is complete, with the addressee's e-mail address already filled in. Figure 8-5 shows Communicator's e-mail window.

After the reader fills in the love letters in the message window — that is, L, O, V, and E — all she has to do is click the Send button, raise her right hand, and wave good-bye to the message. That's it.

Address already filled in   Message window

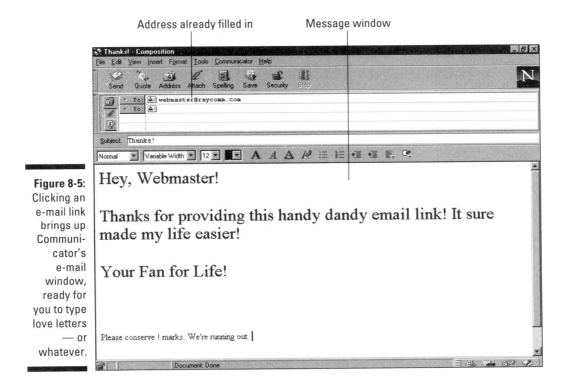

Figure 8-5:
Clicking an e-mail link brings up Communicator's e-mail window, ready for you to type love letters — or whatever.

Hey, Webmaster!

Thanks for providing this handy dandy email link! It sure made my life easier!

Your Fan for Life!

Please conserve ! marks. We're running out.

E-mail links do have some very practical uses on Web pages. First, they let your readers contact you more easily than by more-traditional means. For example, rather than accessing your site, jotting down a phone number, then picking up the phone and calling, readers can just click and link and start typing an e-mail message. And — ugh! — let's not even talk about how much simpler e-mail links are to use than snail mail.

Second, e-mail links are more convenient than opening an e-mail program, starting a new message, and addressing it. E-mail links save your readers time — time they could be using writing you those love letters (you know, L-O-V-E, and possibly XOXO).

Third, e-mail links take very little space on the page — much less space than, say, a form, which you can also use to let readers contact you. An e-mail link can be as short as a word or two or (often and sensibly) as long as your e-mail address. We suppose that the link could take a lot of space if you have a long-winded name and work for a company with an equally enormous name, like victoria.vanhosenheim@mycompanyhasastinkinlongname.com. Now that could take some page space.

You'll find some interesting information about forms in Chapter 14.

If you decide that an e-mail link is the way to go, just follow these steps:

1. **Insert the text you want to make an e-mail link.**

   Common e-mail text includes "contact us," "e-mail us," or "contact me." However, the best e-mail text is the actual e-mail address — so that people will still be able to tell what your address is, even if they print the document. If your readers don't have a visual reminder of your address, they won't be able to figure it out by the link in a printout.

2. **Select the word or words that you want to appear as link text.**

3. **Go to Insert⇨Link, or click the Link button (or press Ctrl+Shift+L).**

   The Character Properties dialog box appears, with the Link tab already selected. You're getting the hang of this — we can tell.

4. **In the Link to a page location or local file field, type** `mailto:` **followed by the actual e-mail address of the person to whom you're sending the e-mail, as in the following example.**

   `Mailto:malcolm@raycomm.com`

5. **Click OK when you finish.**

   Your newly created e-mail link shows up as a regular text link in the Web page.

Chapter 9

Hanging "Visitors Welcome" Signs throughout Your Web Site

. . . .

. . . .

Riiiing … riiiiing. "Hello? Yes, this is Ginger. Hi, Stella. You say you're in town and you're going to drop by in a minute? (pause) Oh, yes. We'd be delighted. Okay. Bye."

Delighted? Did I say that? We'd be as de-lighted as a dead firefly. . . .

Ginger runs frantically around the house picking up dishes, cramming pizza boxes into the trash, flinging undies in the hamper, scraping coffee grounds — or something brown — off the counter, installing a toilet paper roll in the bathroom, clearing a week's worth of mail off the kitchen desk, and (ewww!) dumping the cat's potty box . . . all in an effort to accommodate Stella, the friend who notoriously drops by at a moment's notice.

Sound familiar? Well, we have news for you, folks. The '90s has brought a new breed of dropper-inners, and these folks don't even bother to announce that they're coming. They just drop by, scope out your stuff, and then move on. Hmmm.

In case you haven't guessed, we're talking about *links,* those invisible trails that lead people to your Web site, guide them through different pages in your site, and lead them right out the door again so that they can move on to someone else's site. (The good news, though, is that you, too, can drop in and out of sites.)

When you develop Web pages and publish them, you never know who's going to drop by — and you don't ever get warned that someone's coming to visit. What's more, visitors aren't always people you know. They can be, and often are, complete strangers just checking out your site, seeing what you have, and using any information you make available.

In this chapter, you'll see how to place links purposefully so that readers can easily access your site, visit pages you want them to see, and then leave your site. Placing links purposefully is also called creating navigation, which essentially places a "visitors welcome" sign on pages you want people to see and closes the door on pages that are still under construction.

What Is Navigation?

Navigation refers to the links or sets of links (often called *navigation menus*) that you include throughout your Web site to let people wander through your site in an orderly manner.

Your readers will usually — or at least often — start at your *home page*, which is the main page of your site. Where they go from there and how (or if) they make it back to the home page is your responsibility, as the site developer. A significant aspect of developing a site requires that you allow your readers to easily and effectively find the information they want.

Creating effective navigation is essential because of the inherently unstructured nature of Web sites. It's just a fact that people tend to get "lost in cyberspace" and lose track of their purpose for visiting the Web site. Playing Devil's Advocate here, you could say that letting people get lost will help keep them at your site longer and force them to read through more of the information you provide. Well, yes, possibly. However, when people lose track of which links they've visited and which ones they haven't, they tend to get frustrated and want nothing more than to get out of the maze they feel trapped in.

Therefore, you need to create navigation that will help readers move efficiently through your site. Web sites are generally organized in one of three ways:

- ✔ **Hierarchical:** Presents layers of information, with each layer having multiple topics. The top layer includes the most general and the broadest topics; the next layer includes somewhat less general and more focused topics; the next layer includes even more specialized topics, and so on.

✔ **Linear:** Presents information in sequential order.

✔ **Webbed:** Presents links to multiple pages from multiple pages. This type is the most unstructured and most difficult to effectively present, but you often find it at Web sites because of the ease it provides for linking from page to page.

You may use only one of these types on your Web site, but more than likely you'll combine these options, depending on the type of information you include. The next three sections describe these navigation types, illustrate what they look like, and recommend how you can use each most effectively.

Hierarchical organization

Hierarchical organization ranks sets of topics in order of importance. The result is that readers can move not only laterally through topics of equal importance, but they can also move vertically through the different sets of topics. Hierarchical organization is great for organizing information that easily fits into an outline. For example, information in the following list could logically end up in Web pages organized hierarchically (see also Figure 9-1).

Sparky the Dog	**Fuzzy the Cat**
Good things	Good things
Cuddly	Affectionate
Good with kids	Likes kids
Good eater	Rarely eats off kitchen counter
Funny things	Funny things
Burps loudly	Steals drinking straws from cups
Chases tail on command	Chases spiders up the wall
Drinks out of potty	Carries socks around

Linear organization

Linear organization presents information sequentially and is especially good for providing instructions or procedures. Figure 9-2 illustrates linear organization.

The advantage of using linear organization is that it moves readers through the information in a very orderly manner — almost like herding a bunch of sheep. Through the sequence of links, readers move to the end of the Web site, where, usually, they can link back to the starting page.

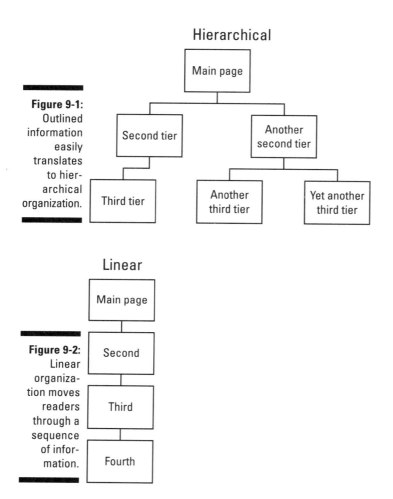

Figure 9-1:
Outlined information easily translates to hierarchical organization.

Figure 9-2:
Linear organization moves readers through a sequence of information.

The disadvantage is that linear organization doesn't give readers an easy way to break out of the sequence. They are forced to complete the sequence — which they may or may not want to do. You should consider whether the order of progress through the site really requires that your readers read linearly. Good opportunities to use linear organization are in sets of instructions — in which readers really shouldn't skip anything — or in, say, product description, when you don't want readers to skip anything.

Webbed organization

Webbed organization provides multiple links between pages. This type is somewhat unstructured, but because it gives readers lots of link options, they can freely roam to the topics of their choice. Figure 9-3 illustrates webbed organization.

Figure 9-3: Webbed organization looks like something spidery that you'd whack off the ceiling — now you see why you can get lost on the Web.

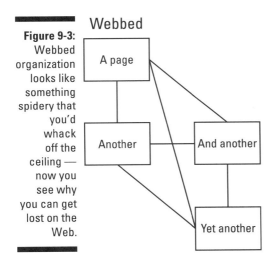

We did say earlier that "roaming readers" lead to the "lost in cyberspace" syndrome, didn't we? Yes, we did, and how observant of you to notice, by the way. Webbed organization does offer readers lots of link options, so many that readers may get so lost and frustrated that they may give up.

Nevertheless, webbed organization does have advantages. Giving readers lots of options to choose from can be a good idea. For example, the links to other pages should always be logical, and often there are lots of logical pages readers can link to. Or the content may lend itself to multiple links — the information may not fit into a sequence or may not have several layers of topics. In these cases, webbed organization is the way to go.

Links for making your readers' lives as easy as possible

Regardless of which organization you choose, you can use other techniques to help readers navigate your site. Here are some ideas:

✔ **Don't change visited link colors.** *Visited links* are ones that readers have already followed, which by default, use a different color than regular text does. Although you can make those links the same color as unvisited links (and some sites do so), by making sure that the visited link color differs from the unvisited link color, you help readers quickly see which links they've visited and which ones they haven't.

✔ **Use descriptive link names.** Make more effective links by providing link names that clearly tell the reader what information they'll find at the end of the link. For example, rather than giving a link a general description like More Information, name it Contact Information, Product Description, or Order Here!

✔ **Use distinctive names for each link.** Give each link a unique name — one that readers won't confuse with other links. When you name your kids or pets, you don't name them Vic, Vickie, and Victoria because the similarities would cause confusion. Likewise, links with similar names can cause confusion. For example, links called What's New, What's Hot, and What's Cookin' may be confusing because they're too similar (not to mention nondescriptive). You can improve these by calling them Today's News, Current Projects, and Projects Pending.

✔ **Link to real information.** Don't include a link to a lame message like "This page is under construction." Think about it. Readers follow links to find specific information or just see what's there. They don't like being fooled into thinking they'll find something and then get slapped with a message that basically says "Psyche! Fooled ya!" Also, because all Web pages and sites are ultimately under construction, the "This page under construction message" is redundant and repetitive . . . which is to say, it says the same thing again and again.

Navigating Navigation Options

After you decide how you want to organize your Web pages, you need to choose the kind of links you want to use. Ahhh, decisions . . . decisions. Don't worry, it's not like going to a restaurant and trying to decide whether to have corn, peas, potatoes, or spinach with your meal; it's more like deciding between the "Dieter's Deeelightful Devoid (of flavor) Deal" and the "Fancy Flavorful All You Can Cram On Your Plate Deal." One navigation option does the job and is pretty standard; in the other one, you can cram as much as you want.

You have two basic navigation options:

- ✔ **Textual navigation:** This option is an effective, though somewhat nonspiffy, navigation type. It includes a word or group of words that readers click on to link to the next Web page.

- ✔ **Graphical navigation:** This option is an effective *and* spiffy navigation type. It most often includes buttons and icons that readers click on to link to the next Web page; it may also include *imagemaps,* which takes navigation to another level.

See Chapter 11 for more information about imagemaps.

Figures 9-4 and 9-5 show the same navigation options using textual and graphical navigation, respectively.

Which option is better for your needs? The following two sections outline the advantages and disadvantages of each.

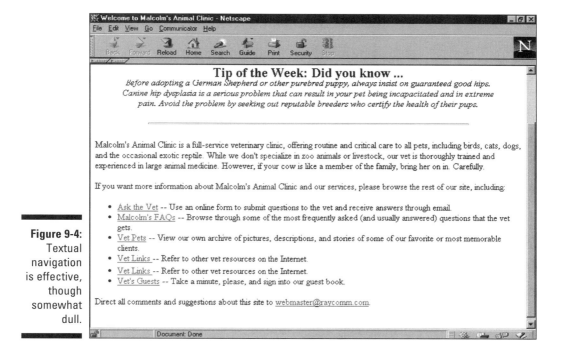

Figure 9-4:
Textual navigation is effective, though somewhat dull.

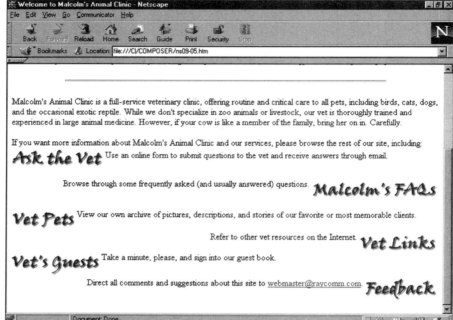

Figure 9-5:
Graphical navigation (in this case with fancy shadowed text-looking icons) is more visually interesting, though more time-consuming to develop.

Textual navigation

Textual navigation is a group of words that describes the information at the other end of the link. Though rather dull, it does have several advantages:

- ✔ **It's easy to use.** Because link text appears underlined and usually in a different color from regular text, readers can easily distinguish the link.

- ✔ **It's inherently descriptive.** Text, particularly when it's informative about the topic on the other end of the link, can often be more descriptive than graphical navigation.

- ✔ **You're not limited on space.** You can make the text as long as you want with as much information as you want — as opposed to being limited to something the size of a button.

- ✔ **It's reliable.** Text links are part of the actual Web page, whereas buttons and icons are not — remember, the graphical file is referenced by the Web page. With text links, you don't have to worry about problems occurring between the Web page and the graphical file.

- ✔ **It's fast.** In the time it takes for a single small image to download, you could also download 15 pages of text. Use a few images, and you're quickly looking at a lot of download time.

So, what are the drawbacks to using textual links? None, really, other than that they're kind of boring. Rather than being colorful and shapely like buttons and icons are, text links are just plain words accented with an underline and usually a different color.

Graphical navigation

Graphical navigation, which often appears as a series of buttons or other images, is an established preference with Web site authors — and for good reason:

- ✔ **It's snazzier than plain ol' text.** Graphics are colorful and shapely and, therefore, more interesting.

- ✔ **It can become part of the page layout.** You can incorporate graphical navigation into your layout just as you would include an image.

- ✔ **It can complement other theme elements in your Web site.** Graphical navigation can use colors, fonts, icons, or shapes consistently through- out your Web site. (You'd have to use sound files to *compliment* the other theme elements, as in, "Nice slim logo you've got there. Those colors sure do look nice!")

Even though graphical navigation seems cooler than textual navigation, it does have a few drawbacks. First, developing effective buttons, bullets, and icons is sometimes easier said than done. For example, squeezing a shape or some text onto an itty-bitty button often produces an illegible or out-of- proportion result or something just amateurish enough to be inappropriate for a professional site.

Second, buttons and icons are not actually part of the Web page, so you not only have to maintain the navigation, but you also must maintain the refer- ence from the Web page to the button or icon. If the reference from the Web page to the graphical navigation doesn't work, readers won't be able to link to other pages.

Third, graphical navigation takes additional time to download. Just as when using images, applets, or JavaScripts, you need to make sure that the benefits they add outweigh the extra download time.

See Chapter 10 for information about using images in Web pages.

Picking Where You Want Your Navigation to Live

Picking flowers . . . picking a shirt . . . picking your nose . . . picking your seat . . . ah, here it is . . . picking where you want your navigation to live.

Think of placing navigation as like opening a business. You can locate your business uptown, midtown, or downtown. When deciding which location is best, you'll likely choose the location that will get the most traffic — the place that's most convenient for potential customers to visit. You can also open branch locations, based on areas that customers might also find convenient.

Placing navigation is similar to locating a business. You can locate the navigation at the top (uptown), middle (midtown), or bottom (downtown) of Web pages, depending on which place is most convenient for readers. And you can have multiple locations — say, with the main navigation at the top and a second location at the bottom — if readers are likely to find additional locations useful.

Also, like a business, having many locations may not be a good thing. For example, just because a business opens three new branches doesn't mean that customers will flock to them — they won't if the need isn't there. Likewise, including multiple navigation locations in a Web page doesn't mean that people will find all of them useful. In fact, people may find them a pain in the butt to wade through.

In deciding where to locate your navigation, you need to consider a few things:

✔ **Uses for each location:** *Uptown navigation* is useful for providing an at-a-glance look at your Web site. People browsing your site can easily see what's in it and easily link to it.

Midtown navigation is useful for providing navigation in long documents. For example, if you publish a newsletter on a single Web page, readers might scroll through a few articles but may not want to scroll all the way back to the top or down to the bottom just to link to a new page. Midtown navigation lets readers wade through the depths of Web pages but lets them also easily swim to other pages. You're likely to use midtown navigation in addition to uptown navigation.

Downtown navigation is useful for medium to long Web pages. For example, if readers are thoroughly engrossed in your Web page (or at least are tolerating it enough to reach the bottom), they will not want to have to scroll all the way to the middle or top just to get to another page. Downtown navigation is extremely handy, particularly when used in conjunction with uptown and midtown navigation.

 ✔ **Length of the Web page:** Just because you have three location options doesn't mean that you use all three in all pages. Short pages usually require only uptown *or* downtown navigation. Medium-length pages may require both uptown and downtown locations. Long pages may require all three. The idea is to provide locations that will be most useful to your readers but not to provide so much that your readers trip over the menus to get to the content.

 ✔ **How readers will use the information:** If, for example, the content encourages readers to link to a page and glance at the cool effects, uptown navigation may be all that's needed. Or if the content, like cutting-edge research, hot news, or soap opera updates, is likely to keep readers clinging to every word regardless of length, provide navigation in the middle or at the bottom of the page so that readers can eventually come up for air.

Putting It All Together

To give you a sample of the thought processes involved in establishing effective navigation, here are a few of the considerations and issues addressed by the Web site staff at Malcolm's Animal Clinic.

First, you organize the Web pages. This site includes a moderate number of pages, each standing on its own fairly well. Because none of the pages include a process or procedure, the clinic ruled out linear organization. That leaves webbed or hierarchical organization to choose from. Some of the clinic's pages could easily fit into an outline, but other pages could logically link to multiple other pages. So, the clinic decided to use both hierarchical and webbed organization (see Figure 9-6).

Taking the uptown express

One fairly handy way to use navigation is to include a minitable of contents at the top of a document. This table can be used to link readers directly to specific places within the same document, relieving readers of having to scroll through a long document just to find the information they're looking for.

If you choose to include a minitable of contents at the top of your Web page, be sure to include <u>Return to Top</u> links throughout the document. In doing so, you let readers take the uptown *express* back to the top of the document — instead of having to scroll all the way back.

See Chapter 8 to find out how to link to specific places within documents.

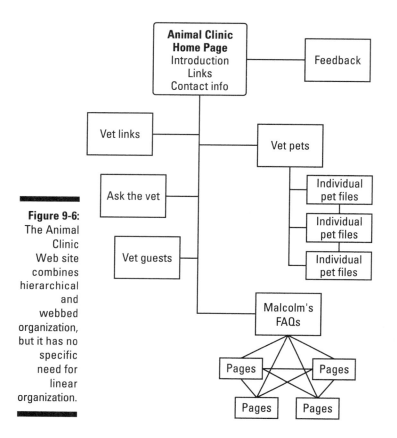

Figure 9-6:
The Animal Clinic Web site combines hierarchical and webbed organization, but it has no specific need for linear organization.

The next step is to decide whether to use textual or graphical navigation. Malcolm's Animal Clinic opted for simple graphical navigational links — the overall site style is fairly clean and sparse, and the only appropriate graphics were simple images with words. The designers determined that the *bandwidth* (amount of time to download) cost of using a bunch of images whose only redeeming quality was replacing words was — just barely — worth it. Figure 9-7 illustrates the clinic's navigation on the tips page.

The final step is to decide where to place the navigation — either uptown, midtown, or downtown. Because the clinic's designers already provide a logo at the top of most pages, they decide to use downtown (bottom) navigation so that they don't mess up the simple, clean logo at the top of the pages. Also, because most pages are short, they decide to include navigation only at the downtown location.

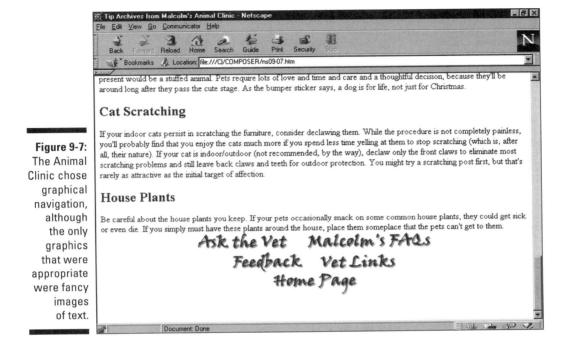

Figure 9-7:
The Animal
Clinic chose
graphical
navigation,
although
the only
graphics
that were
appropriate
were fancy
images
of text.

However, they choose to make an exception to the downtown-only navigation choice. The tips archive page is already fairly long and grows by one tip per week.

Scrolling all the way to the bottom of the page is not a good navigational choice, even though bottom navigation is consistent with the other pages in the site. As a compromise, they decide to use both top and bottom navigation on this one page, putting the top navigation about one paragraph below the logo to keep the appearance fairly clean.

Additionally, the designers add a <u>Return to Top</u> link after each tip to make it easier for readers to get back to the rest of the site after reading the tip. Figure 9-8 shows the navigation used on this long and growing page.

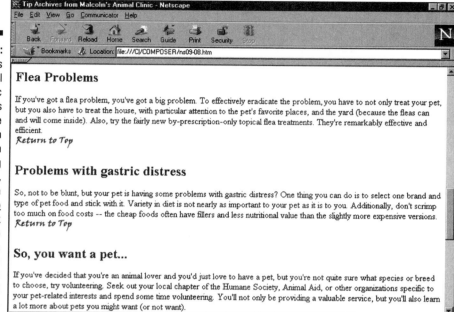

Figure 9-8:
Malcolm's
Animal
Clinic
designers
put multiple
navigation
locations on
this long
page,
including a
Return to
Top link
to help
readers
wade
through the
useful
information.

Chapter 10

Say Cheese!
Adding Pictures and Other Smiling
Things to Your Web Pages

● ●

In This Part

▶ Knowing different uses for images

▶ Finding images to use in Web pages

▶ Making images small

▶ Reducing color depth

▶ Using GIF and JPG file formats

▶ Interlacing images

▶ Making image backgrounds transparent

▶ Adding images to a Web page

▶ Controlling image and text alignment

▶ Specifying space around images

▶ Specifying image dimensions

▶ Using images as Web page backgrounds

● ●

*E*arlier chapters show how to create Web pages, add some cool effects, and even link pages into a unified site. In this chapter, you'll see how to include photos, drawings, illustrations, icons, buttons — practically any kind of image you can imagine — in your Web pages.

This chapter tells you all you need to know to understand image types and to select and include them in your Web pages. Furthermore, you'll find out how to use images and colors as Web page backgrounds and how to modify images to make them suitable for Web pages. So, put on your thinkin' cap, and get movin'!

Distinguishing Image Uses

An *image* is just a fancy term for a graphic — photos, buttons, icons, bullets, lines, drawings, illustrations, cartoons, and so on. In Web pages, images can serve several purposes, ranging from adding a splash of color to an otherwise dull page to filling the background to illustrating a complex concept. Following are specific uses for images in Web pages:

- ✔ **Including a company logo:** You can use images to replace a plain ol' line of text (like your company name) with colorful, spiffy, shaded, or shadowed letters that have a personality all their own.

- ✔ **Establishing a theme:** You can use repeating images, such as backgrounds, icons, bullets, and buttons, throughout your Web site to help make each page part of a cohesive Web site. See Chapter 4 for more information about establishing theme.

- ✔ **Including cool backgrounds:** You can use images as Web page backgrounds, replacing the default white or gray background with one that complements the Web site's purpose and content. See the section "Using Images as Backgrounds" later in this chapter for more information.

- ✔ **Using graphical (button-type) navigation:** Using graphical navigation is a sure way to help your Web site stay visually up-with-the-times. See Chapter 9 for more information about navigation and Chapter 11 for more information about linking from images.

- ✔ **Using thumbnails (itty-bitty images that link to a larger version of the same image):** Thumbnails are a great space and time-saver — via page space and download time. In using a thumbnail, you give readers a choice whether to wait for the larger image to download or just to head right on by. See Chapter 11 for more information about thumbnails.

- ✔ **Including icons and bullets and lines (oh my!):** These Web page extras not only add splashes of color, but also make your pages more visually appealing.

Figures 10-1 and 10-2 show Web pages that use images for a variety of purposes.

Can the Stork Deliver Images?

We have to clear up a few myths:

- ✔ Storks do not deliver images for you to use in your Web pages.
- ✔ Santa Claus doesn't stuff them down your chimney either.

Logo   Illustrate a point

Figure 10-1:
This Web
page uses
images for a
corporate
logo and to
illustrate a
point.

> ✔ You can't tell the gender of your Web pages based on whether the images are "carried high" or "carried low" on the page. (And dangling a nail over your monitor won't tell you this either.)

Well, with that all cleared up, you're probably wondering just where you can lay your sticky fingers on images. Images can come from three places: You can borrow them from a Web site, you can scan your own, or you can create them yourself using image-editing software. You can take these one at a time.

Borrowing images

One of the easiest ways to find images to use is to go Web surfing and look for those marked "free for public use," "okay for you to use," or something similar. Keep in mind that images, like anything else on the Web, were created by someone else; therefore, someone else holds the copyright to them.

Pilfering stuff off the Web without express permission is against the law. Remember that copyright laws apply to Web pages and their contents, just as they do to paper documents and their contents.

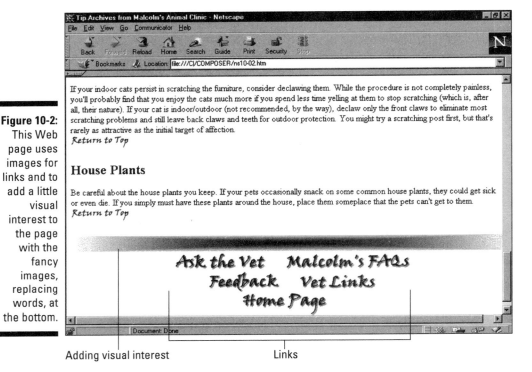

Figure 10-2:
This Web
page uses
images for
links and to
add a little
visual
interest to
the page
with the
fancy
images,
replacing
words, at
the bottom.

Adding visual interest   Links

Any time you find images to use, you should triple-check their public availability. Suppose that you find a great collection of "free" images that includes a picture of Dilbert. Whoever developed the collection had to get the Dilbert picture from somewhere — perhaps from a Scott Adams cartoon gallery. It's more than likely that whoever developed the image used the Dilbert picture without actually having the right to do so. Therefore, even though the person claims his or her images are free for public use, you shouldn't do so — presumably if the Dilbert image is "hot," others are too.

The following locations should give you a good start on looking for images to use.

First, check out the Iconographics collection on the CD that comes with this book and online at `http://www.iconographics.com`. You're welcome to use any of these images for any purpose.

Second, check out the Netscape site for the Navigator Gold Tool Chest. (We assume that this page will hang around, even though it sounds like it was designed for use in conjunction with an older version of Netscape's editor program.) The address is `http://home.netscape.com/assist/ net_sites/starter/samples/`.

Check with software you already have for clip art archives. Most image-editing software comes with clip art, as do many Microsoft programs.

If you need a lot of clip art, check out other commercial collections, such as Diamar (`http://www.diamar.com`) or Artbeats (`http://www.artbeats.com`).

Borrowing images is perhaps the easiest of the options; however, it does have a drawback. You won't always find images that are exactly what you're looking for, and you may end up spending an inordinate amount of time fixing the image to your liking. Then there's no guarantee that you can ever get it just right.

How to borrow images? No problem, just follow this process:

1. **In Navigator, browse to the page that contains the image you want to use.**

   Yes, you can use this procedure on any Web page, no matter what. If you can't get your corporate PR department to release a copy of the company logo for your project and you're willing to take the heat, just pilfer the image from the company home page. (Remember, you're just practicing with these images, not publishing them.)

2. **Right-click (or long-click, Mac users) on the image to bring up the pop-up menu.**

3. **Choose Save Image As from the menu.**

4. **Browse to the location on your hard drive where you want to store the image, provide a new filename if you want, and then click Save.**

   That's it. Now the image is on your hard drive, awaiting your attention.

You might also want to know the following:

- ✔ If you find a site with a whole slew of images and think that it'll take forever to save each one individually (like some of the Netscape pages), try this workaround. When viewing the page in Navigator, choose File➪Edit Page, and then from the new Composer window, choose File➪Save As. This saves the whole page, all graphics included, in the location you specify.

- ✔ If you find a single image you want and need a quicker, easier way to get it, just drag it from the original page into your Composer window. That's it!

Scanning images

If you have photos or drawings of your own that you'd like to include, another option is to scan them. *Scanning* means to take a hard copy version of the image and change it to a computer file. This section gives a high level view of the scanning process. We couldn't stick a scanner on the CD that comes with this book, so we don't know exactly what you have access to. The following information provides generalities about scanning — your mileage may vary.

Scanning is sort of like going to a copy machine, putting your picture on the bed, and pressing the Start button. The copy machine perks and churns for a second or two, and then it spits out a paper copy. With scanning, you basically follow the same process. If you have a scanner and scanning software, you put the photo or drawing on the scanner bed (or perhaps feed it in) and click a button. The scanner perks and churns for a bit, and right before your very eyes, the image appears on your computer screen. After the image appears on-screen, you can crop it (cut out the stuff you don't want), adjust colors, and change the size, among other cool things. After you fuss with it and come up with the final image, all you have to do is save the image as a file. The scanner (and accompanying software) does most of the work for you — you just have to let your creative powers take charge.

The drawback to this option, of course, is that you must have access to a scanner — your own, a friend's, a school's, and so on. But after you have access, the specific procedure isn't difficult. Keep in mind that the computer does most of the work for you. Most of what you have to do includes making the image look like you want it to look after it's in the computer.

If you're looking for additional information on scanners, you might scope out *PCs For Dummies,* 4th Edition, by Dan Gookin, published by IDG Books Worldwide.

Before you decide that this option just can't be right for you because you don't have the money to invest in a scanner, check out the prices. Scanner prices have been plummeting for over a year, and the quality keeps getting better. The scanner we used (Microtek ScanMaker E3) for many of the animal pictures in this book is now (at press time) available through mail order for under $200.

Creating your own images

Another option you have is to create your own images. You can't use Composer to create images. Instead, you need to use image-editing software, like Paint Shop Pro (Windows) or Graphic Converter (Macintosh), which are both conveniently included on the CD that comes with this book.

Though you can create images in any number of other programs, Paint Shop Pro and Graphic Converter are particularly useful because they're easy to use, include lots of formatting and image manipulation options, and save in file formats usable on the Web.

Creating your own images has several advantages. You can develop stuff that's unique to your Web site. You can include colors that fit your site theme (though you should check out the sidebar "Color me blue" later in this chapter for the 216 best Web colors to use), provide intricate details, and do it right the first time.

You also don't have to mess with trying to alter images to meet your needs. The problem with using public images is that everyone else can use the same ones, so your site might end up very (eerily) similar to your competitors'. If you create your own images, you don't have to worry about showing up at the party wearing the same dress as Ms. Jones does.

The disadvantage is that you can spend lots of time creating images — not because they're hard to do but because you can easily get carried away with your creativity. Particularly after you get the hang of your image-editing software, you can sit and create for hours at a time. (We know this from experience, by the way.)

Here are some guidelines to follow when creating your own images:

- **Choose from the list of 216 best colors to use for Web pages.** These colors are good choices because they will always appear solid, without splotches or dots.

  These "best colors" are an issue only if you have broad expanses of colors — like big shapes or backgrounds. Just a little color in text or mixed into graphics isn't going to pose a problem, regardless of the colors you choose.

- **Make them as simple as possible.** Browsers sometimes don't display details effectively — particularly at low resolution settings. Also, details tend to clutter an image, detracting from its overall effect.

- **Make them as small as possible.** Larger images take more time to download, as discussed in the section "Make images as small as possible" later in this chapter.

Keep in mind that you can set Composer so that you can summon the image editor right from the editing window. See Chapter 5 for details.

Images & the World Wide Wait

If you read nothing else in this book, read this: Images are the primary contributor to the World Wide Wait epidemic, where millions upon millions of folks around the world wait F-O-R-E-V-E-R for images to download to their computers. The spread of this epidemic is an enigma — surely people have better things to do with their days than to wait for images to download. It's a wonder Web page images caught on. Still, people sit day after day, hour after hour, waiting for these silly images to download and "dazzle" them.

However, even though modern technology, research, and science can't tell you why this insidious epidemic has caught on, we can speculate about why the problem has grown to overwhelming proportions: People just don't know how to make images so that they download in a minimal amount of time. Image-making techniques have evolved since the age of wood-burning computers. And you, Mr., Mrs., or Ms. Web author, need to use these techniques to make images as efficient as possible so that your Web pages will download faster, look cleaner, and dazzle your readers appropriately.

In all sincerity, if you're a professional graphic designer or work with one, the conceptual shift from preparing images for print to preparing images for online use is significant. It's not unusual for an image destined for print to take about 3.5MB — that's 3,500,000 bytes. By comparison, an image used online that is as little as 35,000 bytes is approaching maximum usable size. Downloading an image that is 350,000 bytes certainly gives readers time to go to the bathroom, get some coffee, drink the coffee, go back to the bathroom, make more coffee, and play with the dog.

The following five sections tell you about techniques you can use to make images more efficient. These techniques are not ones that you'll complete in Composer; instead, you will need an image-editing program such as Paint Shop Pro or Graphic Converter, which are on the CD. For each image, you can use any one or several of these techniques, depending on the results you want.

Make images as small as possible

You can make images as small as possible by *resizing* them — that is, make them physically smaller. Image size is measured in *pixels*, which you can see if you squinch your nose up to the monitor — yeah, that's them, those tiny little dots. For example, an image size that measures 320 x 480 is 320 pixels wide by 480 pixels tall.

Making the image physically smaller results in the file size being smaller. File size is calculated — approximately — by multiplying the image's height, width, and number of colors used. An image that's 300 x 300 x 256 takes up significantly more file space than one that's 30 x 30 x 256. You can't just multiply these numbers and get the file size — there are other technical considerations. However, the file will be significantly reduced just by reducing the height and width.

What is a good image size? That depends.

These have gotta be small:

✔ Images located on frequently accessed pages

✔ Gratuitous images, such as photos of staff members

✔ Multiple images on single Web pages

These can be bigger:

✔ Images that contain information — rather than just glitz

✔ Images located on less-frequently accessed pages

✔ Images that convey concepts or processes

Exactly how you make images smaller varies depending on the software you use. The following steps show you how to do reduce images using Paint Shop Pro; however, the process will be similar in other programs.

1. **Open the image.**

2. **Go to Image⇨Resize.**

   The Resize dialog box appears, as shown in Figure 10-3.

Figure 10-3:
The Resize dialog box lets you change the image's dimensions.

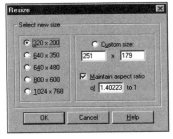

3. Change the image size.

- You can select a predetermined image size from the list under Select new size. Just click the appropriate radio button.

- You can make up your own size by filling in dimensions in the Custom size area. Just fill in the first text field (using pixels), press tab, and then fill in the second text field. If you want to maintain the image's proportions, just click Maintain aspect ratio, and then fill in one of the two size text fields. The other field is filled in for you.

- If you want the fun house mirror effect, don't check the Maintain aspect ratio box, and pick the values for both the height and width. But seriously folks, be careful to check that box for any images that should appear in the right proportions.

4. Click OK.

Reduce color depth

Another technique for making files download faster is to reduce the color depth (which you might have guessed). As mentioned in the previous section, an image's file size is calculated by multiplying the height times width times color depth. In the last section, you reduced the image's height and width, which essentially made the image physically smaller and made the image file smaller as well. In this section, you finish the equation by reducing the color depth.

Color depths are calculated in general ranges — 2 (which is black and white), 16, 256, thousands, and millions. So, if you have an image that uses 240 colors, it will fall in the 256 range; likewise, if an image uses 999 colors, it will fall in the thousands range. You get the idea.

You're probably wondering right about now how you can reduce the color depth and not ruin the image quality. Almost all of the images and pictures in this book use only 256 colors. Although millions of colors will be better for photographs, the reduction to 256 colors retains acceptable quality and dramatically reduces the size of an image.

Remember that many of these Web pages and accompanying images are available on the CD for you to use.

Not all images respond well to having the color depth reduced, but reducing most images to 256 colors usually works well. You may notice some difference, but the quality will likely remain pretty good. Similarly, you can often reduce simple drawings or line art to 16 colors and still have them look good. The results vary depending on the image quality and number of colors used.

Reducing color depth — or at least experimenting with it — is easy. The following steps show you how to do that using Paint Shop Pro, though the process will be similar in other image-editing software.

1. **Open the image.**

2. **Go to Colors⇨Decrease Color Depth.**

   A color pop-up menu appears when you move your mouse over Decrease Color Depth, as shown in Figure 10-4.

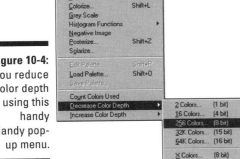

Figure 10-4: You reduce color depth using this handy dandy pop-up menu.

3. **Choose 2, 16, 256, 32K (million), 64K (million), or X million (unlimited).**

   The image should now appear on-screen with the reduced colors. If you don't like the results, go to Edit⇨Undo, or press Ctrl+Z.

   All unavailable choices (such as "reducing" the depth to a value higher than the current value) are grayed out.

Use the right file format

When using images for Web pages, you have two file formats to choose from, GIFs and JPGs, described in the following paragraphs.

GIF (pronounced jif, as in the peanut butter, or gif, as in gift) is the most widely used format and has some distinct advantages over the JPG format. GIF images can be viewed on any graphical browser. In fact, until recently (say, the last couple years) it was the only image file format that browsers could read. The GIF format supports transparent backgrounds (discussed in "Lose the image background") and interlacing (discussed in "Interlace your images"), which make images *seem* to load faster. The disadvantage is that the GIF file format supports only 256 colors, which may or may not be enough to give images the quality appearance you're looking for.

Some colors make better pets than others

Choosing colors to use in Web pages is a lot like owning a nosy dog. You know the kind — the ones that run up and *snorch* you and then pant doggie breath trying to keep your attention. Well, colors in images do essentially the same things to readers — they jump off the page, snorch the readers (okay, maybe in not such a rude spot), and then they continue to howl "look at me; look at me" the whole time readers look at the page.

The most enjoyable household pets are ones that suit the owner's life-style. For some folks, this may mean that the dog is active (but not a *spaz*), plays nice with the kiddies (human and feline), and has a warm disposition to a people-friendly family. For others, this may mean that the dog sleeps 22 hours a day, adopts one end of the couch, and is a footrest to a reclusive couch potato. The point is that pets that match an owner's life-style make happy pets, not to mention happy owners.

Likewise, colors should also match the purpose of the Web site. For example, don't use bright purple and mango-orange twist to convey the traditional philosophies of an accounting firm. This is kind of like a spazzy dog dragging a couch-potato owner down the street. Or don't use drab browns, tans, and greens for a marketing company's logo. This is kind of like trying to take a snoozy dog for a five-mile run every day. The point is that the colors don't match the Web sites' purposes, and the result is that readers are unnecessarily tortured by mixed messages.

How to avoid this dilemma? Choose colors that match the message you're conveying, for example:

- Bright colors convey "I-eat-in-the-car-while-on-my-cell-phone" and "My job is my life."

- Warm colors convey "touchy feely" and "happy, but not ecstatic."

- Earthy colors convey "mellow," "traditional," and "'70s."

- Pastel colors convey "fresh," "creative," and "Easter."

JPG (pronounced jay-peg and also known as JPEG), a more recently available image file format, has a significant advantage: It is highly *compressed*, which means that the file can be mooshed to help speed download time. JPG files are particularly well-suited for photographs — the compression makes the file sizes much smaller than GIF images, and the quality remains significantly better.

JPGs have two disadvantages. The compression sometimes causes images to lose details. Again, the quality, in your opinion, may be just fine. You'll just have to experiment. And people using older browsers won't be able to see JPG images in Web pages. Most readers will be able to view them (say 80 percent or so), but some won't.

The following steps show you how to save files in either GIF or JPG formats using Paint Shop Pro. Again, the process will be similar for other image-editing software, for example, Graphic Converter.

You can use this same process to change an existing image saved in a different format to the GIF or JPG formats.

1. **Open the file.**

2. **Go to File➪Save As (or press F12).**

   The Save As dialog box appears.

3. **Scroll to the directory and folder you want to save the image in.**

   For easier use, save the image in the same folder as the rest of your Web page contents.

4. **If you want to change the name, make the change in the file in the File name field.**

5. **Under Save as type, choose JPG (which is listed as JPG-JPEG-JFIF compliant), or choose GIF (which is listed as GIF-compuserve).**

6. **If you choose GIF, also choose a file subtype under Sub type.**

   Always choose either 89a Interlaced or 89a Noninterlaced. (Don't mess with the 87 options.) See the next section, "Interlace your images," to see how these interlaced and noninterlaced options apply.

7. **Click Save when you're done.**

   That's all there is to it, folks!

Interlace your images

Interlacing refers to how images appear on the screen. Regular (noninterlaced) images come on-screen in one piece. The result is that readers sit around staring at a blank screen until the image pops up. Interlaced images fade onto the screen — the little pixels appear on-screen in waves, with the image appearing progressively clearer as the moments (or minutes, depending on image size) go on. Though interlaced images don't actually download faster than noninterlaced ones, they seem to be faster because readers see the image start to appear on-screen sooner than other images for which the readers wait, wait, wait, and then finally see the image.

To make an image interlaced, you have to use the GIF file format. The following instructions show you how to make an image interlaced using Paint Shop Pro, though you can use the general process in other software.

1. **Open the file.**

2. **Go to File➪Save As (or press F12).**

   The Save As dialog box appears.

3. **Scroll to the directory and folder you want to save the image in.**

   For later reference, save the image in the same folder as the rest of your Web page contents.

4. **Name the file in the File name area.**

5. **Under Save as type, select GIF (which is listed as GIF-compuserve).**

6. **Choose the Sub type 89a Interlaced, as shown in Figure 10-5.**

   If you don't want the image to be Interlaced, choose Sub type 89a Non-interlaced.

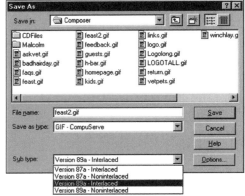

Figure 10-5:
You make images interlaced using options provided in the Save As dialog box.

7. **Click Save when you're done.**

   TaDaaaa!

Lose the image background

In addition to all these techniques you can use to make images download faster, you can also use one handy-dandy technique to make them look cooler. (Yeah, yeah, this is supposed to be a section on improving download time, but we just have to tell you this useful tidbit of information.) You can improve how some images appear by making the background disappear. For example, check out Figures 10-6 and 10-7, which show the same image with and without the background.

Images without backgrounds are called *transparent images,* named so because the background color is set to "transparent" so that the browser's background color shows through. The result is that the images are more interesting because they're not limited to being square or rectangular. Also, as shown in Figures 10-6 and 10-7, image content is more prominent and clear.

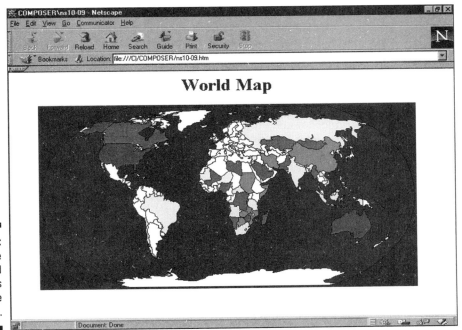

Figure 10-6:
This image background detracts from the presentation.

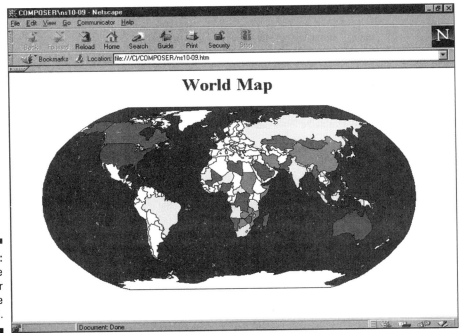

Figure 10-7:
The image looks better without the background.

Not all images can use a transparent background — only ones with a solid-color background will work. Those with multicolored or patterned backgrounds won't work because only one color can be transparent in a GIF image. Also, remember that you can use only those images saved in the GIF file format as transparent images.

The following steps show you how to get rid of pesky backgrounds using Paint Shop Pro. As you'll see, making backgrounds transparent is easy to do and produces results that are well worth the second or two it takes. And, yes, the process is similar in other image-editing software.

1. **Open the file.**

 2. **Make sure the eye-dropper tool (shown at left) is selected.**

3. **Point at the color (background) that you want to be transparent and right-click it.**

   Right clicking sets the background color to the one at which you pointed. Left clicking (normal clicking) sets the foreground color to the one at which you pointed.

4. **Go to File⇨Save As (or press F12).**

   The Save As dialog box appears.

5. **Scroll to the directory and folder you want to save the image in.**

   For later reference, save the image in the same folder as the rest of your Web page contents.

6. **Name the file in the File name area.**

7. **Under Save as type, select GIF (which is listed as GIF-compuserve).**

8. **Choose the Sub type 89a Interlaced or 89a Noninterlaced.**

9. **Click the Options button at the lower-left corner of the dialog box.**

10. **Make sure the GIF tab is selected.**

11. **Choose Set the transparency value to the background color, as shown in Figure 10-8.**

Figure 10-8:
You get rid of the boxy background using options in the File Preferences dialog box.

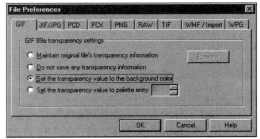

12. Click OK to return to the Save As dialog box.

13. Click Save when you're done.

> Wasn't that easy?! You won't see any difference in the image background, though, until you view it in a browser.

Including Images in Your Web Pages

Gosh, after all that rambling, you finally get to the good stuff — how to include images in Web pages. Hope you still have some energy.

The key idea about Web page images is that they're not actually part of the Web page, or more specifically, they're not part of the HTML document that creates the Web page. Instead, the Web page includes a *reference* to the image file, which is more or less a note to the browser telling it to show the image file along with the other page elements. The result is that the image appears to be part of the page, even though it's located in a separate file.

The next several sections explain how to include images and use image options such as alignment, text wraps, and image size.

Adding an image

The following steps show you how to include images in your Web pages. The process is the same for including any image — whether it's a photo, bullet, icon, or whatever. (Background images are a separate case, though, so those instructions are in the later section, "Using Images as Backgrounds.")

1. Open a Web page in Composer and place your cursor where you want the image to appear.

2. Go to Insert⇨Image, or click the Image button.

> The Image Properties dialog box appears, as shown in Figure 10-9.

3. Click Choose File.

> The Choose Image File dialog box appears, as shown in Figure 10-10.
>
> You can also just type the filename in the Image location text field and move on to Step 5.

4. Scroll to the directory and folder that contain the image file, and choose the image file you want to include.

> If you don't see the file you're looking for, try clicking the down arrow next to Files of type and choosing All Files.

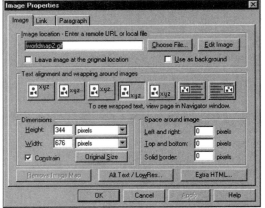

Figure 10-9:
The Image
Properties
dialog box
lets you
easily select
the image
file and
options.

Figure 10-10:
The Choose
Image File
dialog box
lets you pick
out the
image file
you want to
include.

5. Click Open.

You return to the Image Properties dialog box, where the filename now appears in the Image location text box.

6. Click OK.

That's all! The image should now appear in the Web page.

Here are a few words from your sponsor about including images and the Image Properties dialog box:

✔ The Edit Image button (next to the Image location field) invokes your image-editing program so that you can make changes to the image without having to go through the hassle of starting the program in a traditional way. You choose the image-editing program in Composer Preferences. See Chapter 5 for details on setting the preferences.

✔ The Leave image at the <u>o</u>riginal location checkbox specifies that
Composer should not copy the file to the local folder. Unless you're
referencing an identical image from several different files at different
locations, don't check this box. You'll find it easier to upload your Web
pages if you let Composer put everything together for you.

✔ You use the Alt. Text/Lo<u>w</u>Res button for several reasons. First, you can
accommodate readers who can't view images (or choose not to automatically download images). Second, you can provide a *tooltip* (which
describes what the button does) when readers hover their mouse over
the image (in newer browsers). Third, you can provide a description of
the image that's visible while the image loads. After you click the Alt.
Text/Lo<u>w</u>Res button, you see the resulting Alternate Image Properties
dialog box, shown in Figure 10-11. In this dialog box, briefly describe
the image in the Alternate text box. Something like "A picture of Win-
chester the Cat" or "Animal Clinic Logo" is a good choice. Click OK
when you finish.

Figure 10-11:
Adding
Alternate
text lets
readers who
don't view
images know
what they're
missing.

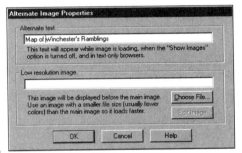

✔ The Low Resolution option, also available from the Alt. Text/Lo<u>w</u>Res
button, lets you provide a *very* small (in terms of file size) supplemental
image of the same dimensions as your regular image. The low res file
loads first so that the readers will see something as quickly as possible.
The main image then loads and replaces the lower-quality image.
Although Netscape Navigator (but few other browsers) supports this
option, you should use low res, particularly if your images are pretty
large. You click <u>C</u>hoose File just as you do for regular images.

Controlling image-text alignment

By default, browsers treat images like one really huge character. No, not a huge character like Frankenstein — a huge character, like a letter that's really tall or really wide (or both!). Basically, browsers just insert an image wherever you put the cursor, without regard to the surrounding text. The result is that the text appears before and after an image as if the image were a plain ol' word. Figure 10-12 shows this default image-text alignment.

You can control this alignment using Composer's neat alignment buttons. So, instead of throwing the image into a bunch of words, you can actually specify how you want the image and text to appear.

The following steps show you how to change the alignment of an existing image and show you the options available. You can use the same basic procedure when including a new image.

1. In Composer, select the image by clicking it.

2. Go to Insert⇨Image, or click the Image button.

The Image Properties dialog box appears.

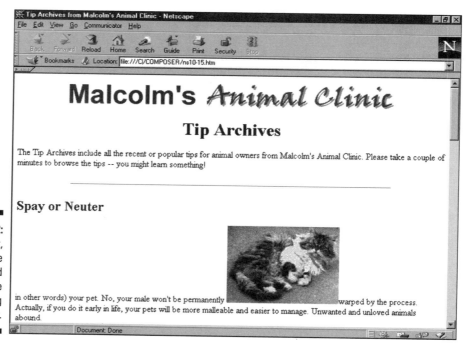

Figure 10-12:
By default, images are just inserted with the surrounding text.

3. **Choose an alignment option from the Text alignment and wrapping around images area.**

The following list shows the alignment and wrap buttons and gives a description of each.

- Aligns the top of the image with the top of the surrounding text.

- Aligns the middle of the image with the middle of the surrounding text.

- Aligns the middle of the image with the baseline of the surrounding text.

- Aligns the bottom of the image with the bottom of the surrounding text. This is the default setting.

- Aligns the bottom of the image with the baseline (bottom of *descenders*, which are the bottoms of letters such as *q* and *p*) of the surrounding text.

- Aligns the image to the left margin and wraps text around the image.

- Aligns the image to the right margin and wraps text around it.

In the final version of Communicator, only the first, third, fourth, sixth, and seventh options work reliably.

4. **Click OK.**

To see the results, you have to view the page in Navigator.

Specifying space around images

After you specify how images and text are aligned, you may want to specify how much space appears between the image and the surrounding text. By default, text appears pretty darn close to images, regardless of how the images and text are aligned. Figure 10-13 shows an example of how crammed images and text can become.

You can specify that more space appears between the two, thereby improving the overall appearance of the image-text combo. The following steps show you how to increase the space between an existing image and accompanying text. You can use the same basic procedure for a new image; you'd just use the process as you're including the image.

1. **In Composer, select the image by clicking it.**

2. **Go to Insert⇨Image, or click the Image button.**

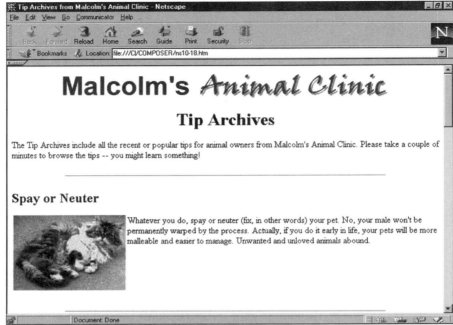

Figure 10-13: The image and surrounding text are crammed together by default.

3. **In the Space around image area, shown in Figure 10-14, fill in the text fields with the amount of space, measured in pixels, that you want to appear between the image and text.**

   The larger the number, the larger the space.

4. **Click OK.**

   Not too hard, eh?

   One final note: You can designate how wide an image border should be. Remember, images that serve as links appear within a border. You can increase, decrease, or delete this border using the Solid border option. Just add a number to specify how many pixels wide the border should be.

Specifying image dimensions

You can also specify how much space an image takes in a Web page. Why go to the trouble? Well, the best way to describe the benefits is to tell you how browsers load Web pages and their associated files. When a browser comes across a page containing an image, it has to figure out where the image goes

Figure 10-14:
The Space
around the
image area
lets you
specify how
much space
should appear
between the
image and
accompanying
text, which is
handy for
improving
image
appearance.

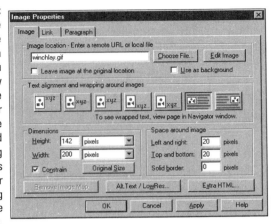

and how much space it needs before it can start displaying other elements such as paragraphs and headings. After the browser decides these things, it starts displaying other page elements and then finishes downloading the image file. The result is that readers sit and stare at a blank Web page while the browser determines where the image goes and how much space it needs.

By specifying image dimensions, you can tell the browser exactly how much room the image needs so that the browser can more quickly display other page elements. The image doesn't actually download faster, but other page elements appear on-screen faster because the browser doesn't have to determine how much space to allot the image. The result is that readers see the image outline (a placeholder of sorts), followed by other page elements, and then followed by the image itself. Readers don't have to stare at a blank screen — or at least they spend less time doing so.

To specify image dimensions, just follow these quick steps, which show you how to specify dimensions of an existing image. You can use the same basic procedure when including a new image.

1. In Composer, select the image by clicking it.

2. Go to Insert⇨Image, or click the Image button.

The Image Properties dialog box appears.

3. **In the Dimensions area, shown in Figure 10-15, verify that the image's Height and Width are displayed and fill them in if necessary.**

By default, the height and width are measured in pixels. If you're stretching an image (like a horizontal rule image) across most of the window, you can specify the number as a percentage of the window.

4. **Click OK.**

You won't see anything different in the browser, but your readers will thank you profusely.

Here are a couple more options for specifying image dimensions:

✔ The Constrain checkbox, located in the Image Properties dialog box, keeps you from accidentally distorting the image. If an image is originally 400 x 500 pixels and you set the Dimensions to 40 x something, Constrain forces that second value to 50. If you don't constrain the value, you can really have a funny looking picture.

✔ Also in the Image Properties dialog box, if the size isn't specified in the Dimensions area or if you've been changing the sizes and want to revert to the original size, just click Original Size, and the original values will return.

Figure 10-15:
The Dimensions area lets you specify an image's height and width.

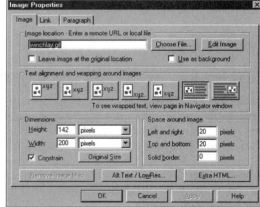

Using Images as Backgrounds

Background images are a special breed. They are referenced files, just like regular images, but they appear behind all page elements rather than as one of the page elements. Figure 10-16 shows a background image.

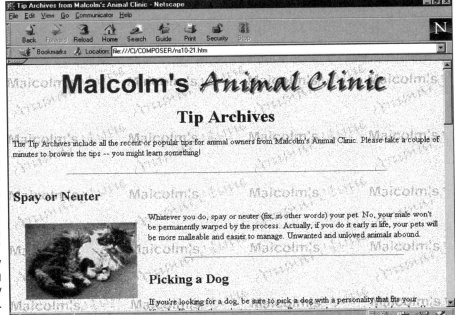

Figure 10-16:
This background image acts as a Web page "watermark," subtly identifying the company name.

The background image in Figure 10-16 is actually a small image that's *tiled*, meaning that the small graphic is repeated to fill the browser window. The result is that you can use a very small background image — which improves download time — and still have the image fill the browser window.

By default, browsers tile an image horizontally and vertically, meaning that the first image appears at the upper-left corner, then fills in across the first row, then the next row, and so on. However, you can be creative with image backgrounds and create a long, skinny image (say, 20 pixels tall by 1000 pixels wide), which forces the image to tile vertically only. So, rather than being repeated across the page, the image is repeated down the page.

For example, Figure 10-17 shows a background image that's actually 10 pixels tall by 1280 pixels wide. It's a two-color image, with a narrow band on the left and a wider band on the right. Admittedly, it's pretty boring — that is, until you use it as a background image, as shown in Figure 10-18.

Figure 10-17:
This image,
which
measures
1280 x 10
pixels, will
tile vertically
as a Web
page
background.

Because background images appear across the entire browser window, you need to keep the following guidelines in mind when choosing an image:

- ✔ **Images should complement, not overpower, Web page contents.** Choose an image that has coordinating colors, patterns, or shapes.

- ✔ **Images should adequately contrast page elements.** If you're using dark-colored text, the background should be light — and vice versa. If you have any doubt whether the background contrasts enough, it doesn't.

- ✔ **Images used to tile vertically need to be at least 1280 pixels wide.** This width accommodates all browsers and screen resolutions, without an unwanted stripe near the right edge of the browser window. Even if the browser window isn't that wide, there's no problem with the long (wide) image.

- ✔ **Images should use simple colors, patterns, or shapes.** If the image is too busy, meaning that it has too many colors, patterns, or shapes, it will obscure the content (not to mention blind your readers).

Including a background image using Composer is a snap. Just follow these steps:

1. **Open a Web page in Composer, and put your cursor where you want the image to appear.**

2. **Go to Insert⇨Image, or click the Image button.**

   The Image Properties dialog box appears.

3. **Click Choose File.**

   The Choose Image File dialog box appears.

   You can also type the filename in the Image location text field and skip to Step 5.

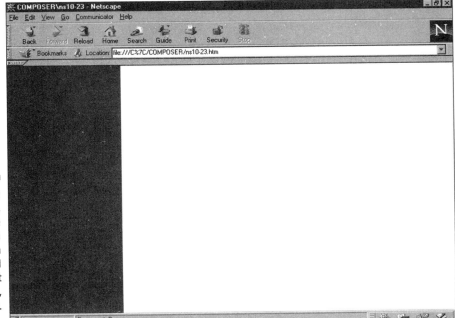

Figure 10-18:
The long, skinny image achieves a two-column background — that's fast to download, too.

4. Scroll to the directory and folder that contain the image file, and choose the image file you want to include.

If you don't see the file you're looking for, try clicking the down-arrow next to Files of type and choosing All Files.

5. Click Open.

You return to the Image Properties dialog box, where the filename now appears in the Image location text box.

6. Select the Use as background checkbox to specify that the image appear as a background, not as an image on the page.

Note that all of the other options vanish when you choose the background option.

7. Click OK.

That's all! The image should now appear as the Web page background.

Color me blue

If all your potential readers were using displays set to show millions of colors, this sidebar wouldn't be here. However, because many (probably most) of your potential readers use computer configurations that display only 256 colors, you need to be careful about the colors you use for page backgrounds or for large expanses of color within images. (Photographs or colored text don't pose the same problems discussed here, so don't worry about them.)

Computer colors are defined as a combination of red, green, and blue colors (called *RGB* colors). You can imagine that you can create a bazillion color combinations using various combinations of red, green, and blue. However, only 216 of these colors look consistently pure on Macintosh, Windows, and UNIX computers set to 256 colors. (The remaining 40 colors are taken by the operating system, so they're not commonly available on all browsers.)

Unfortunately, those 216 colors are not the same colors that you can easily pick off the menus in Composer. What to do? Two things.

First, whenever you're picking a color for use in your Web pages, particularly as the background, choose the "Other" option so that you get the Color dialog box, accessed by going to Format⇨Color and then clicking the Other button.

Second, remember these values for the Red, Blue, and Green proportions: 0, 51, 102, 153, 204, 255. Any combination of these color numbers is reliable. Say that you clicked in the funky rainbow area of the Color dialog box on a color you like. At the lower-right corner, you see that the color values are 2, 50, and 52. These values are close to, but not exactly, the "good" values, so you might find that the color is dithered (looks splotchy) in some browsers at some times. The solution? Compromise a little on the color, adjust the values to 0, 51, 51, and get a reliable color.

Using these guidelines, you can ensure that the colors you choose look great on any browser on any computer.

Chapter 11

Leaping Lizards!
Hopping from Images

. . . .

In This Chapter

▶ Using images as links
▶ Linking from thumbnail images
▶ Creating imagemaps (clickable images)

. . . .

Chapter 8 covers how to include links in your Web pages. Then Chapter 10 explains how to include images in your Web pages. This chapter shows how to use images as links so that readers can click an image and leap to other images or Web pages.

Using image links offers a couple of advantages over using text links. First, you get to include images, which, as we point out in Chapter 10, can add a splash of color or easily illustrate a concept. Second, image links give your page that "up-with-technology" look and feel. At the very least, they can help you keep up — or surpass — those pesky Joneses.

Keep in mind that, although image links are cool and fun, they still have the drawback of added download time — just as regular images do. As you're choosing images to use as links, you may want to check out the image guidelines presented in Chapter 10.

This chapter shows you what image links look like, explains how to make image links and *thumbnails* (tiny images that link to a bigger version of the same image), and shows you how to create *imagemaps* (clickable images that link to multiple places).

Making Image Links

Image links are no different from text links in function — they can link to pages within the same Web site, pages in other Web sites, and to a specified place within a Web page. The only difference is that rather than click a word or group of words, readers click an image to make the link.

You can easily identify image links because the image, by default, has a border around it. Figure 11-1 shows you what an image link looks like.

You can specify that the image link not have a border around it; however, a border acts as an essential visual cue to readers, telling them that the image links to other images or information. If you do not include a border on the image, be sure that something else — either the image itself or accompanying text — makes it clear to your readers that the image is actually also a link. (Yes, readers will be able to tell by looking at the Status bar and moving their cursors over the image, but you probably don't want to make them work that hard. Do you?)

Making an image link is easy, particularly because Composer does most of the work for you. To turn an existing image into a link, do the following:

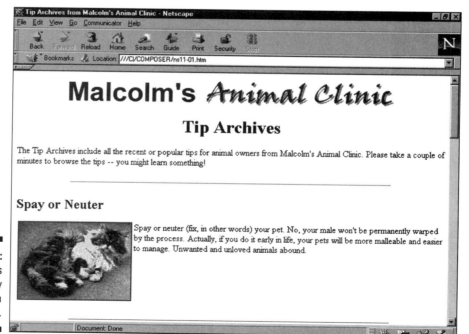

Figure 11-1:
Image links usually have a border.

1. Start with a Web page open in Composer, and include an image.

For more information about including images, see Chapter 10.

2. Select the image by clicking on it.

3. Go to Insert⇨Link, click the Link button, or press Ctrl+Shift+L.

You can also select the image and then right-click your mouse, which is both easy and efficient.

The Image Properties dialog box appears, as shown in Figure 11-2, with the Link tab selected.

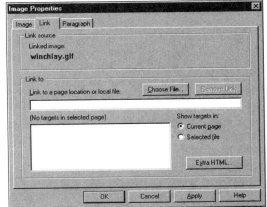

Figure 11-2:
In the Image Properties dialog box, you can take care of all your linking needs.

4. Click Choose File to browse to the file the image should link to.

You can also just type the filename in the area provided, if you happen to know the name.

5. Click OK when you're done.

Your image now appears within a border and will link to the file you specified.

Here are some notes about image links:

✔ Be sure to include *alternative text* (text that describes an image) with every image for readers who choose not to view images or who are using text-only browsers. If you have not yet included alternative text, check out Chapter 10 for more information.

✔ You can also link images to *targets* (specific places within Web pages), which is somewhat more precise than linking to the Web page as a whole. The process for linking images to targets works just about like it does for linking text to targets. You can find more information about targets in Chapter 8.

Making Thumbnails

A *thumbnail* is a small image that links to a larger version of the same image. Though you may think that including two copies of the same image is a waste of time, using thumbnails offers several benefits:

- ✔ **They take practically no time to download.** Because they're small, their files easily and quickly download to readers' computers. Readers don't have to wait to see the image.

- ✔ **They let readers choose to view the larger version.** Readers can view the thumbnail and decide whether they want to wait for the big one to download. You can include several thumbnails on a page without slowing download time too much. Of course, the more you include on a page, the slower the page downloads.

- ✔ **They take up very little page space.** Thumbnails are small, so you can easily incorporate them with other page elements. You can also include multiple thumbnails on a page without crowding other elements or making the page too long.

What's neat is that thumbnails link to full-sized images that are separate files, which means that the full-sized image doesn't have to be downloaded by anyone who isn't particularly interested in it.

Using thumbnails is essentially just linking a small image to a larger image. The following steps explain how to link a thumbnail to a larger image. Before you begin, have two image files ready — one thumbnail image and one full-sized image.

1. **To include a thumbnail image in your Web page, go to Insert⇨Image, browse to the image file, and click OK.**

   Don't forget to include alternative text for readers who choose not to view images or use text-only browsers.

2. **Select the image by clicking it.**

3. **Go to Insert⇨Link, click the Link button, or press Ctrl+Shift+L.**

   You can also select the image, right-click your mouse, and then select Create Link Using Selected.

   The Character Properties dialog box appears with the Link tab selected.

4. **Click Choose File to browse to the file the image should link to.**

   You can also just type the filename in the area provided, if you happen to know the name.

   You may need to select All Files from Files of type to see the image to which you want to link, as shown in Figure 11-3.

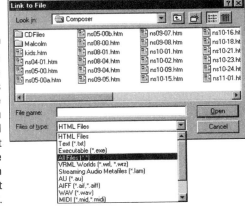

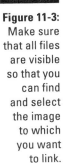

Figure 11-3:
Make sure
that all files
are visible
so that you
can find
and select
the image
to which
you want
to link.

5. Click OK when you're done.

To see whether your thumbnail works, open the Web page in Navigator and click the thumbnail. The thumbnail should link to the larger version of the same image.

Creating Imagemaps

An *imagemap* is a single image that includes multiple links to other images, pages, and sites. Imagemaps provide a great way to enhance your pages — they look cool, and they're easy to use. However, not all browsers support imagemaps, so not all your readers can enjoy your masterpiece.

Imagemaps are commonly used to show geographic areas — that is, the imagemap shows a large area, such as a city, town, or state. When you click the imagemap links, you could link to up-close views of various parts of the map. For example, you can create an imagemap of your town and include links to each of its suburbs so that you can show street names, housing additions, and landmarks. So, rather than babbling on about how to find the Gas-B-Gone Drug Store, you can let readers find it by using the imagemap.

Because Imagemaps — basically because they're cool — have grown in popularity, their uses have expanded beyond showing geographic areas. In fact, they're being used more and more to convey technical information. For example, you can show an image of a car engine with links to information about troubleshooting various engine parts. In this use, imagemaps can help you cut down on paragraphs of text and let readers more easily access information.

Also, imagemaps are frequently used to present a company logo and navigation links. (See Chapter 9 for more about navigation links.) Take a look at Figure 11-4, which shows how Malcolm's Animal Clinic uses an imagemap — essentially a montage of pictures and text — for some interesting links.

The following sections walk you through the process of creating an imagemap, including the how-to stuff you need as well as an example of how the Malcolm Animal Clinic imagemap was put together. Here are the steps you take in the following sections:

1. **Choose a suitable image.**

2. **Select the imagemap type.**

3. **Provide alternative navigation.**

4. **Mark clickable areas.**

5. **Define the links.**

6. **Link to the map.**

Be sure to follow the information in the next five sections in the order provided, particularly for creating your first imagemap.

Figure 11-4: This cool page links to information about cats, dogs, and other animals.

Choosing a suitable image

The first step in creating an imagemap is to choose a suitable image. Not every image makes a good imagemap, you know. The following guidelines should help you pick ones that are most appropriate.

- **Consider whether the content is appropriate for an imagemap.** Will it provide navigation? Will it be an overview of more specific information?

- **Consider whether the image lends itself to multiple links.** Images that show general — rather than detailed — information work best.

- **Choose images that are clutter free.** Images with lots of background fluff are less attractive, more difficult to transform to an imagemap, and harder for the reader to use.

- **Choose images that include easily-definable parts (like the one shown in Figure 11-4).** Having clearly definable parts makes it easier for you to create the imagemap and is more intuitive for your readers to use.

You might also consider whether the benefits of using imagemaps outweigh the time required to create them. They're not difficult to create, but they do take some time. Okay. They take darn near forever to create, particularly for something like the image used in this example. However, for the kiddies (or kiddies at heart), they're worth it.

Malcolm's Animal Clinic created an image to use for an imagemap, combining favorite animal snapshots into one image. This image, shown earlier in Figure 11-4, is simple and uncluttered (look at all the white space), which makes the link areas easy to define and the image itself easy for readers to use.

Choosing an imagemap type

The next step is to choose an imagemap type — or essentially, choose whether the readers' browsers or the *server* (computer where the imagemap resides) determines where the link goes. Think of it this way. When readers click on part of an imagemap, something somewhere has to determine where the click links to. With imagemaps, either the readers' browsers can determine where the click goes or the server where the imagemap resides determines where the clicks go. This difference in where the thinkin' takes place creates two different imagemap types.

- **Client-side imagemaps:** The thinkin' takes place on the readers' browsers. These imagemaps have the advantage of being quicker (because the browser doesn't have to ask the server for information), but not all browsers support them.

✔ **Server-side imagemaps:** The thinkin' takes place on the server computer. These imagemaps have the advantage of being available to all readers (because they're not dependent on browsers supporting them), but they tend to be slower because the browser and server have to iron out what to display. You'll also need some help from your ISP to implement these.

Which one you choose depends on which drawback you're willing to live with. All in all, creating client-side imagemaps is easier because you don't have to drag your ISP guru into the process; you can do all the work yourself. However, if you want absolutely everybody and their dog to be able to view the imagemap, you might want to use the server-side type. The choice is up to you. (Most of your readers will do fine with client-side imagemaps — it's the other 5 percent or so that you'll need to consider.)

Now back to the Malcolm Animal Clinic. The clinic chooses to create a client-side imagemap mainly because it doesn't want to hassle with contacting its ISP. Also, it determines that most of its readers use browsers that support imagemaps.

The following sections show you how to create a client-side imagemap. If you choose to create a server-side imagemap, contact your ISP and ask the following questions:

Do you support server-side imagemaps? _____

What do I need to do to create them? _____

How is creating a server-side map for your system different from the way I already create a client-side map? _____

Do you have some easy way of converting my (functional) client-side map to a server-side map? _____

What else do I need to know, and where do I go for help, if I need it? _____

Providing alternative navigation

The next step to take is to provide alternative navigation. *Alternative navigation* is a separate means of navigation, such as a set of text links or buttons, that your readers can use instead of the imagemap, in case they can't view or choose not to view the imagemap. You're wise to include alternative navigation with every imagemap for two reasons:

> ✔ **Not all browsers support imagemaps.** If you're creating a client-side imagemap, remember that not all browsers support imagemaps and, therefore, not all readers can view them. If readers can't see the imagemaps, they won't be able to link to other information.
>
> ✔ **Not all readers view images.** Remember that some readers choose not to view images and that some readers still use text-only browsers, which don't display images at all. Again, if readers can't or don't view the image, they'll have no way to link to other information.

For these reasons, providing alternative navigation with imagemaps is essential. Take a look at Figure 11-5, which shows how the clinic used alternative navigation.

Marking clickable areas

An imagemap is nothing more that a collection of *clickable areas* (areas that readers click on to link to other information). Clickable areas can be one of three shapes — either circles, polygons, or rectangles. Malcolm's Animal Clinic imagemap, shown again in Figure 11-6, includes each of these clickable shapes.

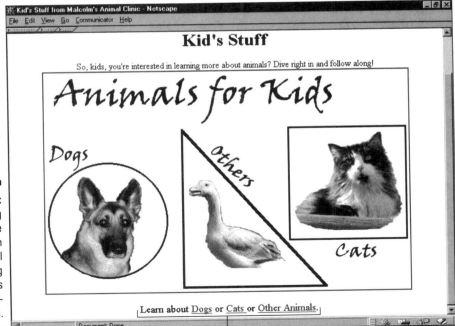

Figure 11-5: Using alternative navigation is essential for letting all readers use image-map links.

Alternative navigation

Figure 11-6:
Clickable
areas in a
client-side
imagemap
can be
circles,
polygons, or
rectangles.

Marking clickable areas isn't hard at all. In fact, it's similar to telling the computer to draw an invisible dotted line where you define the boundaries of the link area. To tell the computer where to draw these boundary lines, all you have to provide are the x,y coordinates — the computer does the calculating and figures the boundaries for you.

The best way to find the necessary coordinates is to open the file in an image-editing program — such as Paint Shop Pro — and hover the cursor over each of the points. Somewhere — probably at the bottom of the editing window — you can see the coordinates of the point where your mouse is located (see an example of coordinates in Figure 11-7); write those down.

If you want to follow along, the imagemap shown earlier in Figure 11-5 is on the CD that comes with this book in the CDFILES folder under the name KIDS.GIF. If you have your own project in mind, no problem — the principles are identical, regardless of the project.

The following steps show you exactly how to figure out the clickable areas for each of the three shapes, using the clinic's imagemap as an example.

Figure 11-7:
Point the cursor at a place in the image and note the coordinates from the Status bar — the dog's nose is at 129,325.

Coordinates   Pointer

Marking circles

Defining a circle (like the one with the dog in it) requires only that you find the coordinates of the center and then the radius (distance from the center to the edge) of the circle. Defining a circle requires a little — but not much — math. Here's the process, assuming that you've opened the image in an image-editing program:

 1. **Select the pointer or magnifying glass cursor.**

   In most image-editing programs, the pointer shows its coordinates in the Status bar of the program. In Paint Shop Pro, you use the magnifying glass cursor for the same purpose.

2. **Move the cursor to the center of the circle, and note the coordinates.**

   In this example, something like 112,269 is close enough. No need to knock yourself out getting *exactly* the center of the circle, unless your reader will be trying to click *exactly* on the edge of the areas.

3. **Move the cursor horizontally to the right edge of the circle.**

   You'll probably get something in the ballpark of 218,269.

4. Subtract the smaller of the *x* (first) values from the second to get the radius.

In this example, you subtract 112 from 218 and get 106. So, your circle coordinates are 112,269,106. Write those down — you'll need them later!

Marking rectangles

Identifying rectangles (or squares) is fairly straightforward. All you do is find the *x,y* coordinates for the upper-left and lower-right corners. The computer figures out the other coordinates.

Here's the process, assuming that you've opened the image in an image-editing program:

1. Select the pointer or magnifying glass cursor.

In most image-editing programs, the pointer shows its coordinates in the Status bar of the program. In Paint Shop Pro, you use the magnifying glass cursor for the same purpose.

2. Move the cursor to the upper-left corner of the rectangle and note the coordinates.

In this example, you get something close to 427,104 for the *x,y* coordinates of the upper-left corner.

3. Move the cursor to the lower-right corner of the rectangle, and note the coordinates.

In this example, you get something close to 650,312 for the *x,y* coordinates of the lower-right corner. Write down those coordinates and keep them safe. You'll need them when finishing the imagemap.

Marking polygons

Polygons — otherwise known as the catchall shape for anything that doesn't fit into other categories — are a little less mathy than circles and a little more tedious than rectangles. To tell the computer about a polygon, you must identify the coordinates of each corner (or *vertices*). If you think about that for a minute, you'll see why the goose in the figure is in a triangle, not in an octagon.

To identify a polygon, use the following procedure:

1. Select the pointer or magnifying glass cursor.

In most image-editing programs, the pointer shows its coordinates in the Status bar of the program. In Paint Shop Pro, you use the magnifying glass cursor for the same purpose.

2. **Move the cursor to a corner of the polygon, and note the coordinates.**

   In this example, you get something close to 245,105 for the top angle.

3. **Move the cursor to an adjacent angle, and note the coordinates.**

   In this example, you get something close to 245,397 for the right angle.

4. **Continue noting the coordinates of each angle.**

   The final angle in this triangle should be something near 502,397. Write down those coordinates. You'll need them when finishing the imagemap.

Defining the links

Finally, after you've marked the clickable areas, you have to define what each area should link to. The steps in this section show you how to define the links from the areas marked in the previous section. This section essentially tells the computer what you discovered about the image coordinates. Table 11-1 lists the HTML tags and attributes you need to define the links. Don't spaz; using the tags and attributes is not hard.

Table 11-1	Tags and Attributes Needed to Define Imagemap Links
Tag or Attribute	*Description*
`<MAP>...</MAP>`	Identifies a collection of links included in a client-side imagemap.
`<AREA>`	Specifies the shape of the link area.
`NAME="..."`	Identifies the imagemap name so that you can refer to it.
`SHAPE="..."`	Identifies whether the link area is a `CIRC`(le), `POLY`(gon), or `RECT`(angle).
`COORDS="..."`	Marks the *x,y* coordinates for the link area.
`USEMAP="#..."`	Identifies the imagemap as a client-side imagemap.
`ALT="..."`	Specifies alternative text.

Following are the steps you use to create the imagemap definition:

1. **In Composer, click your mouse anywhere within the page.**

   We recommend putting the map definition somewhere toward the bottom of the page, just so it's out of the way.

2. **Go to Insert⇨HTML Tag.**

   The HTML Tag dialog box appears, as shown in Figure 11-8.

Figure 11-8:
The HTML
Tag dialog
box lets you
add the
necessary
imagemap
tags.

3. **In the HTML Tag dialog box, add the** ⟨MAP⟩ **tag as well as the** NAME= **attribute.**

   The resulting code will look like this:

   ```
   <MAP NAME="kidsmap">
   ```

   The name you put with the NAME= attribute should be brief and describe the imagemap contents.

4. **Click OK.**

5. **Go to** Insert⇨HTML Tag.

   You'll get real used to this Insert⇨HTML Tag business.

6. **Add the closing** ⟨/MAP⟩ **tag.**

7. **Click OK.**

8. **In Composer, click your mouse between the two** ⟨MAP⟩...⟨/MAP⟩ **tags.**

9. **Go (again) to** Insert⇨HTML Tag.

10. **Add the** ⟨AREA⟩ **tag as well as a** SHAPE= **attribute and the shape coordinates.**

    Your code will look something like this:

    ```
    <AREA SHAPE="CIRCLE" COORDS="112,269,106">
    ```

    The shape value that you fill in depends on the shape you're creating. For example, the SHAPE= attribute in the code could also read SHAPE="RECT" or SHAPE="POLY".

    For the COORDS= attribute, just fill in the coordinates (without spaces in between) that you wrote down when you defined the shape area.

11. **Add a link to the** ⟨AREA⟩ **tag, like this:**

    ```
    <AREA SHAPE="CIRCLE" COORDS="112,269,106"
          HREF="dogs.htm">
    ```

12. **Add alternative text:**

```
<AREA SHAPE="CIRCLE" COORDS="112,269,106"
        HREF="dogs.htm" ALT="Learn about Dogs">
```

13. **Click OK.**

14. **To complete the Animal Clinic imagemap, just complete the same process for the rectangle and polygon.**

    The code ends up as follows (it's really just two lines — therefore two trips to the HTML Tag dialog box):

```
<AREA SHAPE=RECT COORDS="437,104,650,312"
   HREF="cats.htm" ALT="Learn about Cats">
<AREA SHAPE=POLY
        COORDS="245,105,245,397,502,398,245,105"
   HREF="other.htm" ALT="Learn about Other Animals">
```

    Note: If the shapes overlap, the first one defined takes precedence. For example, if a circle is overlaid on a square (visually), you first define the circle and then the square. If a point lies within both the circle and the square, the link associated with the circle will be used, and the other one will be ignored.

Linking to the map

Finally — whew — you get to take your fully-defined imagemap and make it work. You must put the image into the document and then add a teensy bit of HTML code to tell the image it's associated with the imagemap definition. These steps show you how to link the map:

1. **In Composer, go to Insert⇨Image or click the Image button.**

    The Image Properties dialog box appears. Yeah, yeah. You've seen this before.

2. **Use the Choose File button to browse to and select the image file you want to use.**

    For more information about inserting images in your documents, see Chapter 10.

3. **Click the Extra HTML button.**

    You see the Extra HTML dialog box, as shown in Figure 11-9.

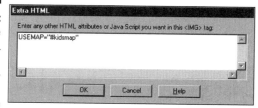

Figure 11-9:
Here's the
Extra HTML
dialog
box —
yippee!

4. **Add** USEMAP="#...", **and fill in the "..." with the name you used for the** NAME= **attribute.**

For example, the Animal Clinic USEMAP= attribute looks like this:

```
USEMAP="#kidsmap"
```

Don't forget the pound sign (#) in the USEMAP= attribute.

5. **Click OK.**

Wowzie! You're done. Now all you do is test the page. Just whiz on over to Navigator, open the page, and try it out by clicking on each shape and verifying that the links go to the correct page!

Part IV
Making Your Web Pages Scream, Jiggle, Gyrate, and Whir

The 5th Wave   By Rich Tennant

"I don't care if you do have a coalition of kids from 19 countries backing you up; I'm still not buying you an ISDN line."

In this part . . .

In this part, you see how to give your Web pages their own personalities. You can make them sing and jitterbug and flash and scroll — right before your very eyes!

In Chapter 12, you see how to add audio, a must see for readers who want their Web pages to make sounds. Then in Chapter 13, you see how Java applets enable you to easily add interactive toys and features to your Web pages. Your readers will really get a kick out of these.

Though these are some of the fancier effects you can include in your Web pages, they're not really any more difficult to include than less flashy effects. In most cases, Composer does the work for you. You just have to be bossy and tell it what you want!

Chapter 12

Adding Toots to Your Web Pages

. . . .

In This Chapter
▶ Adding sound to Web pages
▶ Finding sounds to use

. . . .

*J*ust in case the first 11 chapters in this book don't add enough exciting features to your Web pages, this chapter goes further and explains how to make your pages holler, moo, grunt, or bark at your readers. You'll see how adding sound can give your pages a personality all their own.

Of course, you can always add sounds that actually have a purpose — but heck, why be so stiff and boring if you don't have to? Whatever the content or purpose of your sound clips, this chapter will show you how to incorporate them.

Adding Toots

You've probably guessed, but adding toots and grunts to your Web pages is done pretty much to amuse your readers, with few other practical uses. Most of the sounds you find on the Web are music clips — you know, clips of the themes from "Jaws," "Peter Gunn," "X-Files," "Seinfeld," or other catchy tunes. Yes, they're mostly copyright infringements, as well. The ones that aren't copyright infringements tend to be rude — bathroom sounds, and so on.

However, in rare instances, sounds are used to help readers identify or diagnose problems. For example, you can include sound files to help readers troubleshoot a beeping noise their computer is making. One sound file might indicate what the computer should sound like, and additional sound files might identify weird sounds that computers commonly make right before they bite the dust. Had we only been thinking, we could have recorded some of our own just last week.

What's kind of cool about sound files is that you can specify whether the sound erupts when readers access your page, or you can let readers click a link to activate the sound file. You can even embed a little mini-CD-like control panel in the page. If you choose to just let the sound erupt, keep in mind that you'll be forcing your readers to waaaaait for the file to download. At least with the sound button option, you give them a choice. Figure 12-1 shows a Web page with sound control panels embedded.

Using sound files has some drawbacks. You guessed it — sound files are enormous and take forever to download. In fact, most sound clips require a big bunch of waiting for nothing more than a quick and brief toot. Also, in order to hear the toot, your readers' computers must be reasonably decked out with sound cards and speakers.

How do you know what percentage of your readers have sound cards and speakers? No telling. These fluffier computer doodads are becoming fairly popular; however, a lot of your corporate America readers who have stuffed-shirt computers (ones that can be used only for work, and not play) don't come equipped with sound equipment.

To include sound files in your Web page, use one of these sound file formats:

- ✔ **AIFF (Audio Interchange File Format):** This format is a popular sound file format on the Internet and is supported by most browsers.

- ✔ **AU (or basic Audio):** This format is the standard file format on Sun computers and is widely recognized on the Web. The quality is not as high as is an AIFF file, but an AU file is acceptable for most purposes.

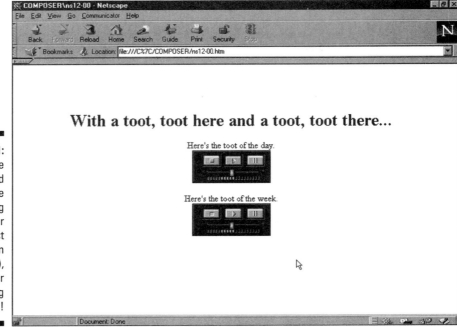

Figure 12-1:
Click the sound buttons (the right-facing arrow is for play, just like on a VCR), and hear something cool!

- ✔ **MIDI (Musical Instrument Digital Interface):** This format is used for synthesized sounds and is a standard in the recording industry. These instrumental files are extremely small and great for background music.

- ✔ **WAV (as in WAVe):** This format is the most common file format on Windows computers and is occasionally recognized on other systems.

If you have a MIDI file that meets your needs, use it. Otherwise, choose AIFF for general use or WAV if your audience is primarily Windows-based.

Finding toots to use

You can find loads of sound files on the Internet — fun sounds, rude sounds, music quips, noises — practically any sound you can think of. Instead of pointing you to specific Web sites that have freebie sounds available, we show you how to search for your own. Why? Searching for stuff on the Internet is a great skill. You can find not only sound files but also video files, images, applets, and JavaScript samples, just to name a few. Also, because of the variety of sounds available on the Web, we don't want to lead you to sites that might — at some point in the future — change from G-rated to X-rated files. Additionally, take a look in the miscellaneous bin at your favorite music store for the musical equivalent of clip art — royalty-free sounds.

The following steps show you a sample search using Yahoo!, a popular Internet directory service that lists Web sites organized by category. If you want more information about directories, check out Chapter 17.

1. **In Navigator, enter** `http://www.yahoo.com`**.**

   The Yahoo! home page appears.

2. **Select a search category by clicking a link.**

   To search for sound files, click the <u>Computers and Internet</u> or the <u>Multimedia</u> link.

3. **Enter a search term (or terms) in the search field.**

   Terms like "sound" or "sound file" work pretty well.

4. **Choose Search all of Yahoo or Search only in. . . .**

   If you're searching for sound files, you'll probably want to choose Search only in . . . to eliminate many of the extraneous files.

5. **Click Submit.**

   Yahoo! perks and churns for a few minutes and then provides you with a list of search results. From there, you can just scroll through the results and follow Web site links that seem to match what you're looking for.

After you find the files of your choice, to store them on your hard drive, just right-click (or long-click, if you're on a Mac) on the link to the sound file, and then choose Save Link As from the pop-up menu.

Putting in the toot

If, despite the warnings about sound files being an enormous pain to download, you still want to put in that blaring toot, this section shows you how.

The first, easiest, and kindest-to-your-readers choice is to link to the sound file just as you link to any file and let readers select it if they want. Linking text such as <u>Select this link to hear my dog</u> to the recording is more than acceptable. See Chapter 8 for more about links.

However, we'll walk you through the process of inflicting the sounds directly on your readers. First, though, take a look at Table 12-1, which shows you the HTML tags and attributes you need to include sound files.

Table 12-1	HTML Tags and Attributes Needed to Include Sound Files
Tag or Attribute	*Description*
`<EMBED>`	Embeds (surprise) something in a Web page.
`SRC="…"`	Identifies the sound file.
`AUTOSTART="…"`	Specifies whether the sound file opens when the Web page is accessed or when a button is clicked. The value can be `TRUE` (automatically starts) or `FALSE` (readers must click a button).
`HIDDEN="…"`	Specifies whether the sound control box is visible in the Web page. The value `TRUE` indicates that the control box is hidden; the value `FALSE` indicates that the control box is visible.
`HEIGHT="…"`	Specifies the control box height.
`WIDTH="…"`	Specifies the control box width.
`<BGSOUND SRC="…">`	Embeds sounds for Microsoft Internet Explorer users.
`LOOP="…"`	Specifies that the `<BGSOUND>` for Microsoft Internet Explorer users should continue playing (loop) or not.

The following steps show you how to include a sound file in your Web page:

1. **In Composer, put your cursor at the top of the page.**

2. **Go to Insert⇨HTML tag.**

   The HTML Tag dialog box appears, as shown in Figure 12-2.

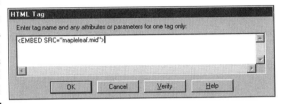

Figure 12-2: The HTML Tag dialog box rears its head again!

3. **Add the** `<EMBED>` **tag as well as the** `SRC=` **attribute to specify the sound filename.**

   Sound files use file formats such as AIFF, AU, AVI, MIDI, or WAV.

   The code, at this point, should look like this:

   ```
   <EMBED SRC="mapleleaf.mid">
   ```

4. **Add the** `AUTOSTART=` **attribute to specify whether you want the sound file to start when the page is accessed or when readers click a button.**

   The value `TRUE` makes the file start when the page is loaded, whereas `FALSE` leaves it to the reader to play the file.

   The code should now look like this:

   ```
   <EMBED SRC="mapleleaf.mid" AUTOSTART="false">
   ```

5. **Specify whether you want to keep a control box from appearing on-screen by adding the** `HIDDEN=` **attribute.**

   The control box gives readers the option to start, pause, and stop the sound.

   The value `TRUE` hides the control box; `FALSE` shows the control box.

   Heeeeeere's some code:

   ```
   <EMBED SRC="mapleleaf.mid" AUTOSTART="false"
           HIDDEN="false">
   ```

6. Specify control box dimensions by adding HEIGHT= **and** WIDTH= **attributes.**

Specify these values as a number of pixels. The larger the number, the bigger the control box.

```
<EMBED SRC="mapleleaf.mid" AUTOSTART="false"
       HIDDEN="false" HEIGHT="140" WIDTH="60">
```

7. Click OK.

If you followed the steps, the sound file control box should appear in your Web page. Go on over to Navigator to check it out. You should see something like one of the control boxes in Figure 12-1.

Here are some notes about sounds you won't hear from just anyone:

✔ As a rule, if your embedded file is hidden, it should be set to Autostart, and vice versa. Visible sound files need not autostart — readers can easily play the sound if they choose to.

✔ If you want to accommodate Internet Explorer users with a background sound, you need to add the <BGSOUND="…" tag and a LOOP= attribute to your HTML document. The BGSOUND= attribute identifies the sound file; the LOOP= attribute makes the sound repeat. You don't have to include these, but not including them may mean that some of your readers won't be able to access the sound file. Again, go to Insert⇨HTML Tag, and enter the tag. Your final code will look something like this:

```
<BGSOUND="mapleleaf.mid" LOOP="infinite">
```

This tag is equivalent to setting the <EMBED> tag to HIDDEN="TRUE" and Autostart="true".

Notice that the Internet Explorer <BGSOUND> tag is separate from Netscape's <EMBED> tag.

Adding moving pictures

Using video in Web pages actually has few practical uses, other than showing off the candid shots of your boss making a fool of himself at the company picnic. Hey, everyone has to see that one, right? In fact, at this point, most videos you see in Web pages are provided merely for grins.

Compared to the "for grins" value and the limited practical uses that video offers, the downsides for including video are pretty hefty. Video files are absolutely enormous and take seemingly an eternity to download. For example, in the time it takes for the video of your boss mooning the marketing staff to download, you could head over to personnel, fill out your resignation, stop by the front desk for a free doughnut, and wave good-bye to the company you just worked for. No kidding, video files are rarely worth the wait.

Another downside is that video doesn't roll smoothly in all computers — particularly older, slower computers. The result is that your boss's moon could look like a bent-over-bunny-hop. (And, no, we don't have this video to show you . . . though we've been asked.) Video clips are definitely intended for readers using high-end computers, equipped with a very good video card.

Just like sound files, you can use a variety of video formats:

- **AVI (Audio Video Interleaved):** These files combine video and audio in a highly compressed, popular multimedia format. This format is a good choice if your audience is mostly Windows-based.

- **MPEG (Moving Pictures Experts Group):** These files are a highly popular video format on the Internet. MPEG is rapidly becoming universally accepted for compressed video of all sorts and is the best choice for heterogeneous audiences.

- **QT (QuickTime):** This format, which is for audio and video, was originally popularized on Apple Macintosh computers but is now commonly recognized on Windows, as well.

You can find tons of video files to use and play with on the Internet. Just take a poke through the Yahoo! directory service (see instructions earlier in this chapter in the section "Finding toots to use").

Chapter 13
Using Java Applets

A Java applet isn't something you add to your coffee. And it isn't some fancy bean grown by Juan Valdez. A *Java applet* is a special application of *Java*, which is (eeek!) a programming language used, among other things, to apply fancy effects to Web pages. Don't be scared off by the techno-babble, though. Java applets are prepackaged for you so that you can add cool Web page effects without having to know a hill of beans about Java, scripting, or programming. You don't have to do a thing other than put the applet in your Web page.

Just what can you do with a Java applet? You can include fancy animations, interactive chat rooms, games, and even such things as limited image-editing capabilities. Figure 13-1 shows a Web page that includes an animated ad banner at the top of a page.

The best way to approach Java applets is to take them in small doses and gradually build up your tolerance. You wouldn't recommend seven double-espresso mochas to a coffee shop novice, would you? Well, by the same token, you want to go slowly and carefully with Java. It's easier that way.

Although Composer won't let you develop your own applets — and developing applets is pretty techie — it does let you easily add prefabricated applets to your Web pages. In this chapter, you'll get a grip on Java and Java applet basics, see how to include applets in your pages, and find out where to go to find new ones.

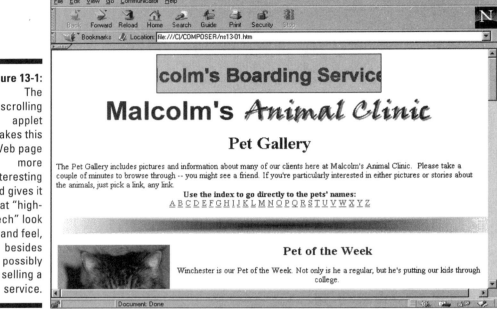

Pet Gallery from Malcolm's Animal Clinic - Netscape

Figure 13-1:
The scrolling applet makes this Web page more interesting and gives it that "high-tech" look and feel, besides possibly selling a service.

Java actually has a ton of uses outside Web page design, but that's far beyond the scope of this book. If you finish this chapter and decide that Java is the greatest thing since caffeine, check into *Java For Dummies*, by Aaron E. Walsh, published by IDG Books Worldwide.

Grinding on Java

Java was developed by Sun Microsystems as a programming language for the Internet, both to enhance Web sites and, more important, to provide a secure environment with which programs over the Internet can be run. Java, and by extension Java applets, can be downloaded to your computer without bringing viruses or malicious or damaging code along with them. The programming language will not let applets come through Web pages and do anything to your hard drive or files, so you have both the power and control of a whole programming language without the danger of messing up your computer.

That security, plus the fact that both Netscape Navigator and Microsoft Internet Explorer support it, make Java a key component of Web pages. Moreover, Java is an open technology — if you're so inclined, you can learn all about Java from completely free sources, without having to purchase an expensive developer's kit or use a proprietary program. Wow!

ActiveX: A Java equivalent, or a bunch of beans?

ActiveX is a Microsoft-designed protocol used to create applets that can be inserted into Web pages. These applets can have basically the same functionality as Java applets, providing extra glitz and glamour and functionality and enabling you to easily access data from your Microsoft applications.

However, ActiveX is primarily a Microsoft-based technology and, therefore, primarily friendly and usable on only Windows-type computers running the Microsoft Internet Explorer browser. With a special add-in for your Netscape browser, you can see ActiveX controls in your Web pages, but that requires the hassle of the extra step of using an add-in.

Unless you have some really overriding reason to choose ActiveX, we strongly recommend using Java, a Java applet, or JavaScript to add special functionality to your Web site. As a rule, Java-related enhancements are more widely accessible to your potential readers than ActiveX controls are.

For more information about ActiveX, head to http://www.microsoft.com/activeplatform/default.asp.

Depending on your perspective, though, Java is an impressive programming language designed for networked applications, the bane of dial-up Internet surfers, a boon to designers of really interactive Web sites, or even, in extreme cases, the future of computing. Pretty impressive claims for a technology that's only a couple of years old, huh? In actuality, it is an impressive language and is, in fact, optimized for networked programs. Java applets and the associated files tend to be fairly large and slow, making the pages that contain them fairly slow, as well. That would make it the "bane of dial-up surfers" and contribute to the "World Wide Wait." Java takes HTML to the next step with the capability to use animations, play sounds, and even control computer games from within a Web browser, so the boon to designers seems accurate, too. Finally, there's a new "future of computing" every year or so, so we'll accept Java being future-oriented as a possibility.

More to the point for Web page designers like yourself, Java lets you include high-powered effects — ones that you cannot achieve using HTML or, by extension, Composer. If you've been surfing the Net, you may have noticed fancy animated banners, or pages with games (Hangman, tic-tac-toe), or interactive discussion sites. These moving, animated, gyrating, interactive, fancy-pants effects are likely programmed with Java.

What Is a Java Applet?

Java applets are little Java programs that do stuff — like animating objects, scrolling text, or masterminding tic-tac-toe — in Web pages. Sometimes the applets work alone, but in many cases, they work in cahoots with other files. For example, a Java applet that scrolls images across the screen requires some image files to work along with the applet to complete the applet function.

As cool as they are, Java applets do have two downsides. First, just like other Web page enhancements such as images and multimedia effects, applets take extra time to download. In fact, for someone connected to the Internet using a modem, a Java applet can easily take a few minutes to download and run. That's certainly long enough to hit users' boredom thresholds and have them moving on to other sites. So, be sure that the benefits (general coolness or something more practical) that an applet adds outweigh the extra download time.

Second, if you're taking the easy way out, you are limited to using applets available for download over the Internet (or perhaps applets that the computer geek next door writes for you). You could go buy *Java For Dummies* and do it yourself, but unless you're a closet computer geek, it's probably more expedient to beg or borrow (but not steal) them.

Not all applets you find on the Internet are available for you to use; they're someone else's creation and belong to that person. Unless an applet is explicitly marked as free to use, don't use it for *anything* other than practice.

Finding applets to use

If you're looking for applets to use in your Web pages, the Internet is *the* place to go. It offers lots of Web sites that have information and sample applets for you to use. For example, the Java home at `http://www.javasoft.com/`, which offers the definitive scoop on Java and related developments, and the Gamelan home page at `http://www.gamelan.com/` give you a full array of Java resources as well as resources about other related technologies, such as JavaScript or ActiveX.

You can also use the Internet to find someone to create a custom applet for you. The Gamelan Web site provides resources for people looking for custom applets — such as names and e-mail addresses of programmers who create applets. Yeah, believe it or not, people do such geeky things for a living.

Figuring out applet anatomy

Applets are nothing more than a compiled file that uses the .class file extension. Because applets are *compiled* — meaning that all the individual instructions to the computer are mooshed into one entity — you can't examine them, tweak them, or fiddle with them. Instead, you have to use them as individual entities. For you, applets make your job easier because all the hard work in developing the applet is done for you.

Applets usually have companions. Often, but not always, applets require you to include additional files, such as images or sound files, to make the applet do its thing. Applets generally contain instructions (like "scroll, please") and look elsewhere for exactly what to scroll. Precisely which and how many files an individual applet requires depends on how the Java program is written, what it does, and what you want it to do.

To get an applet to do its thing, you need to give it instructions. Yes, here's your chance to be bossy. In many cases, you want to provide certain information to applets about what they should do and how they should do it. For example, if you have an applet that makes text scroll, you'll probably have to tell it what text to scroll. "Yo! Applet! Scroll this!" probably won't cut it. It'll take something like <PARAM TEXT="Scroll this!"> to convey the same meaning. Or you might change the direction with something like <PARAM DIRECTION="backward">.

To provide that information to the applet, you just throw in some HTML code with the instructions. Taking a closer look at applet anatomy, examine the following code, which incorporates an applet called ImageTape in a Web page. ImageTape makes a scrolling panel of pictures.

```
<APPLET CODE="ImageTape.class" WIDTH=200 HEIGHT=50>
<PARAM NAME=speed VALUE="4">
<PARAM NAME=img VALUE="images">
<PARAM NAME=nimgs VALUE="4">
</APPLET>
```

By the way, this applet is available at http://www.javasoft.com/ from Sun Microsystems, the company that created Java.

If you don't find that HTML code looks somewhat familiar, you might glance at Chapter 3, which takes a brief look at HTML.

The next couple of bullet points describe the various parts of the same code.

  ✔ The <APPLET>...</APPLET> tags specify to include a specific Java applet by filename, in this case ImageTape.class. These tags further identify the applet's width and height, measured in pixels.

✔ The three `<PARAM>` tags between the opening and closing `<APPLET>`... `</APPLET>` tags specify the name of the folder in which the images are located as well as the number of images to expect in each folder and how fast to scroll the images.

So, the applet and other associated files end up tossed together according to your instructions to give the appearance of one way-cool thing that scrolls images across the screen. Although different applets' anatomies will vary somewhat, they will all include these basic components.

Adding a Java applet to your Web page

Following is the process to include a very simple scrolling image applet in a Web page. You can use these same instructions to include different applets, though the specifics might differ a bit.

1. **Move the** `.class` **file into the same folder as the HTML document that will host the applet.**

   Use the file management tools on your system to move the files. For example, on Windows 95, we used the Windows Explorer to browse to the `.class` file from the CD (in the scroller folder, shown in Figure 13-2), clicked on the file to select it, used Ctrl+C to copy it, browsed to the folder with the Web site in it, and pressed Ctrl+V to paste the file into place.

Figure 13-2: The `.class` files are located in the same folder as the other HTML documents for the Web site, whereas instructions from the developer are in the scroller folder.

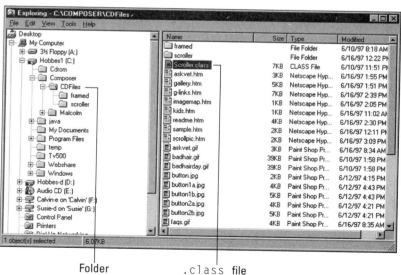

Folder   `.class` file

Using the `.class` file extension works only if you're using Windows 95, Mac, or UNIX. If you're using Windows 3.1*x*, you must open the file on a computer using one of the compatible platforms. Windows 3.1*x* accepts only three-character file extensions.

If you need some extra guidance with moving files around on your system, check out books such as *Windows 95 For Dummies*, 2nd Edition, and *Windows 3.11 For Dummies*, 3rd Edition, both by Andy Rathbone; *Macs For Dummies,* 5th Edition, by David Pogue; or *UNIX For Dummies*, 3rd Edition, by John Levine and Margaret Levine Young, all published by IDG Books Worldwide.

2. **Move any other necessary files into the same folder as the HTML document or into a subfolder of the HTML document.**

   Different applets will require other files or perhaps no files at all.

   The scroller applet requires only an image file called `scroller.gif`.

3. **In Composer, click to position the cursor where you want the applet to be.**

4. **Go to Insert⇨HTML Tag to add the applet tag to your document.**

   The HTML Tag dialog box appears, as shown in Figure 13-3.

Figure 13-3:
The HTML Tag dialog box lets you include HTML tags and attributes to use applets in your Web pages.

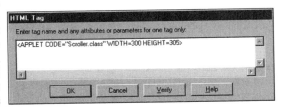

5. **Enter the opening** `<APPLET>` **tag in the dialog box.**

   You can put only one tag at a time into the dialog box, so you enter something like:

   ```
   <APPLET CODE="Scroller.class" WIDTH=300 HEIGHT=305>
   ```

6. **Click OK to close the dialog box.**

7. **Continue adding one tag at a time until all the** `<PARAM>` **tags and the closing** `</APPLET>` **tag are included.**

The remaining tags that this particular applet requires are as follows:

```
<PARAM NAME= picture Value="scroller.gif">
<PARAM NAME=newwidth    Value="225">
<PARAM NAME=newheight    Value="220">
<PARAM NAME=speed    Value="30">
<PARAM NAME=xadd    Value="-10">
<PARAM NAME=yadd    Value="0">
<PARAM NAME=fillpictures Value="false">
<PARAM NAME=bordersize VALUE="40">
<PARAM NAME=bgcolor Value="255">
</APPLET>
```

Whew! (Don't add this.)

8. **After you finish adding tags, test your page in Navigator.**

Be patient when you view the applet for the first time. It often takes what seems like an inordinately long time to get the applet up and running.

Keep your eyes on the Status bar (at the lower-left corner of the Navigator window) for updates on things like "Applet Loading" and "Applet Scroller running."

Figure 13-4 shows an (unfortunately nonanimated) version of the page with the applet.

Following are a few additional notes about including Java applets in your Web site:

✔ **Java applets tend to be kind of picky and, if there are problems, you're unlikely to have any definitive clues about why.** They just won't do what they're supposed to do. One way to make sure that they work properly is to copy the code from a page on which the applets work properly and then make parameter changes, one at a time — testing each change — on the functional code.

✔ **Remember that someone else (the developer) owns the copyright to all those Java applets on the Web.** That is, unless you are specifically given permission to take and reuse the applets, you can't do it. Although borrowing an applet just to learn how to include it in your pages isn't likely to be a big deal, be sure you have permission before including someone else's applet on your Web site for public use.

✔ **If you want to make changes to the parameters, feel free to do so.** Some changes might keep the applet from running (such as changing the `<PARAM NAME=img VALUE="images">` to point to a folder other than the images folder), but others should be fine (such as decreasing the value attribute in `<PARAM NAME=speed VALUE="30">` tag to make the images scroll by faster).

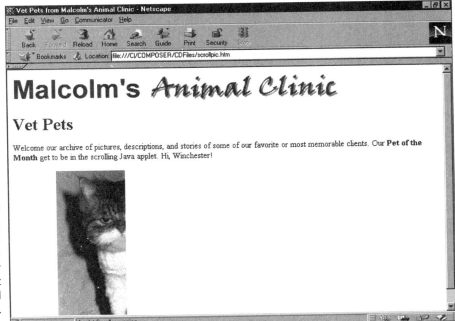

Creating your own applets without (eek!) programming

If you're interested in creating your own Java applets and don't mind a little work, some really cool tools are available to let you create certain types of applets without doing anything that could be considered "programming." Although these development tools will, we're sure, continue to change and evolve, it's not too early to investigate them.

Macromedia (`http://www.macromedia.com/`) has a program called AppletAce that does all the work for you. For example, to create a banner or animated button, you just make selections from menus, and then click a tab to see immediately the fruits of your efforts. After you're satisfied with the results, the program will automatically copy the `.class` files to the appropriate directory, at your instruction, and provide you with HTML code that you can copy and paste into your Web page. It can't get much easier than that. See Figures 13-5 and 13-6, which show the AppletAce program in action.

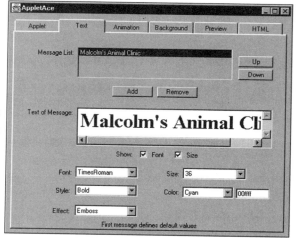

Figure 13-5:
You can easily use AppletAce to develop creative applets.

Figure 13-6:
After you select the text, choose animation effects from the Animation tab.

After you develop the applet to your satisfaction, tell AppletAce to copy the appropriate files, tell yourself to copy the code, and click the upper-right corner of the window to close AppletAce.

If you download and use this program, just click on each tab in turn and follow the instructions — it's even easier than it looks.

Part V

Grad School Stuff: Activity, Interactivity, and Hyperactivity

The 5th Wave   By Rich Tennant

THE MODERN JAMES BOND

The name is bond.com, JAMES bond.com.

In this part . . .

After you finish with this part, your Web pages will have so much activity that you'll have to ask your system administrator to prescribe Ritalin for them. However, activity or not, don't let the title fool you — we're calling this Part "Grad School Stuff" only to distinguish it from the more basic information earlier in this book.

This part focuses on using forms to collect information from your readers (Chapter 14), jazzing up your pages with JavaScript (Chapter 15), and finally dividing your pages with frames (Chapter 16).

Including forms, JavaScript, and frames can add lots of pizzazz to your Web pages and make you look like a Web page guru. And you'll be happy to know that including these is almost as easy as doing any other Web page task. With that, please proceed. . . .

Chapter 14

Squeezing Information Out of People

. . . .

. . . .

Throughout this book, you include features in your Web pages that help you get information *to* your readers. For example, including headings, paragraphs, images, and tables are all methods you can use to tell people what you want them to know. In this chapter, you see how to get information *from* your readers — feedback, answers to questions, contact information, contest entries, product orders, and so on.

Don't think of Web page forms as being similar to those irritating squinched up papers you fill out for your taxes, credit requests, job applications, or Christmas wish lists (hey, some families are more formal than others). Instead, Web page forms can be visually appealing and easy to use. What's more, your readers won't have to spend 32 cents (and climbing) or lick a gooey envelope to send information to you. They can just click a button and — wowzie! — the information makes its way through cyberstreets to a destination you specify.

This chapter introduces you to forms, shows you how to create one, and tells you about different options for getting that all-important information back to you in a format you can use.

What Is a Form?

A *form* is a Web page that contains a collection of places for you (or your reader) to provide information and send it in. In particular, forms are comprised of two parts: the visible part that you can see on the Web page and the invisible (magic, some say) part that makes the form go from readers' computers, down the wire, and to a location you specify. Nothing but Net, as they say.

The part you can see on the Web page is the actual form, and it includes different types of input areas that your readers use to "fill out" and submit it. For example, virtually all forms include Submit and Reset buttons, which let your readers send the information to you or start over on the form if they goof up their answers and want to try again. Also, forms can include checkboxes, radio buttons, text fields, select windows, and textareas, which provide the different ways of presenting questions or information requests. Figure 14-1 shows a Web page form.

You'll find more information about the various buttons and input types later in this chapter in the section "Designing a Form."

The part of the form that you cannot actually see is the part that tells a Web server what you want it to do with the information people submit using the form. A *Web server* is a somewhat smart computer that holds Web page files. These severs basically do nothing until someone wants to access a Web page, at which time the server digs up the file and delivers it to the person requesting it.

In the case of forms, Web servers are in charge of accepting the submitted forms and doing something with them. What's cool is that you just tell the server how you want the information to come back to you, and the server is happy to oblige with no whining or complaining. Basically, you have a couple of options for receiving the information:

- ✔ **You can have the form information submitted to the server and have the server send the information to you via e-mail, where you can process it.** The result is that the server dribbles the results into your e-mail box as people submit information using the form. This is the approach you're most likely to use because it's easier to set up and it's the standard supported by *Internet Service Providers* (*ISPs*), those folks you pay to set up and maintain your Internet access.

- ✔ **You can have the form information submitted to the server, which dumps the information into a database that processes the information for you.** The result is that you can pawn off all the tedious data-processing stuff to a database that'll do the work for you. However, this option requires more setup by the ISP, and for that reason, this option is not always available. If you're doing Web pages or sites for a middling or better size company, this option will be more feasible than if you're running your one-person, evenings-only business over your modem at home.

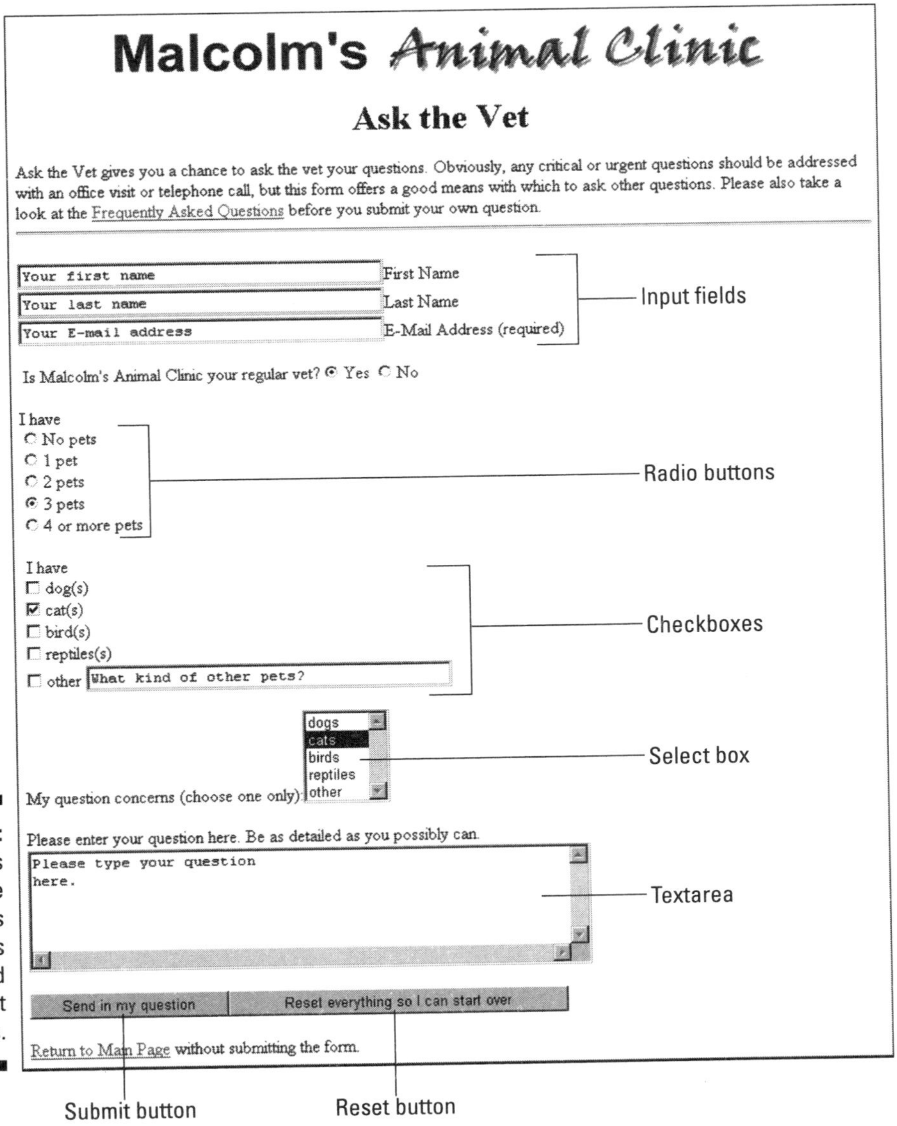

Figure 14-1:
Forms
include
Input fields
as well as
Submit and
Reset
options.

Regardless of which option you choose, the form responses are all processed by the server, which uses a little protocol called CGI. *CGI* stands for *Common Gateway Interface*, and it specifies how programs on the Web server can interact with the server and with information submitted through Web pages. For example, when you complete a form and click the Submit button, there's a little snippet of HTML code in the form (the ACTION= attribute of the <FORM> tag, to be specific) that tells the server to send the results of the form to a specific program. Because of the magic of CGI, the form results actually make it to the program in a usable form. By the way, this program is probably, and *not* coincidentally, located in the /cgi-bin folder on the server.

In many cases, including in the examples in this chapter, that little CGI program just takes the information from the form, massages it slightly, and sends it in e-mail. In other situations, it may add the information into a database, generate a bill, or construct a whole new Web page based on the form responses and send it back out to the reader. Pretty slick, huh? Getting into that kind of fun stuff requires either some programming or that you know, pay, or bribe someone with a fairly techie background. It's not incredibly expensive or difficult; however, it's not likely the most efficient use of your time.

Although having form data added to a database sounds cool and time-saving, there's actually nothing wrong with having the information sent to your e-mail box. You don't have to make big changes to your work flow to accommodate the incoming information, and your ISP is almost certainly

---

Asking your ISP the right questions

If you're unclear about what services your ISP can provide, get on the horn with them and ask some questions. Go ahead and lug out the phone book, find that wee scrap of paper you wrote the number on, or refer to information they gave you when you first signed up for Internet access. And, don't worry. Most ISP folks are more than happy to help, despite the "I won't share my doughnuts" sign on their doors and marketing literature.

When you're on the horn with your ISP, ask the following questions:

✔ Can I use forms on my Web page?

✔ Do you support e-mail and/or database returns?

✔ Where can I find instructions that apply specifically to your environment?

✔ What other information will I need?

By the way, if you can't track down the information you need right now, don't worry about it. You can still develop the form and see how it looks; it just won't work fully without the instructions on how to get the information back to you.

prepared to accommodate sending the results of a form to your e-mail box. The downside is that you have to sort the data yourself, which won't be a huge problem unless you expect zillions of responses to your form.

The examples in this chapter assume that you'll be preparing a form and receiving the data in your e-mail. Though some of the nuances might differ slightly from ISP to ISP, the overall process (and 99.8 percent of your form) will be exactly the same. Ask your own ISP for the specifics when we prompt you to do so.

If you happen to be working in a more technically empowered (had to work that word in) environment, the data from your form might actually go into a database automatically. If so, you'll get to disregard part of the information in this chapter, secure in the knowledge that someone else did the grunt work for you.

Why Use a Form?

A form is the primary means with which you can collect information from your readers — any kind of information. You can use forms to let readers enter a contest, register to win a prize, order products, request services, or just populate your e-mail box with junk mail. No matter what the use, readers go to the Web page, complete the form, and submit it.

In our not-so-humble opinions, a form is a fairly impersonal means of collecting information. You could, for example, solicit similar information and have readers e-mail their responses to you, which gives readers more freedom in answering questions. However, readers might not take the time to answer questions completely or may not phrase answers in a way that's easy for you to process. So, in a sense, using forms can help ensure that you receive complete answers in a form (heh-hem) that you can use.

What can "See Gee Eye" do for you?

CGI programs include all kinds of neat doo-dads that make your server do cool stuff for your Web site, including such neat-o objects as visit counters, guestbooks, and server-side imagemaps. If you're interested in learning more, check with your server administrator and ask the leading multipart question:

What kind of cool CGI programs do you have installed, where do I find instructions, and how can I get started?

For example, Malcolm's Animal Clinic uses a sneaky approach to using a form. Not only does it use the form to answer readers' questions (the providing-a-service aspect), but it also uses the form to gather demographic information about clients. Notice in the following list of form categories, that readers have to answer the demographic questions before they get to ask the vet the $64,000 question. (Sneaky, huh?)

After careful thought and planning, the powers-that-be at Malcolm's establishment decided that the following information is useful for demographic information or essential to answering the question posed.

- First and last names
- E-mail addresses (so that the answer can be e-mailed back)
- Statement specifying if Malcolm is the regular vet (Malcolm will answer those questions first)
- Number of pets
- Reader's particular kind of pet(s)
- What species the question concerns
- Question itself

Although Malcolm's Animal Clinic could just put in an e-mail link and suggest the information people should provide, the clinic decided that the more structured approach of a form will better meet Malcolm's needs and help him provide better answers for his clients. With an e-mail message, Malcolm would be likely to get a lot of "Fluffy looks sick — what do I do?" and he'd have to waste a lot of time sending messages back to the owner to find out if Fluffy is a dog, cat, or iguana. With a form, it's clear that the species information must be filled in.

Planning Your Form

Before you dive into creating a form, you need to do some planning. Yuck, right? Actually, planning your form is just as important as creating it. By planning, you can ensure that you create one that's best suited for your needs, ensure that it's visually appealing to those filling it out, and ensure that you get the information you need. The next two sections help you decide what information you want to collect and how to design the form.

Deciding what information you want to squeeze out of readers

As any statistician or thesis writer will tell you, good survey questions are the key to success. The only way to get the information you seek is to know what information you want and to ask the right questions. That said, here are some rules of thumb:

- ✓ **Only collect information you need.** If you start asking for too much information, people are likely to give up and move on.

- ✓ **Require that your readers click to choose something (rather than fill in blanks) as much as possible.** Although you don't have to decipher bad handwriting from an HTML form, you'll still get to struggle with people's *kreatif speling,* people wandering off topic, or people giving you more information than you'd care to know.

- ✓ **Break the categories down as much as possible.** For example, if you're looking for contact information, provide separate input areas for name, address, city/state/zip, and e-mail address. By separating these, you can ensure that people include complete information and more easily process and use the information after it's submitted.

- ✓ **Check and double-check to make sure you are collecting everything you need.** For example, if you'll be sending e-mail messages to people who complete your survey, make sure you get the e-mail addresses of respondents. Likewise, if you're selling coasters and mouse pads, better get not only the credit card number but also the type and expiration date.

We'd strongly suggest making a list right now of all the information you want to collect. It'll be a good reference as you develop your form. Go ahead! We'll wait.

Designing a form

When designing a Web page form, you have to consider two things:

- ✓ The form elements available for use
- ✓ What you want the form to look like

You can address both these issues by considering the form widgets available to choose from. (*Widget* is the technically savvy sounding term for form elements — you know, the checkboxes, radio buttons, input areas, and buttons mentioned earlier in the chapter.) Here's the lowdown on form widgets, which you're sure to find highly exciting:

✔ **Submit and Reset buttons:** The Submit button is the only absolutely required form button because it lets your readers send information to you. Clicking the Submit button is equivalent to sticking a survey in an envelope, addressing it, affixing a stamp, and carrying it to the mailbox. Clicking Reset (optional, but usually desirable) is like using whiteout to remove all your answers and start over, but without the mess and fuss. Actually, Submit is required and Reset is merely strongly recommended, but they're happier together.

✔ **Radio buttons:** Provide a list of options from which readers can choose one answer. (Think of a car radio. You can choose only one item at a time.) Radio buttons give readers an easy way to fill out information; the options are provided for readers, and all they have to do is select one from the list. Heck, all they *can* do is select one from the list — the browser won't permit anything else.

✔ **Checkboxes:** Provide a list of options from which readers can choose multiple answers or only one. This list is like a grocery list; you can put a check beside anything you need. Checkboxes also give readers an easy way to fill out a form because the options are already provided; all readers do is select the answers they want.

✔ **Select lists:** Are similar to radio buttons — that is, they provide a list from which readers choose one answer. However, select windows help save room on a form because the list of options does not appear on-screen until readers choose to see it.

Each of the preceding widgets is great for you — as both the form developer and information collector. These options keep your readers from volunteering information, misspelling or misstating stuff, or answering a question with irrelevant information. Just remember, an easy-to-complete form is an easy-to-process form.

✔ **Input fields:** Are textareas that allow readers to provide short answers to questions. These are ideal for names and brief information such as e-mail addresses; however, the information you receive is harder to process.

✔ **Textareas:** Are larger areas that allow readers to type longer bits of information. These are ideal for letting your readers make suggestions or comments; however, like input fields, they make information processing more difficult.

Take another look at the Malcolm's Animal Clinic Ask the Vet form, shown earlier in Figure 14-1. Notice how these widgets effectively solicit the information sought.

With these widgets to play with, go ahead and sketch the form. Keep it simple. A single-column format usually works best. Anything more complicated may make the form appear intimidating and increase the possibility that your readers will accidentally skip something.

Creating a Form

The process of creating a form differs very little, especially at the beginning, from creating any other Web page. As a matter of fact, you should start by creating a Web page with all of the text and questions that you'll have in your form. Don't worry about leaving space for the form elements — they'll make space for themselves.

The remaining seven sections walk you through the process of developing your form. Unfortunately, Composer is slightly form-impaired. That is, instead of providing a handy-dandy dialog box in which you can define your form and have the HTML tags and attributes automatically inserted into your file, you must do the dirty work yourself. Oh, and be assured that this is not a Netscape oversight; it's a *feature*.

At any rate, each of the following sections begins with a table that announces and describes the tags and attributes you need to complete the steps. Following each table is a set of instructions. These instructions build from section to section, meaning that you should complete the sections in the order provided. At the very least, complete the section "Creating the basic form" before skipping around to other sections.

For more information about these silly HTML tags and attributes, check out Chapter 3.

If you're pretty comfortable editing text files with Notepad (or SimpleText, vi, or whatever), you might find inserting the form tags somewhat easier if you go ahead and open your soon-to-be-form in the text editor of your choice.

Creating the basic form

Druuuuuuum roll, please! You're about to start your very own first-ever Web page form. Hee hee! You might go ahead and find out about form processing information from your ISP. If you haven't already, check out the sidebar "Asking your ISP the right questions" earlier in this chapter.

Take a look at the tags and attributes described in Table 14-1. These tags and attributes are the ones you use to start your form.

Table 14-1	Basic Form Tags and Attributes
Tag or Attribute	*Description*
`<FORM>...</FORM>`	Encloses the form and tells browsers that all information within and between these tags is part of the form.

(continued)

Table 14-1 *(continued)*

Tag or Attribute	Description
`ACTION=`	Tells the server what program on the server will accept the information in the form.
`METHOD=`	Defines how the information is sent to the server.

To start your form, use these quickie steps:

1. **Open an HTML document.**

   You can either use an existing HTML document or start a new one by including the essential structure tags.

    If you don't have the information you need from your ISP or Web server administrator yet, don't sweat it. Just plow ahead and complete the form. When you get the information, you can go back and add the necessary attributes to the opening `<FORM>` tag.

2. **Put your cursor above the top question in your form.**

   The exact position isn't particularly important, but you'll find the form less confusing if you put the opening form tag on a line by itself above your form questions.

3. **Choose Insert➪HTML Tag.**

   You see the HTML Tag dialog box, as shown in Figure 14-2.

Figure 14-2:
You use the HTML Tag dialog box to enter those silly HTML tags and attributes.

HTML Tag

Enter tag name and any attributes or parameters for one tag only.

OK   Cancel   Verify   Help

4. **Add the opening `<FORM>` tag, like this:**

   ```
   <FORM>
   ```

5. **Insert the `METHOD=` attribute, including the information you receive from your ISP.**

For example, our `METHOD=` attribute looks like this:

```
<FORM METHOD="POST">
```

6. **Add the `ACTION=` attribute, also using the information you got from your ISP.**

   For example, our `ACTION=` attribute looks like the following example. Why? Because the powers-that-be said so, that's why:

```
<FORM METHOD="POST" ACTION="http://www.xmission.com/cgi-
       bin/cgie-mail/~ejray/malcolm/questionmail.txt">
```

7. **Click OK.**

   Notice that instead of seeing the actual tag, you get a funky yellow < or > icon in your document. That icon shows you where the tag is and enables you to see the code as well. Just hover your mouse over the icon to see the actual code in a tool tip.

8. **Click your mouse a few lines below the funky yellow icon, and choose Insert⇨HTML Tag.**

   You see the HTML Tag dialog box again. This dialog box will get pretty familiar before the form is complete.

   And before you ask, no, you can't do multiple form tags at once. One visit to the dialog box, one tag. Second visit, second tag. Third visit . . .

9. **Type the closing `</FORM>` tag, like this:**

```
</FORM>
```

10. **Click OK.**

TaDaaaaa! You just put in the necessary tags to define the HTML form. If you view this page in Navigator, you won't see anything different — yet. You have to add widgets, which are discussed later in this chapter.

For now, check out some additional tidbits about inserting HTML tags directly in your document.

- ✔ If you want Composer to validate your tags — that is, make sure that you put in those angle brackets (< >) and the closing slash (/) — just click Verify in the HTML Tag dialog box before you click OK. Using the Verify option won't find all potential problems, but it will make sure that you've dotted your *i*'s and crossed your *t*'s.

- ✔ If you think you made a mistake and need to edit the tag, just double-click the icon in the document (or right-click the icon and choose Tag Properties) to recall the HTML Tag dialog box. Make the necessary changes, and then click OK.

✔ For a relatively simple form, as in our example, inserting HTML tags through the dialog box is a reasonable solution. However, if you're pretty proficient with a plain text editing program, such as SimpleText (Macintosh), vi (UNIX), or Notepad (Windows versions), you might consider editing your form directly in the text editor rather than wearing a path to the HTML Tag dialog box.

✔ Don't try to double up on the tags. You need to access the HTML Tag dialog box separately for each tag you want to enter. And as the example shows, you even need to access the HTML Tag dialog box twice just to enter opening and closing tags. Sigh.

✔ Note that the closing tag's little yellow icon looks slightly different than the little yellow icon associated with an opening tag. Nothing to do about it, besides marvel at the ingenuity (or inconsistency) of the Netscape programmers.

Adding Submit and Reset buttons

Submit and Reset buttons are almost as vital to your form as the <FORM>… </FORM> tags you just added. These buttons allow your readers to send the form into the server so that you can get the information or to reset their answers so that they can try again to fill out the form.

Traditionally, these buttons are located all the way at the bottom of the form, immediately above the closing </FORM> tag. Actually, this is a pretty sneaky — um, strategic — way of getting readers to answer all questions, because they have to at least wade through all the questions to get to the Submit button at the bottom. Placing the Submit and Reset buttons at the top or middle of the form might result in an unusually large percentage of readers not answering all the questions.

Table 14-2 describes the tags and attributes you use to include the Submit and Reset buttons.

Table 14-2	Tags for Adding Submit and Reset Buttons
Tag or Attribute	**Description**
<INPUT>	Identifies that the widget is an input field of some sort.
TYPE=	Specifies that the input field is, in this case, either a RESET or SUBMIT button.
VALUE=	Specifies what appears on the face of the button.

Both the Submit and Reset buttons are special kinds of `<INPUT>` fields. In the case of the Submit button, the attributes should be `TYPE="Submit"` and `VALUE="Submit"`. The Reset button has attributes of `TYPE="Reset"` and `VALUE="Reset"`.

To put in Submit and Reset buttons, follow these steps:

1. **Click your cursor in your HTML document just before the closing `</FORM>` tag.**

   Remember that you can hover your cursor over an HTML tag to see exactly what the tag contains.

2. **Choose Insert⇨HTML Tag.**

   The HTML Tag dialog box appears, awaiting your code for the Submit button.

3. **Enter the following tag and attributes to create a Submit button.**

   ```
   <INPUT TYPE="submit" VALUE="Submit">
   ```

4. **Click OK.**

   The HTML Tag dialog box disappears, and you have a brand new HTML tag icon in your document. If you want, hover your cursor over the icon to verify that it has the correct tag.

5. **Choose Insert⇨HTML Tag again to insert the Reset button.**

6. **Enter the following tag and attributes for your Reset button.**

   ```
   <INPUT TYPE="Reset" VALUE="Reset">
   ```

   And, again, an additional HTML tag icon appears in your document. That's all there is to it. You just added two buttons to the document. Take a look at Figure 14-3 to see how those tags appear when viewed in a browser.

You might consider viewing your pages in Navigator to see what they'll really look like — just seeing little yellow doohickeys isn't much of a substitute for the real thing. Remember, either choose File⇨Browse Page, or go to Communicator⇨Navigator, or press Ctrl+1, or click the Preview button in the toolbar. Whew!

Keep in mind that only the Submit and Reset buttons will be visible to your readers — the form tags don't show up in the browser.

If you want to change the text on the button, just replace the `VALUE=` attribute with something else. For example, you can change the Reset button text to say, "Oh, crud! Let me start over!"

Figure 14-3:
The little
yellow
doohickeys
in your
Composer
window
represent
the tags
you're
laboriously
entering.

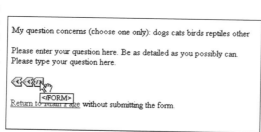

Adding radio buttons

Radio buttons, those choose-one-and-only-one-from-the-list input areas, are similar to other input tags. The primary differences between text input areas and radio buttons are the types and the name fields. Table 14-3 explains the most-common attributes for a radio button input tag.

To insert your radio buttons, use this procedure:

1. **Click in your HTML form to place your cursor.**

   Be sure to put your radio buttons between the `<FORM>`...`</FORM>` tags. Ideally, you'll put the buttons right beside the descriptive text in your dummy form.

2. **Choose Insert⇨HTML Tag to add the radio button.**

   The HTML Tag dialog box appears, as usual. (Getting to be quite a trend, isn't it?)

3. **Type the Input tag for the radio button.**

   To insert a tag to choose Yes or No, as in the sample form, you use a tag like this:

   ```
   <INPUT TYPE="radio" NAME="regvet" VALUE="Yes">
   ```

   In this example, the `NAME=` attribute is a (cryptic) reference to the Regular Vet question from the sample form.

4. **Click OK when you finish.**

5. **Continue inserting radio button tags as needed with Insert⇨HTML Tag.**

   The second tag in this example is for the No response.

   ```
   <INPUT TYPE="radio" NAME="regvet" VALUE="No">
   ```

6. Click OK when you finish.

Check your results in Navigator, as shown in Figure 14-4.

Table 14-3	Radio Button Tags and Attributes
Tag or Attribute	**Description**
`<INPUT>`	The `<INPUT>` tag specifies that there will be an area in the form for readers to provide information.
`TYPE="radio"`	This `TYPE=` attribute indicates that the input field is for selecting one (and only one) option from a list of choices.
`NAME=`	The `NAME=` attribute identifies what you call the information collected in this field. Think of `NAME=` as a label for the whole collection of information — not just the particular radio button. For example, in the sample form shown earlier in Figure 14-1, one name applies to the whole collection of radio buttons, indicating the number of pets the respondent has.
`VALUE=`	The `VALUE=` attribute is the information that will be sent back to you if the radio button is selected. This attribute must be different for each radio button in the set, and you'll make your life easier if you select very descriptive values — such as the choice of "one" if the user chooses the number 1.
`CHECKED`	The `CHECKED` attribute marks one of the radio buttons with a check (or dot in the circle, technically speaking) by default. If you expect that your readers will be likely to choose a particular option, you might add `CHECKED` to that tag to make it easier for them. Conversely, if you want to ensure that the readers have to check something, just omit the Checked attribute from all buttons.

You might consider the following about using radio buttons. Be sure to include descriptive text in your document to accompany the button — little circles in the document without a context don't help the reader much. Also, where you place the descriptive text in regard to the button is very important. If it isn't clear which button the text refers to, the responses to your form can be misleading.

For example, in Figure 14-4, the buttons themselves aren't connected to the surrounding text (yes or no). Just remember, the text between the yellow tag icons is all your readers will have to work from.

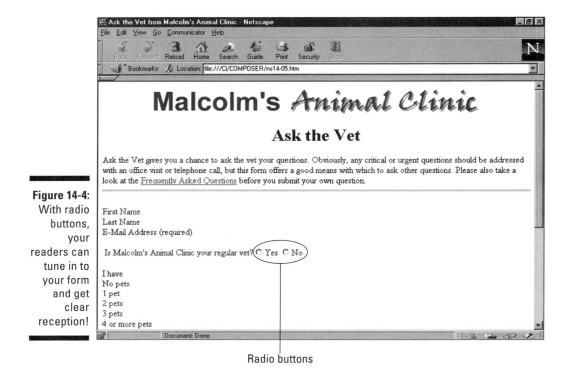

Figure 14-4:
With radio buttons, your readers can tune in to your form and get clear reception!

Radio buttons

Adding checkboxes

Checkboxes, the choose-as-many-as-you-want-from-the-list input areas, pose no particular difficulties. The process is similar to the process used for the rest of the input tags, particularly the radio buttons. Table 14-4 explains the most-common attributes for a checkbox input tag.

Table 14-4	Checkbox Tags and Attributes
Tag or Attribute	*Description*
<INPUT>	The <INPUT> tag specifies that there will be an area in the form for readers to provide information.
TYPE="checkbox"	This TYPE= attribute indicates that the input field is for selecting an item from a list of choices. Technically, you could also use a single checkbox to indicate a Yes or No choice (say, checked is yes; not checked is no), but you might use two radio buttons to elicit the same yes/no answer.

Tag or Attribute	Description
NAME=	The NAME= attribute identifies what you call the information collected in this field. When you're dealing with checkboxes, the NAME= attribute refers to that particular box, not to the whole collection. For example, in the sample form shown earlier in Figure 14-1, each checkbox in the list has a different NAME= attribute.
VALUE=	The VALUE= attribute is the information that will be sent back to you if the checkbox is selected. As with radio buttons, you'll make your life easier if you select very descriptive values. In the sample form, the name and value attributes are the same for each of the checkboxes.
CHECKED	The CHECKED attribute marks your checkbox with a check by default. If you expect that your readers are likely to choose a particular option, you can add checked to that tag to make it easier for them. Conversely, if you want to ensure that the readers have to check something, just omit the CHECKED attribute from all checkboxes.

To insert your checkboxes, use this procedure.

1. **Click in your HTML form to place your cursor.**

   Be sure to put your checkboxes between the <FORM>...</FORM> tags, preferably right next to the descriptive text.

2. **Choose Insert⇨HTML Tag to add the checkbox.**

   The HTML Tag dialog box appears.

3. **Type the <INPUT> tag for the checkbox.**

   To insert a tag for readers to specify if they have a dog, as in the sample form, use a tag like this:

   ```
   <INPUT TYPE="checkbox" NAME="dogs" VALUE="dogs">
   ```

4. **Click OK when you finish.**

5. **Continue inserting checkbox tags as needed.**

   The second tag in this example is for the Cats response.

   ```
   <INPUT TYPE="checkbox" NAME="cats" VALUE="cats">
   ```

6. **Click OK when you finish.**

   Check your results in Navigator, as shown in Figure 14-5.

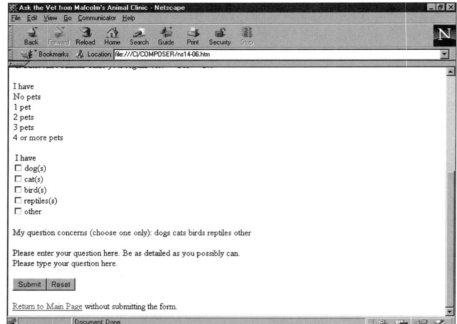

Figure 14-5:
Check out these checkboxes!

Adding select lists

Just call these Ms. Versatile! Select lists can be very much like radio buttons because they can allow only one response from a list. They can also be like checkboxes and allow multiple responses. More than anything else, however, select lists have the great advantage that they can take much less space in your HTML document than either radio buttons or checkboxes. Table 14-5 explains the most-common tags and attributes for a select list.

Table 14-5	Select List Tags and Attributes
Tag or Attribute	**Description**
`<SELECT>...</SELECT>`	The `<SELECT>...</SELECT>` tags, which are paired tags, require both an opening and a closing tag that bracket the list of items.
`NAME=`	The `NAME=` attribute identifies what you call the information collected in this field. Think of `NAME=` as a label for the whole collection of information. For example, in the sample form shown earlier in Figure 14-1, one name applies to the response to the "what's this question about" question.

Tag or Attribute	Description
MULTIPLE	The MULTIPLE attribute is necessary to allow more than one selection from the list. If you omit the multiple attribute, your readers will be able to select only one item from the list. (In other words, without the MULTIPLE attribute, the select list functions like the style or font selections from the Composer menus.)
SIZE=	The SIZE= attribute indicates how many selections are visible at one time. If you omit this attribute, only one item will be visible, as with standard drop-down menus (like the font or style selections in Composer). If you're allowing multiple selections, you should probably consider making the select list somewhat larger than 1. If you make the select list larger, it'll look kinda like Figure 14-6.
`<OPTION>`	The `<OPTION>` tag (or, more likely, tags) goes (or go) between the opening and closing `<SELECT>`…`</SELECT>` tags and indicates one choice in the list.
VALUE=	The VALUE= attribute specifies the information that will be sent back to you if the option is selected. This attribute must be different for each option in the set, and you'll make your life easier if you select very descriptive values — such as the choice of "cat" if the user chooses "cat."
SELECTED	The SELECTED attribute marks an option as a selection by default. If you expect that your readers are likely to choose a particular option, you might add CHECKED to that tag to make it easier for them. Conversely, if you want to ensure that the readers have to check something, just omit the attribute from all options.

Figure 14-6 shows you what a select list looks like.

You need to be sure that you have the select options listed in your document before you start on the list. To insert a select list, use this procedure:

1. Click in your HTML form to place your cursor.

Be sure to put your select list between the `<FORM>`…`</FORM>` tags.

2. Choose Insert⇨HTML Tag to add the opening `<SELECT>` **tag.**

You're an old pro at this by now.

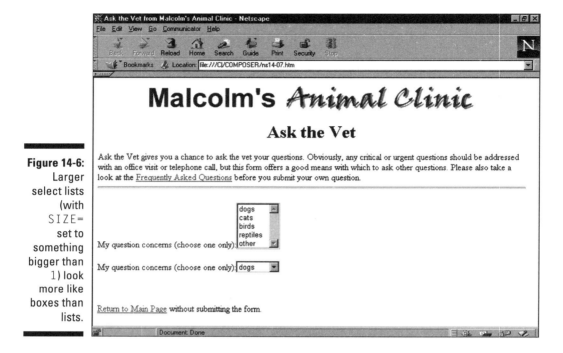

Figure 14-6:
Larger
select lists
(with
`SIZE=`
set to
something
bigger than
1) look
more like
boxes than
lists.

3. **Type the opening** `<SELECT>` **tag and attributes.**

   To insert a tag for a basic select list use a tag like this:

   ```
   <SELECT NAME="concerning">
   ```

   You could, but don't need to, also include other attributes from Table 14-5.

4. **Click OK when you finish.**

5. **Click at the end of the list, and choose Insert⇨HTML Tag to add the closing** `</SELECT>` **tag.**

6. **Type the closing** `</SELECT>` **tag.**

   Remember, no attributes go in a closing tag!

   ```
   </SELECT>
   ```

7. **Click at the front of one of the options to place the cursor.**

8. **Type the** `<OPTION>` **tag and the** `VALUE=` **attribute.**

   Generally, you need to put in only the option tag and the value attribute. You can also include `SELECTED` to specify which option should be selected by default.

   ```
   <OPTION VALUE="dogs">
   ```

9. **Click OK when you finish.**

10. **Continue inserting** <OPTION> **tags as needed by selecting** **Insert⇨HTML Tag.**

    Check your results in Navigator.

Keep the following tips about select lists in mind as you create your masterpieces:

✔ The only descriptive text necessary beside a select list in your document is text that explains the overall category. Because the select list contains the information the readers will choose, you have no reason to enter further explanations.

✔ Revising or changing tags is easy. Just double-click the yellow icon in the document, or right-click the icon and select Tag Properties. Make the necessary editing changes, and then click OK again.

Adding text input fields

Inserting text input fields, in which your readers can type short bits of information such as names and e-mail addresses, is similar to adding special buttons. Table 14-6 provides a list of input field tags and attributes, as well as a description of each.

To insert your text input field, use the following procedure:

1. **Click in your HTML form to place your cursor.**

   Be sure to put your input area between the <FORM>...</FORM> tags.

2. **Choose Insert⇨HTML Tag to add the text input form tag.**

   The HTML Tag dialog box appears, awaiting your code.

3. **Type the** <INPUT> **tag.**

   In the sample form, shown earlier in Figure 14-1, Malcolm used an input tag like the following:

   ```
   <INPUT TYPE="text" NAME="firstname" SIZE="40"
           MAXLENGTH="40" VALUE="Your first name">
   ```

4. **Click OK when you finish.**

   Check your results in Navigator, as shown in Figure 14-7.

After you have your input area as you want it, you must repeat this process for each text input field you want.

Table 14-6	Input Field Tags and Attributes
Tag or Attribute	**Description**
`<INPUT>`	The `<INPUT>` tag specifies that there will be an area in the form for readers to provide information.
`TYPE=`	The `TYPE=` attribute indicates that the input field is for typing text into, as opposed to providing a list of choices.
`NAME=`	Think of `NAME=` as a label for the information. The name attribute identifies what you call the information collected in this field. The first three input tags in Figure 14-1 use names of `firstname`, `lastname`, and `email`, respectively. Each input area in your form must have a unique name.
`SIZE=`	The `SIZE=` attribute is optional, but handy. By specifying the number of characters wide, you can ensure that fields line up properly and provide enough visual space so that readers don't have to move the cursor around to see what they typed.
`MAXLENGTH=`	The `MAXLENGTH=` attribute, which is also optional, specifies the maximum actual length of the data collected. If you set `maxlength` for `firstname` to 5, Eric can fill in his name, but Deborah can't fill in hers. Generally, you want `maxlength` and size to be the same, but technically they don't have to be.
`VALUE=`	The `VALUE=` attribute is the context visible in the input field when your readers first see the form (or after they click Reset to return to the default values). We often put in something to help readers know what to type, but the field is optional if you want to omit it.

Here's a little additional information about text input fields:

✔ If you want to make sure that your fields line up neatly on-screen, put the input areas to the left of the descriptive text (as in Figure 14-7). Otherwise, your fields won't be in a line — they'll be kind of random looking.

✔ Remember to use a New Line Break (Shift+Enter or Insert⇨New Line Break) after each input tag and related descriptive text. If you just press Enter, you'll have too much vertical space between items. If you don't do anything, the Input items all end up on the same line.

✔ Revising or changing text input areas is easy (and necessary, if you get a little quick on the draw with the OK button). Just double-click the yellow icon in the document, or right-click the icon and select Tag Properties. Make the necessary editing changes, and then click OK again.

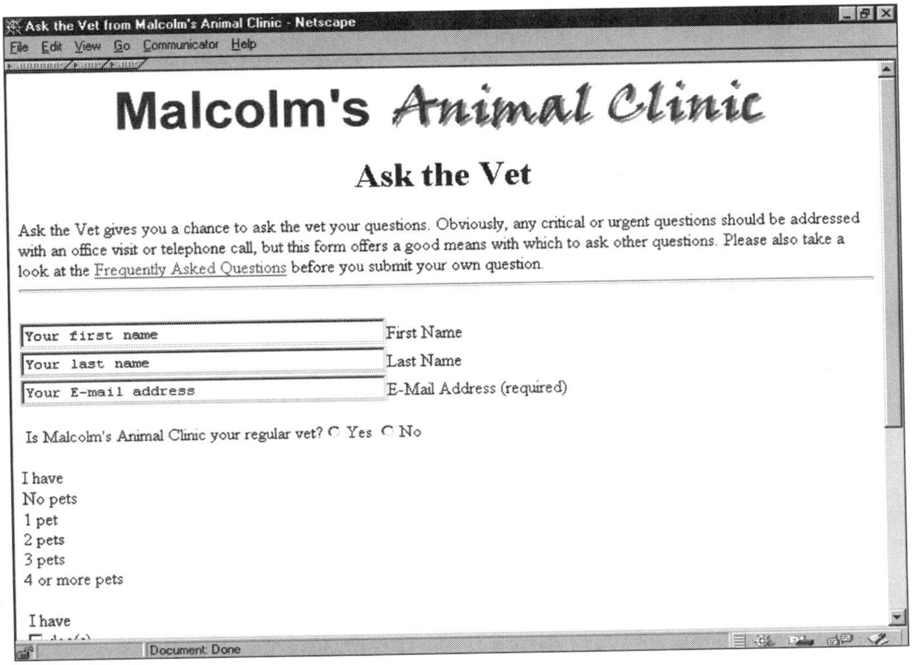

Figure 14-7:
Text input
fields are
outstanding
for letting
your
readers
talk — but
not too
much.

Adding textareas

A textarea is just an open part of a form in which your readers can put a longer or free-form response. Questions that merit a textarea for the response include: "Please list all the ways you liked this page" or "What are the various merits of your favorite political philosophy?"

The actual tag and attributes for a textarea are straightforward. Table 14-7 lists the most-common options.

Table 14-7	Textarea Tags and Attributes
Tag or Attribute	*Description*
`<TEXTAREA>…</TEXTAREA>`	The `<TEXTAREA>…</TEXTAREA>` tag requires both an opening and closing tag that bracket the information.
`NAME=`	The `NAME=` attribute identifies what you call the information collected in this field. If the reader will be entering a free-form question, the name "question" is a logical choice.

(continued)

Table 14-7 *(continued)*

Tag or Attribute	Description
ROWS=	The ROWS= attribute specifies how many rows high the textarea will be.
COLS=	The COLS= attribute specifies how many columns wide the textarea will be.

To insert a textarea, use this procedure:

1. **Click in your HTML form to place your cursor.**

   Be sure to put your textarea between the <FORM>...</FORM> tags.

2. **Choose Insert⇨HTML Tag to add the opening** <TEXTAREA> **tag.**

3. **Type the opening** <TEXTAREA> **tag, and add the** ROWS= **and** COLS= **attributes.**

   To insert a tag for a basic textarea, use a tag like this one:

   ```
   <TEXTAREA NAME="question" ROWS="5" COLS="60">
   ```

   The NAME="question" attribute refers to the free-form question that readers of the sample form page will be submitting.

4. **Click OK when you finish.**

5. **Click just after the opening tag, and choose Insert⇨HTML Tag to add the closing** </TEXTAREA> **tag.**

6. **Add the** </TEXTAREA> **tag.**

   ```
   </TEXTAREA>
   ```

7. **Click OK when you finish.**

8. **If you want sample text to appear within the textarea field, put it between the** <TEXTAREA> **opening and closing tags.**

   In the sample form, the text included is:

   ```
   Please type your question here.
   ```

   Check your results in Navigator, as shown in Figure 14-8.

That's it! Pretty good looking form, isn't it?

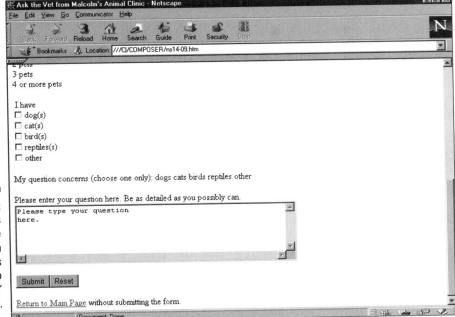

Figure 14-8:
Textareas
provide
more room
for readers
to write to
their hearts'
content.

Case study: Just where does a form go, anyway?

Presumably, you've checked with your Internet Service Provider or local system administrator to find out how to get the results of your form back, but it may be helpful to walk you through what happens to the sample form in the journey from the reader's browser back to our e-mail accounts.

We followed the instructions from our ISP. First, as we completed the form, we inserted an extra — hidden — form tag:

```
<INPUT TYPE="hidden"
  NAME="success" VALUE="http://
  www.xmission.com/~ejray/
  malcolm/qsuccess.html">
```

This tag points to an HTML document on the server that the reader will see after successfully completing and submitting the form. We

had to create this document and put it on the server, just as with the rest of the documents on the site.

Second, we created a response template. As per the instructions, we made a plain text file, not an HTML document, using a text editor (Notepad, 'cause we're primarily Windows 95 users).

The response template is actually the file that the ACTION= attribute of our form points to, as in this example:

```
<FORM METHOD="POST"
  ACTION="http://
  www.xmission.com/cgi-bin/
  cgie-mail/~ejray/malcolm/q-
  mail.txt">
```

(continued)

(continued)

In the file, we listed each of the NAME= attributes from the whole form. Within the response template, we included an e-mail address to which the form would be mailed. We put this file on the server as well.

Thus, when readers complete the form and click Submit, they see an HTML document that we created, advising them of success. The information goes to the server, is inserted in the response template, and then mailed to us. We get an e-mail message that looks somewhat like the following:

```
Janet Rowe
auser@aol.com


Malcolm's Client: Yes


Has three pets.
```

```
Has     dogs
    cats



specifically


The question concerns dogs

What's the best way to treat a
    nose rash on
a dog?
```

Remember, the instructions and process recommended by your ISP might differ considerably from the process we followed. This is only an example, and you'll have to follow the instructions from *your* ISP or Web server administrator for it all to work right.

Chapter 15

Gimme Some JavaScript — Straight Up!

. . . .

In This Chapter

▶ Defining JavaScript

▶ Adding JavaScript to an HTML document

▶ Adding text using JavaScript

▶ Printing date last modified using JavaScript

▶ Making text appear in the Status bar

▶ Validating forms

▶ Invoking image gyrations

▶ Finding more information and resources on JavaScript

. . . .

*I*n Chapter 13, we introduce you to Java applets, those prepackaged Java programs that you can easily include in your Web pages. As we mention in Chapter 13, these applets are built with the Java programming language, which is a means of *caffeinating* your Web pages so that they bounce, shimmy, shake, and ooze with excitement.

JavaScript isn't actually related to Java, other than the fact that JavaScript also lets you add pizzazz to your Web pages. In fact, JavaScript also lets you add functional (not just snazzy) capabilities to your pages. For example, JavaScript enables you to validate form input to make sure that the fields are filled out properly, make notes and descriptions appear in the browser's Status bar, and even play sounds on command. Well, they're *mostly* more functional than snazzy capabilities.

JavaScript isn't standard HTML, so keep in mind that a number of your potential readers may not be able to take advantage of the JavaScript features that you add. If readers are using fairly recent versions of Netscape Navigator or Microsoft Internet Explorer, though, they'll be able to see the JavaScript effects.

You don't have to be a programmer to use JavaScript, but if you *are* a programmer, you have a bit of a head start.

This chapter walks you through the basics of JavaScript, including how to put it in your Web pages, how to adapt and modify existing JavaScript code, how to write a little on your own, and where to look for more information. Rather than wade through exhaustive (and exhausting) detail about JavaScript, you'll find examples and snippets of JavaScript code that illustrate what you can do with the code.

You can slip the examples provided — both in this book and some on the CD — right into your Web pages without modification. If you want to tweak them, you're welcome to do so, but just using what's here will get you started. This chapter can't possibly tell you *everything* about JavaScript — that's way out of the scope of this book. To take full advantage of JavaScript programming potential, you need to be a programmer-type, be able to find a programmer-type, or invest in *JavaScript For Dummies Quick Reference,* by Emily Vander Veer, published by IDG Books Worldwide, Inc.

What Is JavaScript?

JavaScript is a vaguely HTML-ish scripting language developed by Netscape and built into Communicator. By *scripting language,* we mean a watered-down programming language (eek!) that lets you write instructions — a script — to tell the Web browser or HTML document how to behave. For example, you can write a (very brief) script to print text in the Status bar of the Navigator window — giving the information you want to provide rather than just letting the browser print boring old URLs down there. This scripting language was developed to give Web authors — like yourself — more control over page layout and design and appearance, comparable to the control you'd have with a real multimedia authoring tool.

JavaScript does have two disadvantages. It's not standard HTML, and it's pretty much a Netscape- and Internet Explorer-specific application. Both of these disadvantages mean that not all your readers can take advantage of the JavaScript effects you include. Again, though, if you include the JavaScript as shown in this chapter, other readers won't have funny characters or strange icons pop up on their screens; they won't even know that a JavaScript is lurking, sight unseen.

What else can JavaScript do?

In the context of making great Web pages, you can think of JavaScript as offering you three separate capabilities. First, you can just add little snippets of JavaScript code to your HTML document to augment the existing HTML. You can use a little JavaScript to verify that readers complete specified blanks on a form, a line of JavaScript to open a new window, or a line of JavaScript to put messages down in the Status bar of the window. This use — treating JavaScript as an extension to HTML — is the easiest and generally the most practical use.

Second, you can use JavaScript for little programs within your Web pages. Recall those madlib thingies — you know, the silly stories you make up by supplying nouns, verbs, and adjectives that someone then uses to

construct a (usually rude) story? Well, JavaScript scripts are out on the Internet that do just that; you fill out a form and supply the nouns, verbs, and so on, and the JavaScript presents your new little (still generally rude) story incorporating all of the elements you provide. We're not going to walk through this particular process, but that's an idea of the range of power JavaScript offers.

Third, on a more practical level, you can use JavaScript to animate images, create customized tutorials, or automatically generate whole new pages based on responses to a form. Though these are fairly practical JavaScript uses, they are somewhat complicated and outside the scope of this book.

The following sections show you how to incorporate snippets of JavaScript into HTML documents. In particular, they show you how to do the following:

- Add text and file modification dates to a Web page, which you can do by using other methods, but doing these in JavaScript is handy. What's more, these examples show you a good way to get a running start with JavaScript.

- Put neat descriptive text in the Status bar of the browser window link (rather than only the URL).

- Verify the contents of an HTML form — that is, make sure people don't leave essential form fields blank. For example, if you let people order Gas-B-Gone by filling out a form, you can use JavaScript to ensure that they fill out the credit card number before submitting the form.

- Make images used as links change when readers move their mouse over the images. For example, have a button with red text replace a button with black text when the mouse is over the image.

So that the examples that follow will make more sense, you might go ahead and check out the JavaScript code following the next paragraph. This snippet will give you enough to begin to see how the pieces fit together. (Think of the snippets of code in this chapter as being a pair of pliers and a screwdriver; that is, you have enough tools to be able to get into trouble, but you can't construct a whole house with them.)

In particular, this JavaScript snippet does three things: Prints "Hello!" (without quotes) in browser windows, prints the date and time on which the document was last changed and saved (modified), and puts the word "Goodbye!" (also without quotes) in the Status bar of browser windows. The three things that do something are JavaScript commands, whereas `document.lastModified` is a property of (information about) the current document that JavaScript can check into. The `<!--` and `-->` tags are comment tags that hide the script from browsers that don't understand JavaScript, and the `<SCRIPT>` and `</SCRIPT>` tags indicate that the whole mess is a script. Whew!

```
<SCRIPT>
<!--
document.write("Hello!")
document.write(document.lastModified)
window.status="Goodbye!"
-->
</SCRIPT>
```

Adding JavaScript to a Web page

When you add JavaScript to a Web page, you can't just open the page in Composer and push a couple of buttons. You have to add the JavaScript to the HTML document that creates the Web page and tell Composer that you've added some funky code. Otherwise, Composer may look at the funky code and assume that your cat sat on your keyboard.

The process for adding JavaScript using Composer is *basically* the same regardless of the specific script you include. The following sections explain how to add text, print document information, place text in the Status bar, validate forms, and jazz up some images — some of the most practical uses for JavaScript.

If you're really planning to get into using JavaScript in your HTML documents, you might strongly consider using a text editor to put in the JavaScript code. Composer's treatment of JavaScript code is somewhat cumbersome and awkward.

If you specify a text editor in your Communicator preferences, you can select Edit⇨HTML Source to get down to the bare essentials of your HTML document. See Chapter 5 to see how to specify a text editor in Communicator.

Adding text

The following example adds simple (and somewhat underwhelming) JavaScript to a Web page. In particular, it adds "Malcolm's Animal Clinic" using the `document.write` JavaScript method. Yeah, yeah, yeah. You can put this text in using other, easier techniques — for example, just typing it — but this example is an easy one for showing the scripting process.

1. **To start a new page in Composer and save it on your disk, go to File⇨New⇨Blank Page (or press Ctrl+Shift+N), and then go to File⇨ Save As. But you knew that.**

   Having a blank slate makes it much easier to see what's going on and to throw out mistakes without a guilty conscience.

2. **Type your very first-ever, unprecedented, ground-breaking JavaScript code.**

   ```
   document.write ("Malcolm's Animal Clinic!")
   ```

   The code tells your document to write (print/output/produce) the text "Malcolm's Animal Clinic!"

3. **Click immediately before the beginning of your JavaScript statement (on the same line), and select Insert⇨HTML Tag.**

   The HTML Tag dialog box appears and awaits your input.

4. **Enter `<SCRIPT>` (the opening script tag) in the dialog box, and click OK.**

5. **Click immediately after the end of the JavaScript statement (on the same line), and select Insert⇨HTML Tag.**

6. **Enter `</SCRIPT>` in the dialog box, and click OK.**

   You see your JavaScript code in the document window, bracketed by the cute little yellow tag icons, as shown in Figure 15-1.

7. **Save your document.**

8. **View your document in Navigator.**

   In the browser window, you see only the text from within the quotes, as in Figure 15-2.

Pretty impressive, huh? You fledgling JavaScript programmer, you. Remember this process any time you get the hankering to slip a little JavaScript into an HTML document.

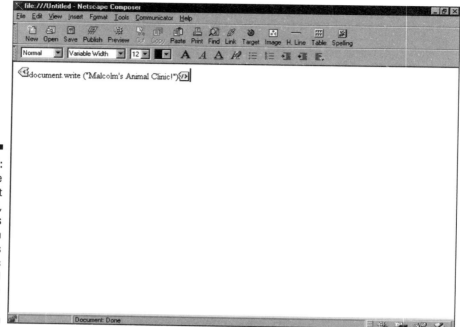

Figure 15-1:
The
JavaScript
statement,
which is
visible in
Composer's
window, is
bracketed
by style
tags.

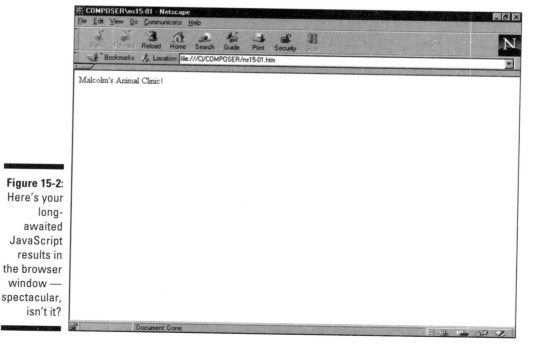

Figure 15-2:
Here's your
long-
awaited
JavaScript
results in
the browser
window —
spectacular,
isn't it?

Here's the rest of the story about this particular use of JavaScript:

✔ If you view the document's HTML source code, you'll notice that the only real difference between what's visible in Composer and the real HTML code is the difference between the clever yellow tag icons in Composer and the <SCRIPT>...</SCRIPT> tags. Aha, you say, if I wanted to, I could enter JavaScript manually through a plain text editor! You're right! Just remember the <SCRIPT>...</SCRIPT> tags around the JavaScript code.

✔ If there is a possibility that anyone reading your page will have an older browser or a browser that isn't JavaScript-enabled, you have to make a special adjustment — otherwise your JavaScript code will appear in its naked glory in the reader's browser window. (Ewww! Naked JavaScript!) Use a text editor (not Composer) to enter <!-- immediately after the first script tag and before the JavaScript code. Then enter --> after the code and before the closing script tag. Doing so hides the code from older browsers. This example (seen from a text editor), looks like the following:

```
<SCRIPT>
<!--
document.write ("Malcolm's Animal Clinic!")
-->
</SCRIPT>
```

Sounds like a lot of trouble to accommodate old technology? *Hint:* Only newer versions of Netscape and Internet Explorer support JavaScript. Your boss's browser may very well not support JavaScript. After you finish your pages, go ahead and manually edit each of the pages containing JavaScript to add the <!-- and --> comment tags.

Manually, you say? Well, yes. Composer won't let you add comment tags through the Insert HTML dialog box, so you have to use a plain text editor to put those in. Just choose Edit⇨HTML Source to bring up your text editor. (Chapter 5 tells you how to set a text editor.)

Printing document information

Document information is data about the document, such as its size and date last modified. This information is handy to have — the date last modified in particular, because it saves you the trouble of remembering to update the date last modified each time you change your document. Just put in this bit of code one time, and you never have to worry about it again. The following steps show you how to print the document's date last modified using the document.write JavaScript.

1. **Click to place the cursor at the point you want the last modified date of the document to appear.**

2. **Enter the following statement (all on one line):**

```
document.write("This document last modified on " +
        document.lastModified + ".")
```

As in the previous example, `document.write` prints text in the HTML file when viewed in a JavaScript-enabled browser. The text within the quotes prints exactly, and the `document.lastModified` property provides the date.

You're welcome to change anything between the " " but must leave the remaining information exactly as is.

3. **Click immediately before the beginning of your JavaScript statement (on the same line), and select Insert⇨HTML Tag.**

The HTML Tag dialog box appears and awaits your input.

4. **Enter `<SCRIPT>` (the opening script tag) in the dialog box, and click OK.**

5. **Click immediately after the end of the JavaScript statement (on the same line), and select Insert⇨HTML Tag.**

6. **Enter `</SCRIPT>` in the dialog box, and click OK.**

7. **Save your document.**

Pretty spiffy, huh? You might consider putting the statement in small type and burying it down at the bottom of the page, just so it isn't too obtrusive. See Figure 15-3 for an example.

In a non-JavaScript browser, such as most versions of Mosaic, nothing at all appears where other readers see the last modified statement. That's why we used the `document.write` function to print the accompanying (descriptive) text as well. We could have used regular HTML to do the text and JavaScript for the date, but that might result in text such as "This document last modified on" appearing in older browsers, which wouldn't do anyone any good. Better to have it completely omitted than to have it mangled.

Here is some gossip about printing document properties (and pay attention; we promised not to repeat this information, so we can say it only once):

If you want to automatically provide the last modified date for documents and have the date available to all browsers, you can accomplish the same thing through something called a *Server-Side Include,* in which you make the Web server do the work and add the date as the page is served. You need to ask your server administrator for the specifics because they depend on the server software. The Server-Side Include method has a downside, though: Dates appear only when the document is distributed by the server, so the date isn't visible, for example, when you test the document locally.

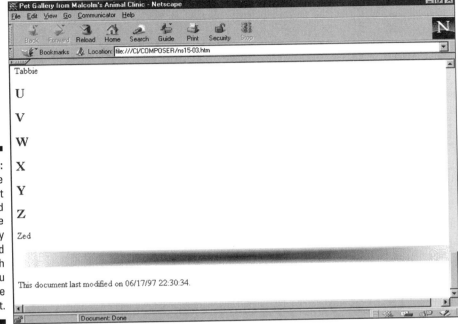

Figure 15-3:
The date
last
modified
will now be
automatically
updated
each
time you
update the
document.

Making text appear in the Status bar

The Status bar — the bottommost portion of the browser window — is a useful place to put information for your readers. If you've spent any time surfing the Web, you've probably noticed that URLs appear in the Status bar whenever you move your mouse cursor over a link. You can use JavaScript to control the Status bar and put messages in it. For example, on a link pointing to our home page, `http://www.raycomm.com` generally appears in the Status bar when the mouse is over the link. However, using JavaScript, we can change that to "Visit the RayComm Home Page," as shown in Figure 15-4.

If you want to get really fancy, you can enhance your page so that when readers move their mouse over the Status bar, they see a specific message rather than a URL (because showing something like `askvet.html` or `http://www.xmission.com/~ejray/malcolm/askvet.html` isn't particularly helpful to readers). More useful to your readers would be to show a description such as "Choose this link to ask the vet a question." To enter a specific message and update the Status bar, you must add another attribute (specifically, a JavaScript function) in the HTML link code.

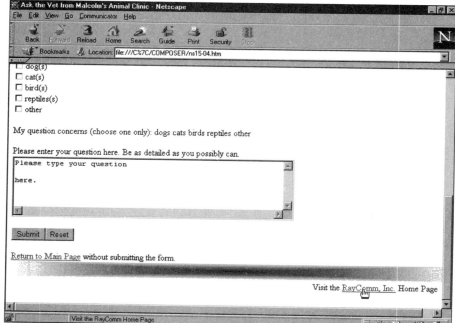

Figure 15-4:
The
Status bar
includes
text that
describes
what the
mouse
points to.

Actually, two JavaScript methods work together to make the Status bar change happen — one to change the Status bar when the cursor is over the link and the other to change the Status bar back when the cursor is not over the link. Here's what the JavaScript code looks like:

```
onMouseOver="window.status='Pick me!';return true;"
onMouseout="window.status=''"
```

onMouseOver (a funny abbreviation for when the mouse pointer moves over something) puts the words "Pick me!" in the Status bar — rather than the URL of the link. onMouseOut (for when the mouse moves away from something) makes the Status bar go blank again. If you leave the onMouseOut bit out, the Status bar will read "Pick me!" until the reader moves the cursor over a different link.

Rather than putting these JavaScript commands in a separate script block of your HTML document, as in the previous section, you can place them in the link text. Here's the process:

1. In Composer, open a document with a link that needs to be jazzed up.

2. **Right-click a link, and select Link Properties from the pop-up menu.**

    Alternatively, you can highlight the text of the link and select Format⇨ Character Properties (Alt+Enter) and click the Link tab, or select the link and click the Link button from the toolbar.

3. **Click the E̱xtra HTML button to bring up the Extra HTML dialog box.**

4. **In the dialog box, enter the following JavaScript code to set up a function to change the Status bar, as well as a second function to erase it.**

```
onMouseOver="window.status='Choose this link to see
        other questions!';return true;"
onMouseout="window.status=''"
```

    Be careful with the single and double quotes — they must appear exactly as they do here or it won't work. Additionally, the only place you can put a line break is just before `onMouseOut`. Although HTML doesn't care about line breaks, JavaScript most certainly does.

    Edit the text between the single quotes as you choose. You can use this same code as many times as you'd like in any document, substituting appropriate text for the "Choose this link to ask a question!" part.

5. **Click OK to close the Extra HTML dialog box, and click OK again to close the Properties dialog box.**

    That's all there is to it. Just save the document and try it out in the browser to see the fruits of your labors — your fruits should look similar to Figure 15-5.

    Check out `GALLERY.HTM` on the `CDFILES` folder for a working example of this script.

Validating forms

Using JavaScript to validate forms is a good idea because it ensures that the reader's input is complete enough to meet your needs. For example, in the form created by Malcolm's Animal Clinic, readers are expected to provide their e-mail addresses. If they don't provide an e-mail address, they can't get an answer. Malcolm is worried about the possible bad publicity caused by failing to answer questions because of a missing address (which would make him look bad), so he decides to use JavaScript to validate the form.

You can have a form validated on the server, through CGI programming, but that sometimes costs money and sometimes requires that someone with fairly keen programming skills write a program to process the incoming data. Malcolm is happy with the e-mailed form results and is willing to accept a less-than-perfect solution to the validation problem, believing that something quick and easy and *now* is better than nothing.

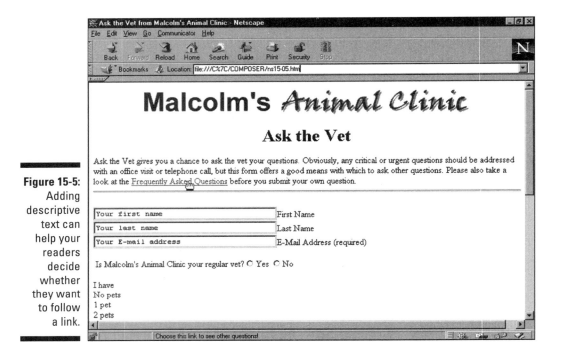

Figure 15-5: Adding descriptive text can help your readers decide whether they want to follow a link.

To validate the results of the e-mail field on the form, the information provided must meet two criteria: The field cannot be left blank, and it must include an "at" sign (@), because Internet e-mail addresses always have one.

To completely and thoroughly validate the form, Malcolm would need to do some more checking — for example, to verify that no spaces are placed after the @, that at least three letters and one period are after the @, and so on. With enough time, a completely precise validation scheme can be constructed. However, for this instance, complete validation just isn't worth it. Just making sure that the reader didn't overlook the field and put in something that vaguely resembles an e-mail address is enough for now.

After some deep thought, Internet surfing, and consultation with the local programming geeks (who also happen to have pets), Malcolm's validation function looks like the following:

```
function validate(form) {
   if ((form.email.value == "") ||
   (form.email.value.indexOf('@') == -1))
     alert("Please Enter Your Address");
     }
```

After the developers define the validation function at the top of the HTML document, they have to include an additional attribute in the form tag for the e-mail input. Those two parts together validate the form. Here's the process for inserting the function and for modifying the form tag in an existing form.

Because Composer tends to be a little too helpful with formatting commands — and, thus, messes up the script code — you need to do part of this editing in your text editor. Here's the process:

1. **In your text editor (not in Composer), open the form that you want to validate.**

2. **Find the** `</HEAD>` **tag within the code.**

3. **Immediately before the** `</HEAD>` **tag, add the following tags:**

```
<SCRIPT>
<!--

-->
</SCRIPT>
</HEAD>
```

4. **Right in the middle — between the** `<!--` **and the** `-->` **— add the following JavaScript code, pressing Enter at the end of each line.**

```
function validate(form) {
    if ((form.email.value == "") ||
    (form.email.value.indexOf('@') == -1))
      alert("Please Enter Your Address");
      }
```

   You don't absolutely have to press Enter at the end of each line, but doing so makes the code much easier to read and troubleshoot.

5. **Save your document and open it in Composer (or continue in the text editor, whichever is easier).**

6. **Move down your document to the form tag you want to validate, and double-click the yellow icon that contains the form tag to validate.**

   Remember, you can hover your cursor over the form tag to see the contents.

   If you'd rather, you can click once on the icon to select it and then right-click and choose Tag Properties.

   If you're editing the plain HTML code in your text editor, just find the form tag you want to validate.

7. Add a JavaScript statement to tell the browser to execute that validation function when the reader finishes filling out that field.

onBlur is the JavaScript statement that refers to the act of tabbing or clicking out of an input field. The attribute reads:

```
onBlur="validate(form)"
```

When you finish, the HTML Tag dialog box should look similar to the example in Figure 15-6. If you're editing the plain code in a text editor, your HTML tag will look like the contents of the dialog box.

Figure 15-6:
Here's how the validation attribute appears in the HTML Tag dialog box.

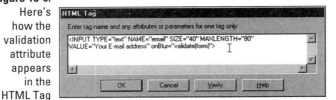

8. Click OK to close the HTML Tag dialog box.

That's it! You just set validation for that form with JavaScript.

9. Save and then try out the validation in your browser.

Place the cursor in the e-mail field, and then press Tab to leave the field. If the field is blank or if there is no @, you receive a JavaScript alert telling you to fill in your address. Pretty slick, huh?

Read on for a couple more comments about validating fields:

✔ Note that for most somewhat complex functions — such as validating forms — you must provide the script at one point in the document and the function that activates that script at another point. It's easy, particularly when you're in the flurry of developing documents, to forget one or the other and then have problems figuring out why the script doesn't work. Go slow, cross your *t*'s and dot your *i*'s. And be careful not to dot your *t*'s and cross your *i*'s . . . or your eyes.

✔ If you want to validate the form more carefully, you can do so. As the validation stands now, the script checks to make sure that the field input is a possible e-mail address — that the field isn't blank and contains an @ sign. For cases in which you need more-complex or more-thorough validation, that's also easily done by using a little-more-comprehensive JavaScript function. Check out *JavaScript For Dummies Quick Reference* for more information.

Getting fancy with images

The final fancy JavaScript trick covered in this chapter is making images appear to change when you move the cursor over them. This trick is often used with images that are used as links — making the text change colors or replacing the text with a picture as the mouse pointer goes by.

Yeah, sure, it's kinda gimmiky but not a bad trick, all things considered. Before you start, you need a Web page with two buttons that are used as links. You also need two more images that are the exact size as the first two but with different colors — so that the image swapping will be visible. We've used two images with black text and red text. The red text buttons appear when the cursor is over the image.

The images can be of any size, but the images you'll be swapping must be exactly the same size as the ones they replace. Ours happen to be 100 pixels wide by 30 pixels high. The names are `button1a.jpg` (for the black version of the first button), `button1b.jpg` (red text version of the first button), `button2a.jpg` (black version, second button), and `button2b.jpg` (red version, second button).

The following steps show you how to add this cool JavaScript to your Web page. Don't be scared off by the number of steps; in fact, we included so many steps to help keep you from getting lost or overlooking details. With that, here are the steps:

1. **In your text editor, open the form that you want to validate.**

2. **Find the `</HEAD>` tag within the code.**

3. **Immediately before the `</HEAD>` tag, add the following tags:**

```
<SCRIPT>
<!--

-->
</SCRIPT>
</HEAD>
```

4. **Right in the middle — between the `<!--` and the `-->` — add the following JavaScript code, pressing Enter at the end of each line.**

```
pictureson = new Image(100, 30);
          pictureson.src =   "button1b.jpg";
picturesoff = new Image(100, 30);
          picturesoff.src = "button1a.jpg";
storieson = new Image(100, 30);
          storieson.src  = "button2b.jpg";
storiesoff = new Image(100, 30);
          storiesoff.src = "button2a.jpg";

function img_active(imgName)
{
 imgOn = eval(imgName + "on.src");
 document [imgName].src = imgOn;
 }

function img_inactive(imgName)
{
 imgOff = eval(imgName + "off.src");
 document [imgName].src = imgOff;
 }
```

This ugly blob of code sets up which buttons are used in which contexts. The two buttons are for Stories and Pictures, so the first four lines of code set up the images to use for `picturesoff` (no mouse cursor) and `pictureson` (with the cursor over the image) and similar settings for stories. The function `img_active` line (and the four following lines) swap the colored image for the original one. The `img_inactive` line (and the following four lines) swap the original image back into place.

5. **Save the document, and then open it in Composer.**

6. **Click the first image (pictures, in our example) to select it and click the Link button, or go to Insert⇨Link (Ctrl+Shift+L).**

7. **Click the Extra HTML button to bring up the Extra HTML dialog box.**

8. **In the dialog box, add the following code:**

```
onMouseover = "img_active('pictures')" onMouseout =
          "img_inactive('pictures')"
```

This code specifies that the `img_active` function happen when the mouse moves over the link and that the `img_inactive` function happen when the mouse moves away from the link. The word pictures in the code work with the previous snippet of code to specify which pictures are swapped. Because the code specifies the pictures button, it's the pictures files that should be swapped.

9. **Click OK to close the Extra HTML dialog box, and then click OK again to close the Link Properties dialog box.**

10. **Select the second image and click the Link button, or go to Insert⇨Link.**

11. **Click the Extra HTML button to bring up the Extra HTML dialog box.**

12. **In the dialog box, add the following code:**

```
onMouseover = "img_active('stories')" onMouseout =
        "img_inactive('stories')"
```

This code is identical to the code from the previous button, except the word stories have been substituted for pictures because this is for the stories button.

13. **Click OK to close the Extra HTML dialog box, and then click OK again to close the Link Properties dialog box.**

14. **Save your document and try it out in the browser.**

If you're having problems or think you might have introduced a typo in the code, just open up GALLERY.HTM from the CDFILES folder that comes with this book and check out the original code. Each one of the buttons we used is there.

Here are some additional comments about this fancy and slightly convoluted process:

✔ Although short snippets of JavaScript code can be entered directly in the Composer window (and bracketed with script tags), the Composer editor introduces some odd characters and formatting that preclude entering extensive raw JavaScript code. Putting it in through a text editor is much easier. Adding bits of code to existing tags works consistently well through Composer, although you can add little bits and pieces in the text editor.

✔ If you like this effect, you can add additional buttons by providing more figures, duplicating these two lines of code:

```
pictureson = new Image(100, 30); pictureson.src  =
        "button1b.jpg";
picturesoff = new Image(100, 30); picturesoff.src =
        "button1a.jpg";
```

In the new lines of code, you have a couple of edits to do. You need to replace "pictures" with a new name and the two .jpg filenames with the new filenames and finally insert new code in the Link tags, again replacing "pictures" with the appropriate new name.

Finding More Information and Resources

This chapter has provided only a small sampling — make that a very small sampling — of JavaScript and its capabilities. If you're intrigued with the possibilities of how JavaScript can be used to enhance your documents, we can recommend the selections of resources in this section in addition to other ...For Dummies books mentioned earlier in this chapter.

If you're looking for online resources, check out the Netscape site, which is always the definitive source for JavaScript information. Start at http://home.netscape.com/ or at http://developer.netscape.com/library/documentation/ for the Netscape JavaScript documentation.

Other JavaScript pages abound on the Internet. If you're looking for sample code or general information, try connecting to Yahoo! (http://www.yahoo.com/) and searching for JavaScript. A fairly high-end but extremely useful site is at http://www.gamelan.com/, with information about both Java and JavaScript and lots of other relatively technical resources. If you need specific help with a specific issue, try going to AltaVista (http://www.altavista.digital.com). When there, just enter a search string with all of the key phrases, such as "JavaScript onMouseOver alert" if you're looking for information about how to use JavaScript to flash an alert dialog box when you pass your mouse over a specific object on the page.

Whew! Was that a chapter, or what?

Chapter 16
Eeek! Your Browser's Been Framed!

· ·

· ·

*G*ads! I've been framed. "Here I sit with nothing but borders, all around. Can't go through them, or over them, or . . . Wait! That view in the frame next door. It just changed. And the other one, it changed, too. What's going on here?"

This abbreviated transcript of an HTML document's *thoughts* within a frame has been brought to you by Better Organization and Linking to Organize Great Net Advancements (BOLOGNA).

For more information about framing HTML documents and what to do with them after you've framed them (besides hang them on the wall), read on.

What Are Frames, Anyway?

Frames divide your browser window into multiple parts, each of which can accommodate a separate HTML document. Whether the frames are vertical or horizontal, each frame contains one HTML document and can function as a completely separate browser window.

Before you go running off and adding frames to your Web pages, you ought to know two things. First, frames are not standard HTML, meaning that many browsers don't support them. If your readers use a fairly recent version of either Netscape Navigator or Microsoft Internet Explorer, you'll be fine. However, if they rely on an older browser or a browser that rigidly expects standard HTML, your readers may have some difficulty.

Check out "Accommodating browsers without frames" later in this chapter to see how you can use frames, even if they aren't supported by some of your readers' browsers.

Second, Composer won't actually create frames for you. You must add the frames manually to the HTML code. (No eeek-ing, folks. Adding frames is easier than it sounds, not to mention that we'll show you how.)

Why did we include this chapter on frames if Composer won't do it for you? Well, frames offer several benefits that you might be interested in having in your pages. Frames make Web pages and sites more visually interesting. For example, instead of having one wide-open window, frames can divide windows into separate parts. Or you can use different background colors or images in each window. These effects, shown in Figure 16-1, make pages more interesting.

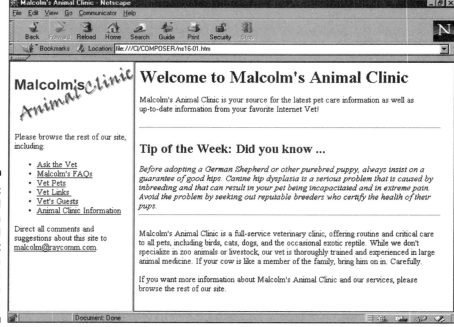

Figure 16-1: Framed pages can help add interest to an otherwise typical Web site.

Frames also enable you to set off important elements such as logos, navigation menus, or copyright notices from the content. Furthermore, you can specify that these elements appear on-screen at all times, regardless of what content is showing. Figure 16-2 shows a three-frame site that divides the window into logo, navigation, and content.

Keeping copyright notices and corporate logos visible throughout all parts of your site can really help establish a corporate identity as well as remind your readers of where they are. Using frames to keep the corporate logo visible is a good idea, particularly in cases where a company is providing information of general interest on the Web.

Finally, frames can, if done correctly, improve site navigation. For example, in many nonframed pages, readers must scroll to the bottom or top of pages to find the navigation menu. By using frames, you can improve navigation by keeping the menu on-screen in a consistent place at all times. Readers won't have to scroll or look for the navigation menu because it appears in the same place on every screen.

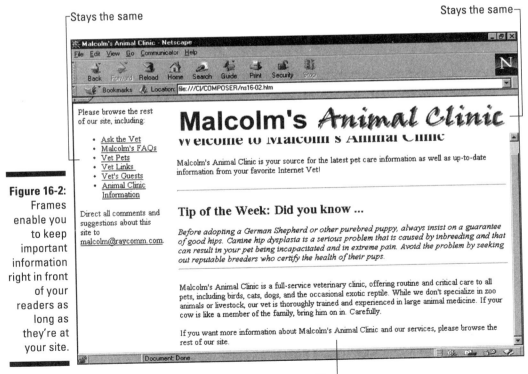

Figure 16-2: Frames enable you to keep important information right in front of your readers as long as they're at your site.

Designing Frames

Before you start creating frames, you should take a few minutes to design them. By planning ahead, you can make sure that they'll all fit on the screen (at all resolutions), that they'll work as you intend, and that you'll be able to implement them easily, without time-consuming trial and error.

In general, don't include more than, say, two or three frames because any more than that will look lousy. Unfortunately, many Web page designers get a little carried away with frames and put four, five, or six of them on a screen, making it remarkably difficult to identify or use information. Figure 16-3 shows a compelling example of what *not* to do (names and files were changed to protect the guilty).

Use the following quick steps to sketch your frames and avoid the "Top 10 list of lousy framed sites."

1. **Sketch a browser window, and draw lines roughly where you want the frames to appear.**

   The Malcolm Animal Clinic Web site includes two vertical frames, one for content and one for navigation.

2. **Create an alternative frame design.**

   For example, add an additional (small) frame for animations and special effects and another frame to ensure that your company name remains visible to all visitors. We call this alternative design Plan B.

   The instructions throughout the rest of this chapter use the Animal Clinic's original frame design, which features two frames. To take a peek at how the four-frame Plan B progresses, check out the sidebars "Malcolm's Plan B frameset" and "Malcolm's Plan B frames," both later in this chapter.

3. **Add names to your sketch, giving informative names to each frame, so that you can refer to them easily later.**

   The Animal Clinic frames are named toc and main for the original sketch and toc, main, effects, and logo for the alternative sketch. Stick to short and descriptive names that you'll easily remember.

4. **Determine each frame's size for both your original and alternative ideas.**

   You can specify size three ways:

   • Specify the size either in precise numbers of pixels or in a percentage of the overall window size.

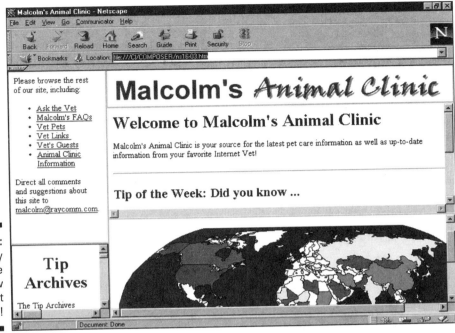

Figure 16-3:
There really
ought to be
a law
against
this!

- Specify the size of one frame and let the other take the remaining space.
- Have each frame take a specific relative fraction of the window or of the remaining space — for example, two each at $1/2$ or one at $1/2$ and two each at $1/4$.

Obviously, the frames together should add up to the total window area. That is, if you are designing a two-frame layout like the original Animal Clinic sketch, the width of the first frame plus the width of the second frame should total the width of the window. (Don't want drafts and chilly breezes, right?)

If you're going to use an image within a frame, make the frame size equal to the image size — or at least be sure the image fits within the frame.

Figure 16-4 shows frame sizes for the Animal Clinic alternative site.

If you're still waffling about sizes, don't worry about it. Anything you do at this stage can be changed later, but you'll find the creation process much easier if you're *just* creating and not trying to plan at the same time. Walk, then chew gum, we always say.

Figure 16-4: Malcolm's Plan B (more complex) frame sketch shows four frames and corresponding measurements.

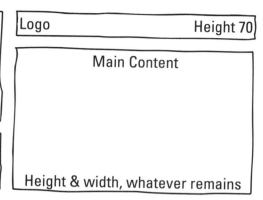

Table of Contents		Logo	Height 70
		Main Content	
Width 160			
Effects			
Height 120		Height & width, whatever remains	

Creating Frames

At the beginning of this chapter, we told you that Composer won't actually create frames for you; you have to insert the frames in the HTML code. You can, certainly, use Composer to create the documents that fill the frames, but we'll get to that in a minute.

Creating frames is a six-step process:

1. **Create a frameset document that sets up the frame structure.**

2. **Add the frames.**

3. **Add alternative text, which accommodates people who aren't quite with the times and use a browser that does not support frames.**

4. **Test and troubleshoot frames to make sure you didn't goof.**

5. **Add content.**

6. **Include links between frames.**

The following six sections walk you through these steps.

Creating a frameset document

A *frameset* document (also called a *layout* document) sets up the frame structure. In essence, it describes to the browser those frame sketches, with sizes.

Table 16-1 shows you the frame tags and attributes you need to create a frameset document.

For more information about tags and attributes, refer to Chapter 3.

Table 16-1	Tags Used to Set Up Frame Layout
Tag or Attribute	*Description*
`<FRAMESET></FRAMESET>`	The `<FRAMESET>` tag replaces the `<BODY>` tag in your layout document and establishes the location and sizes of the frames.
`ROWS=`	This attribute for the `<FRAMESET>` tag establishes the rows contained within the frame, in percentage, pixels, or as a proportion of remaining space.
`COLS=`	This attribute for the `<FRAMESET>` tag establishes the columns contained within the frame, in percentage, pixels, or as a proportion of remaining space.
`FRAMEBORDER=`	This attribute turns off borders for all frames contained within this `<FRAMESET>`. You could also turn off the borders in each frame individually, but turning off the frames here is easier.
`BORDER=`	This attribute specifies the width of the border in pixels. If you want invisible borders, set `FRAMEBORDER=NO` and `BORDER=0`.

The following steps show you how to create a frameset document for a two-frame page. In particular, the examples with the steps show you how to create the Animal Clinic's two-frame page. To complete the following steps, you need to use a plain text editor. Here are our recommendations:

✔ If you're using Windows, use Notepad (not Wordpad, you Windows 95 people).

✔ If you're using a Mac, use SimpleText or TeachText, depending on your particular operating system version.

✔ If you're using UNIX, use vi, emacs, pico, or any other editor you find easy to use. If you don't find any editors on UNIX particularly easy to use, we've got a lot in common.

1. Open the text-editing program of your choice.

The actual process depends on your platform and on the program you choose. As long as you can save plain text files without any formatting, you'll be fine.

2. **Type basic structural tags to identify the document as an HTML document.**

   These tags are some of the ones that Composer does automatically for you. They actually appear in any Composer document you create. If you want to see for yourself, open one of your documents in Navigator and go to View⇨Page Source.

   ```
   <HTML>
   <HEAD>
   <TITLE></TITLE>
   </HEAD>
   </HTML>
   ```

3. **Fill in the title of your document between the opening and closing** <TITLE>...</TITLE> **tags.**

   In this example, "Malcolm's Animal Clinic" is the document title because this frame layout document will be the home page for the site.

   Whenever you have to type information at a specific position within the document, you may see the example code with some bold text and some plain text. The bold text is what you should type, and the plain text represents text that already exists in your document.

   ```
   <TITLE>Malcolm's Animal Clinic</TITLE>
   ```

4. **Put in a** <FRAMESET> **opening and closing tag pair, after the closing** </HEAD> **tag and before the closing** </HTML> **tag.**

   ```
   </HEAD>
   <FRAMESET>
   </FRAMESET>
   </HTML>
   ```

   At first, a single <FRAMESET>...</FRAMESET> set will suffice to set up two frames. Later in this section, we discuss multiple <FRAMESET>...</FRAMESET> tags.

5. **Add the** COLS= **attribute to the** <FRAMESET> **tag.**

   ```
   <FRAMESET COLS=>
   ```

6. **Specify frame widths.**

   In this example, the left frame should be specified at exactly 160 pixels wide, and the right frame should occupy the remaining space — as determined in the sketch we drew. The left frame will include an image that is 160 pixels, which is why specifying the width of the left pane in pixels is necessary.

```
<FRAMESET COLS="160,*">
```

7. **Add the** FRAMEBORDER=NO **and** BORDER=0 **attribute to the** <FRAMESET> **tag.**

```
<FRAMESET COLS="160,*" FRAMEBORDER=NO BORDER=0>
```

These attributes specify no borders for all the frames within the <FRAMESET>...</FRAMESET> tags, which often makes for a cleaner and nicer looking page. It takes two attributes to turn off the borders because Microsoft Internet Explorer and Netscape Navigator use different commands to control frame borders.

8. **Save your document.**

As you save the document, be very sure to put it in the same folder as the rest of your Web site and to name it with an .htm or .html extension. A name such as frames.htm will make it easier to track what's happening throughout the rest of the process of developing frames.

If you're using a program like Word or Wordpad to develop your document, check to make sure that the file type is set to text, ASCII, or DOS text.

You can't see anything yet, so there's no need to view your document in Navigator.

Here are some other notes about frames:

- You can specify frame widths in pixels — as in the preceding example — in percentages or in terms of remaining space. Additionally, if you're developing multiple parallel frames (striping the window), you can include all of the instructions together. For example, to specify that the first frame should be 50 percent of the window and the second frame should take the remainder, use an attribute like COLS="50%,*". Or if you want the first column to be 150 pixels, the third to be 50 percent of the window, and the second to take the remaining available space, use COLS="150,*,50%".

- If you want frames to be horizontal — in rows, not columns — use ROWS= in place of COLS=.

- You can't combine ROWS= and COLS= in the same frame set tag, however. To find out how to have both columns and rows, check out the sidebar "Malcolm's Plan B frameset."

Malcolm's Plan B frameset

If you want to set up asymmetric frames within other frames, as in Malcolm's alternative idea, you must insert multiple `<FRAMESET>` tags. Within each `<FRAMESET>`, you provide parameters in which the frames will fit. However, instead of filling those slots with frames, you can also fill them with an additional `<FRAMESET>` statement that further subdivides the space.

For example, Malcolm's Plan B site would require a total of three `<FRAMESET>` tags to establish the overall left/right division. You would divide the left pane for the table of contents and the multimedia pane and then divide the right page into the logo pane and the content pane. So the code would look like the following example (we put descriptions between the lines so that you can more easily see what's going on — don't type the descriptions).

```
<FRAMESET COLS="160,*"
   FRAMEBORDER=NO BORDER=0>
```

This line makes two columns, one at 160 pixels, the other taking the rest of the space.

```
<FRAMESET ROWS="*,120"
   FRAMEBORDER=NO BORDER=0>
   </FRAMESET>
```

This line makes two rows within the left pane of the first `<FRAMESET>`. The bottom row is 120 pixels high; the top takes the remaining space. Note the closing tag — don't forget it!

```
<FRAMESET ROWS="20%,*"
   FRAMEBORDER=NO BORDER=0>
   </FRAMESET>
```

This line makes two rows within the right pane of the first `<FRAMESET>`. The top row takes 20 percent of the available space; the bottom row takes the remaining space. Again, this line has a closing tag.

```
</FRAMESET>
```

The closing `</FRAMESET>` tag closes the opening `<FRAMESET>` tag, so each of the opening tags has a corresponding closing tag. Although it looks horribly confusing, if you build it one piece at a time with a sketch to refer to, you'll find that these framesets are really easy to build.

Adding the frames

Adding frames in an existing layout document (with `<FRAMESET>` tags in place) is fairly straightforward. All you have to do is insert one frame tag for each frame and add attributes. Table 16-2 describes the frame tags and attributes.

Table 16-2	Tags Used to Fill and Format Frames
Tag and Attribute	*Description*
`<FRAME>...</FRAME>`	This tag summons the content for each of the frames designated in the `<FRAMESET>` tag. If you specify six divisions for frames within a `<FRAMESET>` tag, you'll have six `<FRAME>` tags.
`SRC=`	This attribute for the `<FRAME>` tag includes a URL, just like an anchor tag and identifies which HTML document will fill that frame. `SRC="content.htm"` or `SRC="http://www.xmission.com/~ejray/malcolm/jazzed/toc.htm"` are acceptable SRC attributes. If you omit the SRC attribute, your frame will be sadly, tragically, empty.
`NAME=`	This attribute for the `<FRAME>` tag gives the frame a name, so you can refer to it. "Yo!" and "Hey, You!" don't work as well for frames as they do for your friends. Left, content, logo, main — those are good frame names if you're playing the name that frame game.
`FRAMEBORDER=`	This attribute turns off borders for this frame. However, if the frame shares a border with an adjacent frame, you'll have to turn off the borders for both frames.
`BORDER=`	This attribute specifies the width of the border in pixels. If you want invisible borders, set `FRAMEBORDER=NO` and `BORDER=0`.
`SCROLLING=`	By specifying `YES`, `NO`, or `AUTO`, you determine if and when scrollbars appear on the edges of your frame. Yes requires the scrollbars at all times, No forbids them at all times, and auto applies scrollbars only if there's something to scroll. Web developers often specify `SCROLLING=NO` in an index or table of contents frame and then make sure that all the text will be visible. This approach gives a cleaner looking frame, but if you specify no scrolling and then summon a longer chunk of text than can fit in the window, your readers won't be able to see it.
`NORESIZE`	This attribute keeps users from resizing the frame by clicking and dragging on the frame border. Aha! You didn't know that was possible, did you? If you're specifying a frame size in pixels and specifying `SCROLLING=NO` to make sure that you get the appearance you want, you should also probably specify `NORESIZE`.

(continued)

Table 16-2 *(continued)*

Tag and Attribute	Description
MARGINHEIGHT=	This attribute specifies the vertical margin, above and below the content of the frame, in pixels. You can, and probably should, omit this. Particularly given the non-WYSIWYG nature of Web pages, specifying the margin isn't likely to do exactly what you want. If you do want to define a margin rather than let the browser automatically determine it, go back and add it later after you're sure that the frames work properly.
MARGINWIDTH=	This attribute specifies the horizontal margin, to the left and right of the frame content, in pixels. All the qualifications about the margin height apply to this one as well.

Now that you've seen the possibilities, use the following steps to implement your frames.

1. **Make sure that you have a layout document open in a text editor.**

   The layout document contains the <FRAMESET> tags to establish the areas in which frames will appear.

   Just as in the preceding section, you can use any text editor you choose.

2. **After the opening <FRAMESET> tag, insert a <FRAME> tag.**

   ```
   <FRAMESET COLS="160,*"  FRAMEBORDER=NO BORDER=0>
   <FRAME>
   ```

3. **The <FRAMESET> in this example calls for two frames (one at 160 pixels wide and the other filling the remaining space), so insert a second <FRAME> tag.**

   ```
   <FRAMESET COLS="160,*"  FRAMEBORDER=NO BORDER=0>
   <FRAME>
   <FRAME>
   ```

   You should insert <FRAME> tags for each specified frame at this point so that you don't accidentally forget one of them.

4. **Add the SRC= attribute, along with the file source, to the first <FRAME> tag.**

   This SRC attribute brings a specific file in to fill the frame. You can add either an attribute to point to an existing file or just make up a name and later create the file. Either way, in this example, the table of contents `<FRAME>` (at the left) is called `toc.htm`.

```
<FRAMESET COLS="160,*"  FRAMEBORDER=NO BORDER=0>
<FRAME SRC="toc.htm">
```

You can also put in a complete URL to point to a document on a different server or somewhere else within your Web site. However, we're keeping everything together within a single folder, so you just need to include the filename.

5. **Add the** `NAME=` **attribute, along with a reference name, to the same** `<FRAME>`.

```
<FRAMESET COLS="160,*"  FRAMEBORDER=NO BORDER=0>
<FRAME SRC="toc.htm" NAME="toc">
```

Strictly speaking, a name isn't necessary, but if you're going to get fancy with your frame navigation later, you should name your frames with something short and simple.

6. **Add the remaining attributes to your** `<FRAME>` **tag.**

The only additional attributes Malcolm's contents frame needs are those to disable scrolling and resizing, because either scrolling or resizing will mess up the effect. The `MARGINHEIGHT=` and `MARGINWIDTH=` attributes aren't really necessary.

```
<FRAMESET COLS="160,*"  FRAMEBORDER=NO BORDER=0>
<FRAME SRC="toc.htm" NAME="toc" SCROLLING=NO NORESIZE>
```

7. **Insert a** `SRC=` **attribute for the second** `<FRAME>`.

See, you'd already almost forgotten it, hadn't you? Again, you can point to any valid URL, but pointing to a file within the same folder is the simplest and best solution, at least for the example Web site.

```
<FRAME SRC="toc.htm" NAME="toc" SCROLLING=NO NORESIZE>
<FRAME SRC="main.htm">
```

8. **Add the** `NAME=` **attribute to the** `<FRAME>`.

```
<FRAME SRC="toc.htm" NAME="toc" SCROLLING=NO NORESIZE>
<FRAME SRC="main.htm" NAME="main">
```

In case you're wondering, it's just coincidence that the frame names are similar to the URLs. The name can as easily be `content` or `big` or `right` — whatever works for you.

9. **Optionally, add other attributes to the** `<FRAME>`.

For this example Web site, no additional attributes are necessary. It's only the toc `<FRAME>` that really requires fancy formatting.

10. Save the document.

The precise procedure will vary for different platforms. Again, though, be sure to put it in the same folder as the rest of your Web site with an `.htm` (or `.html`) extension.

Figure 16-5 shows the framed page that the example site calls for, using placeholders in the `toc.htm` and `main.htm` files so that you can see what's going on.

Good for you! The next step is adding alternative text so that people using browsers that don't support frames can still view your pages. Read on!

Accommodating browsers without frames

Can you believe it? Some people still use browsers that don't support frames. It's kind of hard to believe considering how cool frames are, but those laggers are still out there. And being the accommodating person that you are, you want to make sure that those people can access the information you provide. (Of course, "those people" has the same connotation as your mom when she disapprovingly refers to your significant other — you know, "That Kenny," "That Carlo," "That Catherine," or "That Kim" . . . to name a few.)

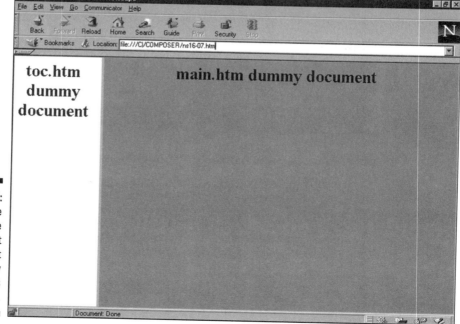

Figure 16-5:
The example frameset document now includes frames.

Malcolm's Plan B frames

Yup. Even Malcolm's alternative frame plan now has frames included. Following is the code for the alternative frames, complete with all four `<FRAME>` tags, one for each separate chunk of text. The only tricky part here is to make sure that each `<FRAME>` tag lands within the correct `<FRAMESET>` tag. That is, if a `<FRAMESET>` establishes places for two frames, you must put two `<FRAME>` tags between that opening and closing `<FRAMESET>` tag.

```
<FRAMESET COLS="160,*"
   FRAMEBORDER=NO BORDER=0>

<FRAMESET ROWS="*,120"
   FRAMEBORDER=NO BORDER=0>

<FRAME SRC="toc.htm" NAME=""
   SCROLLING=NO NORESIZE>

<FRAME SRC="effect.htm" NAME=""
   SCROLLING=NO NORESIZE>

</FRAMESET>

<FRAMESET ROWS="20%,*"
   FRAMEBORDER=NO BORDER=0>

<FRAME SRC="logo.htm"
   NAME="logo" SCROLLING=NO
   NORESIZE>

<FRAME SRC="home.htm"
   NAME="main">

</FRAMESET>
</FRAMESET>
```

All kidding aside, no matter how much you like frames, you should really be nice and accommodating for all your readers, frame-fans or not. Beyond just being nice, you should accommodate those people for one very practical reason: If you don't, they won't be able to access the information you provide. Without accommodations, when those people link to your framed site, they see a completely blank window. And because you never know who might try to visit your site, you're better off being safe than sorry. Like, you wouldn't want "That Kim" to miss your page titled "My ex is a fleabag," would you?

Anyhoo, all of the text for nonframed browsers goes within `<NOFRAMES>`...`</NOFRAMES>` tags. Logical, huh? This tag specifies the text that will be seen by browsers that cannot display frames. Everything between these tags will be ignored by a frame-capable browser (which includes, realistically, a pretty high percentage of the browser world) and be seen by all older or less-sophisticated browsers.

Before you dive into using `<NOFRAMES>`...`</NOFRAMES>`, give some thought to how you want to accommodate your nonframed readers. You have several choices:

✔ **You can develop a complete HTML document within the nonframes section of your layout document.** That has the advantage of providing your readers with the content they need immediately — without missing out. Of course, that gives you an additional document to maintain and, unfortunately, it is a document you're likely to forget to maintain. You see, if you're using Navigator to browse your site, you don't ever see the `<NOFRAMES>`...`</NOFRAMES>` pages, and you'll quickly forget that you created them.

✔ **You can put in a small placeholder document that links to the rest of your site.** For example: "Hi! Welcome to my site. Click here for the table of contents." That minimizes your labor (and gets you out of the text editor and back into Composer more quickly). It's sensible to make that link point to the content that would otherwise appear in the main frame — it cuts your effort slightly.

✔ **You can just forget it and leave your nonframe-capable readers hanging.** Keep in mind that more and more browsers are capable of handling frames, and it's probably pretty likely that your readers will be able to see the frames. The question for you is really, "How important to you are the nonframed readers." If only 10 percent of your readers cannot view frames (a reasonable estimate), are you willing to live with not showing/selling/explaining something to them?

The following steps provide something for those people not using a frame-capable browser:

1. **Make sure that you have a layout document open in a text editor.**

   The layout document contains the `<FRAMESET>`...`</FRAMESET>` and `<FRAME>`...`</FRAME>` tags to establish the frames.

   Just as in the preceding section, you can use any text editor you choose.

2. **After the final closing** `</FRAMESET>` **tag, insert the** `<NOFRAMES>`... `</NOFRAMES>` **opening and closing tag.**

   ```
   </FRAMESET>
   <NOFRAMES>
   </NOFRAMES>
   ```

3. **Between the** `<NOFRAMES>`...`</NOFRAMES>` **tags, insert the HTML code you want the nonframed readers to see.**

   The Animal Clinic example included a very small placeholder document between the tags, as in the following code:

```
<NOFRAMES>
<H1 ALIGN=CENTER>Welcome to Malcolm's Animal Clinic</H1>
<P ALIGN=CENTER><A HREF="noframes.htm">Please visit our
site</A>
<P ALIGN=CENTER>
If you have any problems or questions, please
<A HREF="mailto:malcolm@raycomm.com">contact us</A>.
</NOFRAMES>
```

The code produces a page like Figure 16-6 in a nonframe-capable browser.

If you want to hand code the HTML, you're welcome to do so. However, you may also just create the page in Composer, and then go to View⇨Page Source (or Ctrl+U) and highlight the HTML code. To copy the code, press Ctrl+C. Return to this document and paste the code. That's probably the easiest solution.

There you go! You just created a framed site (although still without any real content) and accommodated the browsers that cannot display frames. The next step is to flesh out those frames, remembering to create the document to which you just pointed your nonframed readers.

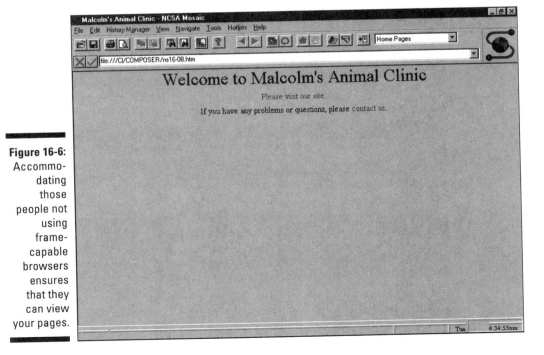

Figure 16-6: Accommodating those people not using frame-capable browsers ensures that they can view your pages.

Testing and troubleshooting frames

After you complete your frames, you should test and, perhaps, troubleshoot them. It's important that you test framed documents carefully, especially before you complicate things by adding a bunch of content about your ex being a fleabag. As you noticed while creating the frames, they're complex and offer lots of opportunities for boo-boos. So, catching your mistakes before adding content makes creating frames easier in the long run.

Here's the high-level process of troubleshooting your frames. (We assume that you have the basic making-a-page process down, but if you need a reminder, head for Chapter 6.)

1. **Use Composer to create dummy documents, all within the proper folder, with the correct names.**

   We prefer to use different colored backgrounds and minimal text within the documents so that we can see what's going on. Figure 16-7 shows the `main.htm` dummy document.

   Using content-free HTML documents — the kind you can create in your sleep — makes it easier to see what's going on with your frames and saves you the hassle of managing content at the same time that you're checking out your frames.

   Using the "correct" names just means that you should use the same names that your `<FRAME>` tags will be looking for. If you use `SRC= "toc.html"`, you need to create a dummy document and save it with the name `toc.html`.

   After you create dummy pages with the correct names and verify that they work individually, you're ready to try out that layout document.

2. **In Navigator, open the layout document (probably called** `frames.htm` **or something similar).**

   Hold your breath. If everything worked as planned, your document should appear with frames intact. Figure 16-8 shows how the Animal Clinic page incorporated background colors to help set frames apart.

Now then, what if it isn't as you expected? More to the point, what if nothing happens? If nothing at all happens, you probably made some little picky mistake that muddled everything up. Things to check include:

- **Correctly paired tags:** Do you have a closing `</FRAMESET>` tag for every opening one?

- **Frame tags:** Do you have a `<FRAME>` tag for every document that you plan to load? Are the tags between the appropriate `<FRAMESET>`... `</FRAMESET>` tags? Do they all have correct `SRC=` attributes?

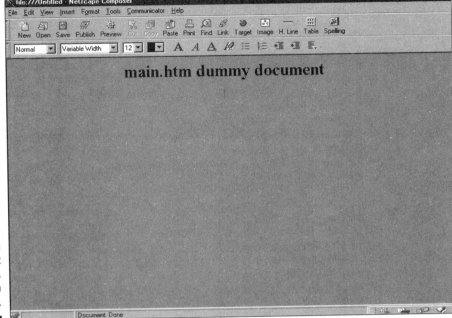

Figure 16-7:
Develop
individual
documents,
like the
`main.htm`
document
shown here,
within
Composer.

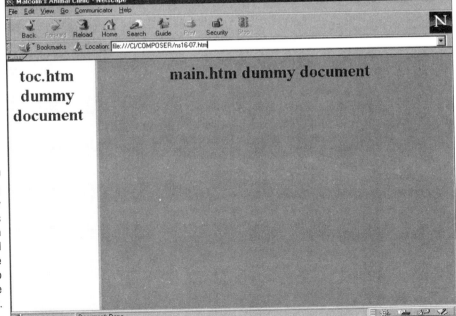

Figure 16-8:
Dummy
documents
with
background
colors make
it easier to
see how the
frames work.

- **Body tags:** Did you remember to *omit* the `<BODY>...</BODY>` tags from your document?
- **Source files:** Are all the files you reference located in the same folder as the layout document, and do they all work individually?

If you find something to change, go back to your text-editing program, make the change, save your changes, and reload the document in Navigator to see the results.

Reloading and retesting framed documents are sometimes a little challenging. To get the layout document to reload, click your mouse in the Go to line, and then press Enter. If you are sure you made a change and saved the layout document but the change doesn't seem to show up in Navigator, try exiting and restarting Navigator. If you just need to reload one of the framed documents, click in the appropriate frame, and then click the Reload button.

If none of these solutions make your frames work properly, simplify your layout document as much as possible. For example, save the document under a different name (so that you don't mess up your hard work), delete all `<FRAME>` tags except one and all `<FRAMESET>...</FRAMESET>` tags except one pair, and then see if that works. Finally, add elements back in one at a time.

When the different pages all show up correctly in your browser, you're ready to replace the dummy content with real content, which you can certainly handle on your own at this point. (Note that you can reuse this frameset document, just editing a copy as necessary, and save yourself the trouble of making a new frameset document.)

Adding content

Adding content to framed pages is just like adding content to nonframed pages. You open the document in Composer and start adding text, images, tables — whatever you want. However, you can be a bit more creative when using frames with how and where the content appears. Following are a few cool ideas you may want to use:

- If you create a frame that is not resizable and is fixed to a specific size in pixels, you can get really creative with a background image. A background of the same size as the frame will not be tiled, so you can use the image to apply a watermark effect or to insert a picture, rather than just a pattern.
- Be careful not to overfill a frame that is set to be nonscrollable. Any text that doesn't appear in the visible portion of the frame will not be accessible. It's often a good idea to combine images — not text — with nonscrolling frames because you can be more confident of the results.

✔ As you insert images and multimedia elements, be careful not to put in too many items. A framed page is inherently visually busy, and too many images will only exacerbate the problem. Additionally, it's easy to get carried away with images and stuff and end up with an incredibly large (= slow to download) collection of files.

Linking frames

Believe it or not, the process of making a layout document and filling each of those frames with something is the easy part. The more challenging part is providing useful content that takes advantage of frame capabilities and makes it easier — not harder — for readers to find the information they need. This section gives you some of the information necessary to effectively use frames.

If you have experimented with your new frames (or browsed through framed sites on the Web), you've probably noticed two ways you can link documents in frames:

✔ **Clicking on a hyperlink in one frame brings up a document in a different frame.** This is handy for using navigation and content frames, where readers click a link in the navigation frame and the content appears in the — well — content frame.

✔ **Clicking on a link in one frame brings up a document in the same frame.** This is handy for links to related material from documents within your "content" frame.

By default, the new page appears within the same frame. If you want the new page to appear in a different frame, you have to specify which frame the new document should appear in.

To create either of these two link options, you use the two attributes described in Table 16-3.

Table 16-3	Attributes Used to Control Linking within Framed Documents
Attribute	*Description*
NAME=	This attribute, to the <FRAME> tag, labels the frame so that links can be directed to it.
TARGET=	This attribute, in the <A> tag (for a link), <AREA> tag of an imagemap, or <FORM> tag, guides the resulting page into a different frame.

Possible targets include any frame that you name with a NAME= attribute and a few special names (yes, they really do all start with an underscore character):

✔ _blank to target a new window

✔ _self to target the same frame

✔ _parent to target the window or frame that contains the current frameset (erasing the visible frames in the area)

✔ _top to target the current window, erasing all frames in the window

Now then, here's the procedure for targeting a frame from a regular hyperlink.

1. In Composer, load the document that contains a link you want to target into a different frame.

You can add a new link or modify an existing link. In our example, we're editing the toc.htm document from Malcolm's site to target the link into the main windows.

Note that we are directly editing the file and that the frames are not visible. You cannot easily view a framed set of documents and then switch over to editing a single one of them, so we loaded the toc.htm document directly into Composer by choosing File⇨Open Page (Ctrl+O), browsing to the file, and selecting Open in Editor from the dialog box.

2. Select the text you want to use for the anchor, and then choose Insert⇨Link (Ctrl+Shift+L), or click the Insert Link icon.

If you want to add a target attribute to an existing link, select the existing anchor and right-click; then choose Link Properties from the resulting pop-up menu.

You see the Character Properties dialog box with the Link tab visible, as shown in Figure 16-9.

3. Add (or just verify) the Link to filename.

4. Click Extra HTML to summon the Extra HTML dialog box.

You use the Extra HTML dialog box to add the TARGET= attribute.

5. Type the TARGET= attribute.

The actual target name you type depends on what you named your frame. In Malcolm's site, the main window is called, logically, "main," so the target link looks like the following.

```
TARGET="main"
```

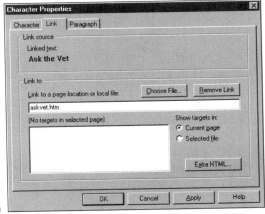

Figure 16-9:
Use the
Character
Properties
dialog box
Link tab to
edit links and
direct them
into specific
frames.

6. **Click OK to close the Extra HTML dialog box, and then click OK again to close the Character Properties dialog box.**

7. **Save your document.**

That's it!

To test the target, you need to open up your layout document (or reload everything if it's already open). Click the edited link, and you should see the new document appear in the target window. Wow! Now that's pretty cool.

Following are a few more notes about targeting frames:

✔ To target frames from `<FORM>` or `<AREA>` tags, just include the attribute in the tag as you would a regular link tag. For example, you may want the results of a form submission or the links from an imagemap to appear in a specific frame.

✔ If a link from your table of contents takes your readers to a page that's on a different Web site (or even just a page you don't want too closely tied to the rest of your site), you should use the `TARGET="_blank"` attribute to call up a whole new window.

✔ A good time to use `TARGET="_top"` is when you want to take your readers out of the frames, but without giving them the appearance of leaving your site. For example, Malcolm may choose to provide a parallel site for people who just don't like using frames (not a particularly bad idea, by the way) and can use `TARGET="_top"` to make a link fill the entire window.

✔ To experiment with frames, use the sample files found in the `CDFILES/framed` folder on the CD that comes with this book.

Part VI
The Part of Tens

The 5th Wave   By Rich Tennant

"He's our new Web Bowzer."

In this part . . .

This part provides you with a bunch of lists:

- ✔ Chapter 17 gives you 10 steps to a great Web site.
- ✔ Chapter 18 gives you 10 tips for a great Web site.
- ✔ Chapter 19 gives you 10 (well, 7) cool things about Netscape Communicator.
- ✔ Chapter 20 gives you 10 sites with the latest information about developing Web pages.

So why not just call this part, "40 Miscellaneous Tidbits of Information?" Well, we can't count that high with our shoes on, and, besides, you'll probably find the groupings we provide pretty helpful. Enjoy!

Chapter 17
Ten Steps for Great Web Sites

. . . .

In This Chapter

▶ Taking a few steps toward Web site greatness
▶ Getting the hang of the overall process

. . . .

To the tune of *White Christmas:*

> "I'm dreeeaming of a greaaaaat Web site
> Just like the one the Joneses have.
> May its background glisten; and have nothin' missin'
> so the do de dum de do da. . . ."

So, you want to make a great Web site? Believe it or not, just *creating* a
Web site involves a series of steps. But don't be scared off. These steps
are intended to make things easier, not make things more complicated. The
best part is that after you complete the steps, you'll have a real, live Web
site that you can hug and pet and squeeze and name George.

Step 1: Analyze Your Readers

And you thought creating Web pages was a private sort of affair! Well, it is.
However, if you're planning on publishing your pages, you will indeed have
an audience. *Readers* refers to the people who visit your Web site and read
the information in your Web pages.

As we discuss in Chapter 4, readers fall into one of three categories: decision makers, techie types, and casual surfers. Your job is to determine what
your readers need:

✔ **What information to provide (and not to provide) in your Web site:** For example, if your readers browse your site because they're looking for general information about your products, give them information about your products. If they browse your site to learn about the technology and tools you use, tell them about the tools. If they browse because they want to contact you, be sure to include all your contact information and an e-mail link. Or if your readers want to actually purchase something from you on the Web site, provide an order form.

✔ **What kinds of effects you should (and should not) use:** For example, if you know that your readers have newer browser software — ones that can handle fancier effects — you can include some of the cooler effects, such as tables, forms, applets, and JavaScript. However, if you suspect that your readers might have older browsers or text-only browsers, your best bet is to stick to Web page basics, such as paragraphs, headings, and lists.

✔ **What kind(s) of Web site organization and navigation to use:** For example, if you know that your readers will most likely just graze through your site, organize your site so that readers can easily flip back and forth to pages and possibly access navigation at the top and bottom of pages. On the other hand, if your readers will most likely use your site to follow a procedure or find out how to do something, organize your site so that readers can readily work through a sequential set of steps.

For more information about types of organization, check out "Organize Your Topics," coming up next, or you can refer to Chapter 9, which discusses organization types in more detail.

Step 2: Organize Your Topics

Now that you've figured out roughly what your audience wants to see in your Web site, the next step is to organize the information. Web site organization can be described as one (or a combination) of these strategies:

✔ **Hierarchical:** This organization is used to provide several major topics of equal importance or to present several topics and subtopics.

✔ **Linear:** This organization is used to provide procedural information.

✔ **Webbed:** This organization is used to provide information that can be easily accessed from several different Web pages within the site.

Step 3: Develop Web Site Contents

The next step is to develop your Web site contents — that is, start drafting the information in HTML documents. A good place to start is just by "dumping" information into HTML documents and then going back and figuring out the specifics of headings, paragraphs, lists, and so on.

As you're developing content, you should keep an eye on document length. Sure, you have all the room in the world in your HTML document, but keep in mind that the longer a document, the more your readers will have to scroll to find information. In some cases, such as instructions, reference information, specifications, or information that the reader might want to print, long pages are perfectly acceptable. However, information that your readers are likely to glance at and move on is best provided in shorter documents.

A good guideline for creating HTML documents of an appropriate length is to create a new document for each topic (or even subtopic).

Step 4: Determine Web Site Theme

The next step is to figure out your Web site *theme*, which is just a fancy term for making sure that your HTML documents flow together to create one unified Web site. You can create a unified theme several ways:

- ✔ Use a consistent background color or image.
- ✔ Use a consistent scheme for text, links, and logos.
- ✔ Use consistent navigation tools. For example, include the same navigation options from page to page or develop your own cool navigation buttons and use them on each page.
- ✔ Use a logo on each page. You may want to use a big logo on the home page and a smaller version of the logo on other pages.
- ✔ Use a graphic in the logo (make it a small graphic, though).
- ✔ Use a header or footer on each page that identifies you or your company.

Figure 17-1 shows a Web page with several theme-bearing elements.

Logo

Background color

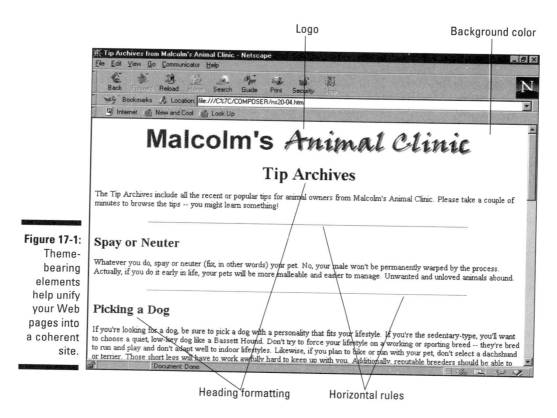

Figure 17-1:
Theme-
bearing
elements
help unify
your Web
pages into
a coherent
site.

Heading formatting   Horizontal rules

Step 5: Select Images

Now you get to the fun part of selecting images. Chapter 10 covers the fact that images should have a purpose in your Web pages; they can help establish theme, provide a logo, be informational, serve as a background, or provide icons and bullets.

When selecting images to use, keep in mind that large images seem to take forever to download and that each image should be worth the wait, from your reader's perspective.

Step 6: Develop Navigation Tools

What you need to think about now is establishing your navigation tools — that is, getting your readers from one page to another. Here's what you need to do, in this order:

1. **Decide whether you want to use text links or graphical links.**

   Text links are adequate for most needs; they're easy to find, easy to read, and informative (as long as you don't do that "click here" nonsense). Graphical links are flashier and add snazz to your pages, but they're often time-consuming to create, and they do add to the download time for the page.

2. **Determine where you want to put navigation — top, bottom, middle, or some combination.**

   Remember, you should include at least one of these locations consistently on each page; you can include additional navigation locations as needed on a page-by-page basis.

3. **Develop your navigation tools.**

   If you decide on textual navigation, go ahead and set those up. If you decide on graphical navigation, get busy creating those cool buttons.

4. **Place the navigation tools in each page.**

5. **Establish the links.**

6. **Test the links. And test again.**

 For more information about navigation, check out Chapter 9.

Step 7: Polish Web Pages

At this point in the process, you should have HTML documents that include (pretty much) all the content you want to include, organization that works well for the intended purpose, one or more theme-bearing elements, images (at least picked out), and navigation. Your job now is to polish your work and make it shine! Remember to do the following:

- ✔ Make sure that the information suits your audiences' needs.

- ✔ Make sure that the overall organization is easy to use and meets your audiences' needs.

- ✔ Make sure that all your links work.
- ✔ Make sure that your forms work. (Check with your server administrator for details on getting your form to work, or check when your form should work but it doesn't.)
- ✔ Make sure that graphics appear as you want them to (and make sure that they're worth the wait).
- ✔ Make sure that the theme-bearing elements appear on all pages.
- ✔ Make sure that you include informative headings.
- ✔ Make sure that you use bulleted and numbered lists where possible.
- ✔ Proofread your work — look for typos and spelling errors (and remember Composer's spell checker, discussed in Chapter 5).

Step 8: Put Your Web Site "Out There"

After you finish your site (or enough for the time being), you'll probably want to make it available to other people. Generally, you do that by copying the files — both the images and the HTML documents — to a Web server that you have access to. The exact procedure for putting your Web site out on a Web server differs somewhat depending on the server configuration, but generally it requires only that you give Communicator the same information your Webmaster gave you, push a button, swig down some coffee, and then call your friends and have them check out the site. See Chapter 5 for the specific step-by-step instructions for uploading your Web pages and suggestions for coffee (black, no sugar, — unless real cream is available, then coffee with the works.)

Step 9: Submit Your Web Site to Directories and Search Engines

After you put your Web site "out there," you should do everything you can to lure readers to it. You can help draw people to your site by making it available to them through Web directories and search engines.

A *directory* is a list of Web sites organized by category. Think of a directory as those hangie signs in your local grocery store that provide a general list of foods you find in each aisle. For example, the hangie sign might say, "canned fruits and canned veggies," and from that list, you can expect to find things such as canned green beans, corn, spinach, asparagus, pears, apples, and that yummy fruit cocktail stuff. Likewise, a Web directory provides you with general categories (such as computers, people, places, culture, humanities, business, education, entertainment, government, and health) that point you to Web sites that contain specific information about the topic.

A *search engine* is a computer program that sends out "spiders" or "crawlers" that do nothing all day but sniff out new Web addresses. When they sniff out a new address, they catalog it in a database, thereby making it available to people who use the search engine. Think of a search engine "spider" or "crawler" as being like a cat living on a farm. It goes out every morning seeking little critters, finds a critter, and then brings it back to your doorstep for you to do something with. It's a dirty job, but someone (or something) has to do it, right?

Submitting your Web site to either a directory or a search engine is easy. Just use these quick steps:

1. **Make sure that you're connected to the Internet.**

2. **Open Navigator.**

3. **Enter the URL of a directory or search engine.**

    Note: See Table 17-1 for URLs to some common directories and search engines.

4. **In the directory or search engine, look for a command such as "Add URL," "Add Site," or "Submit URL."**

5. **Enter your Web site URL (enter the exact URL — check with your server administrator to find out for sure).**

6. **Follow all other instructions provided by the directory or search engine.**

That's it! You can submit your URL to as many directories or search engines as you want, but generally submitting it to just a few is adequate.

Table 17-1	Directories and Search Engines		
Directory	**Address**	**Search Engine**	**Address**
Yahoo!	http://www.yahoo.com	AltaVista	http://www.altavista.digital.com
Lycos	http://www.lycos.com	Webcrawler	http://www.webcrawler.com

Step 10: Maintain Your Site

Now, this is the easy part. (Thank goodness, right?) At the very least, you should visit your site every two weeks to make sure that everything's in order. In particular, you should do the following:

1. **Check links (especially those that link to pages outside your site).**

2. **Make sure that all elements appear as they should (graphics, alignment, navigation tools, and so on).**

3. **Update information to ensure that you're providing the most timely information.**

4. **Update the "date last modified" text.**

5. **Re-upload pages that you've made changes to.**

Chapter 18

Ten Tips for Great Web Sites

A *great* Web site can mean different things to different people. For some, a good Web site provides just the information they're looking for, every time they surf the site. For others, a good Web site is coherent and easy to navigate. For others, a good Web site burps and grunts on command. For yet others, a good Web site might just be one that doesn't crash their computers.

The fact is that great Web sites are really a combination of all these things. This chapter provides ten ways you can help all your readers enjoy and benefit from your site. You'll find some of this information covered in more detail in other chapters; however, we wanted to compile this "Deb and Eric's" top ten list of what's most important so that you can see the key points at a glance.

Pay Attention to Who's Reading Your Stuff

If you want your readers to pay attention to what you're saying (that is the point, isn't it?), you need to pay attention to your readers' needs. The important concept here is that *you* have to identify what your readers want, and then give it to them.

Here are some other ideas to consider as you develop your Web site:

- ✔ **Provide information that's appropriate to readers' needs.** Determine what information your readers will want to know based on what they're going to do with it. If you want them to purchase your products, provide readers with information that will help them make informed decisions. If you want them to use your services, explain your services and the uses so that readers can see how they can benefit. Providing information your readers want is one of the best ways to keep them coming back for more.

- ✔ **Provide details, but don't flood readers with unnecessary information.** For example, don't provide a bunch of technical descriptions if your readers aren't familiar with or don't care about the techie stuff or if they're already knowledgeable on the topic. Flooding your readers with information they don't care about or don't need to read will not help you get your point across.

- ✔ **Provide images only where they help present information better than text alone.** Remember that images, even small ones, take time to download to readers' computers. Make all images worth the wait.

- ✔ **Provide your readers with the option to choose what they do and do not see.** For example, if your readers are likely to be surfing to your site from a slow dial-up Internet connection, don't include multiple movies and animations for them to have to wait for and view before they can get to the point.

If you want more information about determining who your readers are, see Chapter 4.

Chunk Information

A great way to help readers wade through your Web pages is to *chunk* information into smaller, manageable pieces. Chunking is an invaluable tool to help your readers scan your pages for the information they want.

You can chunk information several different ways:

- ✔ Chunk long sections of text into smaller paragraphs.
- ✔ Group related paragraphs under one informative heading.
- ✔ Create shorter Web pages that cover only one topic.
- ✔ Place graphics close to (or adjacent to) related text.

Use Informative Headings

Using informative headings is an effective way to help readers find information on your Web pages. Headings can provide a great deal of information in a small amount of space, if you create them correctly. When creating headings, you should consider the content of the information that follows and try to summarize it in a few words. That way, readers can glance at your Web pages and easily see what's in them. Where do you put these informative headings? Every time you change topics, you should include a new heading.

What's an informative heading? We like to think that the headings in this book are informative. If you read the heading, you have a pretty good idea of what's in the section. If the head for this section were "Good Headings" or "Using Headings" or even just "Headings," you wouldn't have the information the current title provides. We hope.

Chapter 6 tells you all about making headings — informative ones, of course.

Put the Most Important Information First

Always put the most important information at the top or beginning of pages and sections. Whether the readers are just cruising the Web, looking for specific information, or wanting to see what's in your site, they are not going to read every page word for word.

In fact, readers' reading patterns are likely to look something like this: read . . . read . . . read . . . read . . . skip . . . read . . . yawn . . . blah . . . blah . . . blah . . . blah . . . big blah . . . neat applet . . . blah . . . cool picture . . . blah . . . blah, basically just skimming the contents of your site, not reading word for word. By putting the most significant information first, you increase the chance that readers will actually read and comprehend your most important points.

The first corollary to this is to cut to the chase. Don't try to sound intelligent or like you have the world's largest vocabulary. Remember, your page remains on the reader's screen only until she gets bored or distracted. Then, click, you're gone.

Use Bulleted Lists for At-a-Glance Reading

Oh, you're making a list, and you're checking it twice, twice. Gonna find out how to make a list right. La deee daaaa deee da da deee dum.

Lists. Lists. Lists. Everyone makes lists. Even Santa Claus. Using bulleted lists in Web pages is essential for helping readers glean a lot of information in a short amount of time. Even short paragraphs that do a good job of chunking information can benefit from lists. Take a look at Figure 18-1, which shows the same information presented first in paragraph form and then in a bulleted list.

Here are some tips for creating effective lists:

✔ Put the most important information first (readers may not read all list items and may miss important points if they're near the bottom).

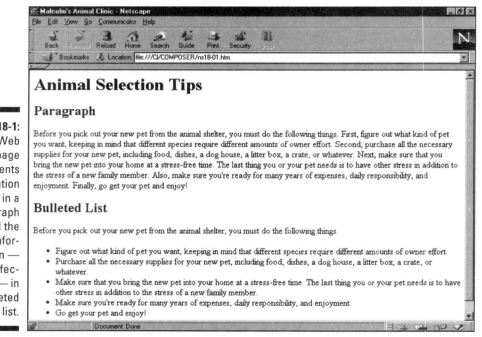

Figure 18-1:
This Web page presents information in a paragraph and the same information — more effectively — in a bulleted list.

✔ Start each bullet with the same part of speech (nouns, verbs, adjectives, gerunds, and so on).

✔ Include no more than about seven items in the list (longer lists can be just as difficult to read as paragraphs).

Chapter 6 tells you how to create lists.

KISS Your Web Pages

If you've ever done any Web surfing, you've probably noticed that some sites go completely overboard using too many colors, graphics, patterns, fonts, and alignments. The result is that, yes, you remember the site, but you remember the site because it screamed "I'm a cluttered mess!" not because you found the site particularly useful or readable.

Web sites can become cluttered in all sorts of ways — too many fonts, colors, graphics, wild backgrounds, alignments. Figure 18-2 shows a cluttered Web page, which is not only hard to look at but also not easy to use.

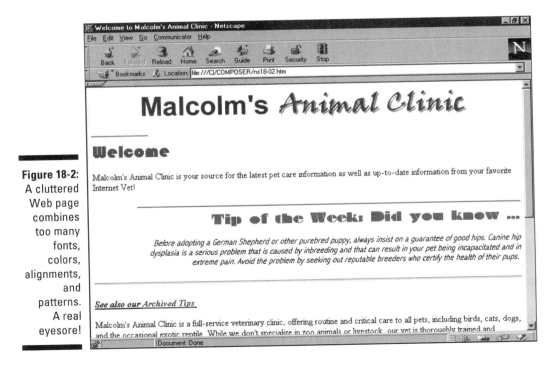

Figure 18-2: A cluttered Web page combines too many fonts, colors, alignments, and patterns. A real eyesore!

Why are messy sites bad? Think of it this way. Remember when you were a kid and your mom constantly bugged you about cleaning your room? She might have said, "How do you ever find anything in this mess?!" Or possibly, "What's that stench coming from your room?" Or better yet, "Why must you ruin the new paint job by hanging all those atrocious posters on the wall?" Your answer to this, of course, was probably that your room was a secret science project and cleaning it would wipe out years of hard work.

Then the problem was that after your mom convinced you to clean your room, the task was completely overwhelming. "It could take days . . . even weeks," you may have thought. And it did take forever to clean the mess, the clutter, the debris, the dishes, the whole nine yards. But when you finished, your room was clutter free, you could find clean socks and undies at a moment's notice, the bedspread coordinated nicely with the drapes (now that you could see the bedspread), and you were happy to invite even crabby ol' Mom to see your room.

Now that you're experienced in clutter removal, you've probably decided that it's much easier to start with a clean room and keep it clean than it is to hire a bulldozer to take care of the mess every so often. Well, folks, the same goes for Web pages.

As you're developing your Web pages, remember one principle: *Keep It Simple, Silly* (or, *KISS*)! In keeping your Web pages simple, you can provide your readers with uncluttered information that is easy to find, easy to navigate, and — better yet — easy to remember as a usable source of information. If for no other reason, you should create your page so that it's simple just because it's easier to maintain that way. But you already learned that from Mom.

Avoid Using Silly Directives

While surfing the Web, you're sure to come across directives such as "click here," "see above," or "see below." You have to admit that these are not a bit helpful. For example, "click here" is completely useless because the link is already announced with an underline and possibly a different text color. Unless that particular link is the very first link your readers have seen in their entire lives, saying "click here" is just repetitive, redundant, and saying the same thing over and over.

As for the "see above" and "see below" directives, you have to keep in mind that by nature, Web pages are not intended to be read linearly. The "see above" or "see below" directives won't mean a thing to someone who's just passing through your pages — "see above" referring to a different page will have no relevance if someone lands directly on the page with the "see above" reference.

Make the Most of the Space You Have

You've probably noticed by this point that Web pages are not the most spacious places to put information. A graphic, a couple of headings, a little descriptive text, and — boom! — that page is already pretty long. However, even within the confines of Web pages, you can create nifty layouts and designs using the text and graphics that you have. Often, being a little creative can also save valuable space.

Here are some examples of creative layouts that use space wisely:

- ✔ Instead of having your text and paragraphs span the width of the page, try using a two-column format.

- ✔ Instead of placing graphics after a related paragraph, use a two-column format or text wrap to put text and graphics next to each other.

- ✔ Instead of trying to describe difficult concepts using paragraph after paragraph, try showing that concept in an illustration or table.

- ✔ Use frames to separate navigation objects from the part of the text that will be read or viewed.

- ✔ Segregate tangential information into a second page and link to it, just as we pull tangential information into a sidebar that you can read or skip (but you wouldn't dare, would you?) if you choose.

Provide Timely Information

A great way to ensure that your readers return to your site is to provide timely information. *Timeliness* refers to providing information that is current, updated, or new for your readers. After all, readers won't keep returning to your site if the information never changes.

Sites are composed of two types of information:

- ✔ *Static information* includes general information that tends not to change — things like a company name, logo, contact information, copyright information, and mission statement. Unless you work for Dilbert's company, in which a case mission statement is dynamic information.

- ✔ *Dynamic information* includes information that changes frequently or can be updated to provide readers with the latest and greatest — things like pricing, schedules, calendars, links to outside Web resources, and date of last revision.

Frequently updating dynamic information can help you keep your readers coming back for more. For example, keeping prices, schedules, and outside links up to date encourages readers to use your site as a long-term resource. Keeping an events calendar current helps readers plan their schedules. And keeping that date of last revision updated lets readers know how recent the information is and helps them obtain the information they're looking for.

Check out Chapter 4 for more about timeliness as well as static and dynamic information.

Polish Your Work

Polishing your work should be the last task you complete before publishing your Web pages and sites. No matter how careful you are when developing your pages, you're bound to have mistakes in spelling, punctuation, and grammar, not to mention those pesky typos.

Will a few little itsy-bitsy mistakes ruin your Web site? Ummm. Yes. Think of it this way. A Web site provides information to your readers just like an advertisement, brochure, article, manual, or résumé does. You wouldn't dare let, say, a brochure be sent out to potential customers with even the tiniest mistake because the customer might see that mistake as representative of the quality of the work you do. Same with a résumé. Same with the other documents. Don't think for a minute that just because you're using the latest-and-greatest way-cool technology, mistakes won't be noticed . . . and remembered.

Also, be careful about leaving a draft site out on the Web, even if you don't expect to have links made to it. Someone is likely to find it, or, worse, an Internet search engine will find it and index it for all to see. If it's a draft, don't publish it on the Web. If you must publish it on the Web so that someone can take a look at it, remove it as quickly as possible.

Chapter 19

Ten (That Is, Seven) Cool Things about Netscape Communicator

In This Chapter

▶ Seeing some of the best aspects of Communicator

▶ Seeing some of Composer's coolest features

You're probably wondering why we waited until Chapter 19 to tell you about Netscape Communicator's best features. Actually, many of them are mentioned throughout this book, but numerous cool Composer features extend to Communicator as well. This chapter sums up the coolest, latest, and greatest features so that you can have them at your fingertips — coolness at a glance, you might say.

After you read — or even just skim — this chapter, you'll realize that only seven cool features are mentioned, which doesn't mean that Communicator ran out of features to talk about. This chapter includes the features that are most relevant to you, Mr. or Ms. Web author. If you want more information about Communicator, you might check out *Netscape Communicator For Dummies*, by Paul Hoffman, published by IDG Books Worldwide.

With that, take a browse through this chapter and stand (or sit) in awe at all of Communicator's greatness.

An All-in-One Package

Communicator is a big Internet toolbox that includes the full spectrum of Internet capabilities — e-mail, Web page authoring, Web browsing, and discussion groups. The advantage to having all these capabilities in one software program is that you don't have to spend forever starting the different programs. Instead, you can switch between Communicator's components and take care of all your Internet needs.

Say good-bye to bouncing back and forth among six different programs all day long, and say hello to Mr. Component Bar, who ties Communicator features together.

Style Sheets

Style Sheets, although they're kinda beyond the scope of this book (okay, so we ran out of pages), are awesomely cool. Frankly, they're still new enough that they could flop like a bad dive, but they do have a lot of potential.

What are they? *Style Sheets* let you establish formatting rules for your documents and store those rules separately from the rest of the document. Then instead of hauling each individual document up in Composer and making sure that all of the first-level headings are aqua, you just tell the document to "Use this Style Sheet!," and Navigator makes sure that all headings are formatted according to the rules you specified, including having the first-level headings shown in aqua.

Formatting headings is only the beginning of Style Sheet capabilities. For example, you can specify margins and alignment. Or you can specify things like the background color for individual sections of text.

The drawbacks? Not many browsers support Style Sheets yet, and the browsers that do support Style Sheets don't support them thoroughly or well.

Kiosk Mode

Kiosk mode is a clever little trick — it lets you make everything but the document window disappear, leaving nothing but an HTML document in a box. Instead of seeing standard things like the title, button, and status bars, your readers see nothing but the Web page.

The advantage to kiosk mode is that, for some purposes, Web pages look better without all the clutter. For example, Web page displays that you see at conferences or museums often use kiosk mode to make the page as big as possible — and inviting — to passersby. Also, you can use kiosk mode for presentations. Rather than preparing your presentation with software like Microsoft PowerPoint, you could just develop a spiffy Web presentation and turn on kiosk mode.

Check out the documentation at the Netscape site (`http://home.netscape.com/`) for the specifics of activating kiosk mode, if that's something that you'd find useful.

Drag-n-Drop or Copy-n-Paste Image Import

This is a goodie, folks! No more days of adding a bunch of long-winded code to include a simple image. And, heck, Composer goes a step further than a one-click image addition (though it does that, too). You can now copy and paste things like images right into your Web page, or you can just drag and drop from another program right into your Web page. These features are a must for anyone who needs to quickly and easily develop HTML documents or to quickly assimilate a variety of files into a single Web page.

One-Button Publishing

Many of you may be intimately familiar with the perils of publishing Web pages. In the olden days — that is, six months or more ago — you had to manually upload your files to the server, meaning that you copied the Web site files from your computer to the server computer. And you had to get the FTP connection working, select which files to upload, make sure you were uploading them to the right place on the server, and — gritting teeth — hope like heck it all would work.

Communicator — well, Composer, actually — lets you publish your Web pages by just clicking a button. Yes, you still have to fill in and verify some Internet Service Provider information, but you don't have to mess with a separate program and select from a cryptic list which files you want to publish. What's more, Composer automatically uploads all the files associated with a Web page, meaning that it digs out all the stuff that you included on the Web page and publishes that, too.

Chapter 5 reveals the specifics of this one-button publishing, in case you're interested.

A Wizard and Some Templates

One short link away from the Communicator package are the Web page Wizard and some very handy templates, all of which can help make developing Web pages a snap. (Specific instructions lurk in Chapter 5.)

The Wizard walks you through developing Web pages — one step at a time. It tells you what options you have and then lets you select what you want to include in the page and how you want to do it. You sacrifice some control and a lot of flexibility, but you get a cool Web page in five minutes or less. It's easy!

Netscape also provides a variety of templates to choose from that give you a good starting place for your Web page development efforts — complete with neato designs and ideas for extras to include. All you have to do is replace the existing text with your own information. That's it!

JavaScript

Naw, do tell! It's cool, we tell ya. Okay, so it's kinda finicky and a little complex for mere mortals and daily use. However, it really adds a lot of power to your Web pages, including dozens of ways of implementing bells and whistles in addition to some more practical applications. For example, you can validate forms, control some aspects of layout, and even set up searchable pages.

Chapter 15 gives you the scoop about JavaScript, describes some uses, and shows you how to include it in your Web page.

Chapter 20

Ten Cool Web Sites to Find More — Lots More — Information

In This Chapter

▶ Finding some awesome resources on the Web

▶ Visiting our Web site for updated or modified information about Composer

*E*arlier chapters in this book provide good "starting-point" information about Web publishing, HTML, Java, JavaScript, and so on, but those chapters don't provide all the information available on the topics, particularly on the high-end technologies. (If we provided all the information on these topics, you'd have to hire a forklift to lug around this book.) To round out the information in this book, this chapter points you to some Web sites that can give you more information about those topics. So if you decide you need to know it all, check out the sites in this chapter.

Also, because the content of these sites is updated regularly — often daily — they can offer you the latest and greatest information and answer most questions you might come up with.

Table 20-1 gives you a quickie list of the Web sites this chapter visits:

Table 20-1	Web Addresses for More Information
Web Address	**Name**
http://home.netscape.com	Netscape Corporation Home Page
http://www.netscapeworld.com	NetscapeWorld Home Page
http://www.w3.org	World Wide Web Consortium
http://www.htmlhelp.com	Web Design Group
http://www.stars.com	The Web Developer's Virtual Library

(continued)

Table 20-1 *(continued)*	
Web Address	*Name*
http://www.webreference.com	webreference
http://www.gamelan.com	Gamelan
http://www.microsoft.com/ie	Microsoft Internet Explorer
http://www.raycomm.com	RayComm

To visit any of these sites, fire up Navigator and type the address in the Location line. You'll find more information about using Navigator in Chapter 2.

Netscape

Visit http://home.netscape.com to find the latest and greatest information straight from Netscape Corporation. On this home page, you can find everything from the latest product updates to free Internet access (temporary, not permanent), links to Netscape-related articles and columns, hot news headlines, and upgrade information.

NetscapeWorld

Visit the NetscapeWorld Home Page by linking to http://www.netscapeworld.com. *NetscapeWorld*, an IDG Books Worldwide sister publication, has the hottest online articles on topics including HTML, Web publishing, CGI, Dynamic HTML, as well as other related topics. Find out about the latest Web technologies and solutions to common Web development questions. This is a great site to visit as you advance your Web publishing skills!

World Wide Web Consortium

Go to http://www.w3.org and find the latest information on HTML in its purest form. Find the latest specification updates and announcements as well as sample code to fiddle with. Also, you can find out a bit of Web history and see how the W3 Consortium shapes the Web-publishing world. Visit this site for the definitive answer to just about any question about the HTML specification.

Web Design Group

Visit the Web Design Group site, `http://www.htmlhelp.com`, for information on a wide variety of HTML and Web topics. This site boasts of providing information that's nonbrowser-specific, nonresolution-specific, creative, and informative. At this site, you can follow links to frequently asked questions (with answers provided, of course), a Web authoring reference, as well as information and articles about Web design and related topics.

The Web Developer's Virtual Library

Visiting this Web site, `http://www.stars.com`, opens the doors on an HTML-Web development library with some of the most useful information available — without the hassle of lugging around tons of books! Find scads of links to articles and information about the Internet, software, multimedia, Web authoring, and HTML, among others. Also, use its handy-dandy glossary of Web-related terms!

webreference

Yes, we capitalized this one correctly — the webreference site, `http://www.webreference.com`, is a great source for Web-related book reviews, expert "workshops" on the latest Web technologies, conference locations and topics, and general information about Web software and technology.

Gamelan

Visit the Gamelan site, `http://www.gamelan.com`, for information on advanced Web page topics such as Java, ActiveX, JavaScript, and VRML (Virtual Reality Markup Language). This site includes scads of useful tips, tricks, and articles to help you advance to the latest and coolest Web skills. Also, link to the Developer Direct Internet Technology Store, which is an online store from which you can purchase all sorts of tools, software, and (heh-hem) books.

Microsoft Internet Explorer

Go to http://www.microsoft.com/ie to check out what Netscape's competition is up to. This Web site includes information about Internet Explorer — Microsoft's equivalent to Communicator — which will be useful if you're trying to accommodate those readers who use that product. (Again, there's the "those readers" reference — like your mom talking about your ex.) So, if you're interested in what Microsoft is up to these days, you can find out all sorts of tidbits. We won't brag about them too much — they *are* the competition, you know.

RayComm

We welcome you to visit our Web site (http://www.raycomm.com) for information and updates about this book. Just follow the Our Projects link to find out about changes or additions to Composer that you might find useful. Of course, we welcome you to browse the rest of our site, too. We're kind of partial to the photos of Ashleigh (go to What's New and follow the Ashleigh Sarah link), but you may be more interested in finding out about us, our projects, or our services. Roam around!

Part VII
Appendixes

The 5th Wave   By Rich Tennant

"Hold your horses. It takes time to build a
home page for someone your size."

In this part . . .

The looooong and winding book (dah dah, dah dah) thaaat leeeeeds, to this part. . . .

Hope we write better than we sing. It sounded good when we thought of it. Anyhoo, Appendix A gives you a glossary with quickie definitions of all of the new, different, or interesting terms we use in this book, and Appendix B describes the handy dandy software and files that are on the CD. So, if you read the whole book (and didn't look up any words) or if you accessed files from the CD, you may not need the information this part provides.

Otherwise, dive right in and enjoy. Short, sweet, and to the point.

Appendix A
Glossary

. . . .

AIFF (file format): Audio Interchange File Format (AIFF) is a very popular sound file format on the Internet. It is supported by most newer browsers. *See Chapter 12.*

Alignment: Alignment describes where paragraphs, headings, tables, graphics, applets, and so on, appear on a page. By default, browsers display these elements using left alignment (arrayed against the left margin); however, you can also specify that these elements appear in the center or along the right side of the page. *See Chapter 6.*

Alternative navigation: Alternative navigation is a separate means of navigation, such as a set of text links or buttons, that your readers can use instead of an imagemap (see Imagemaps). It's essential to include alternative navigation to accommodate the readers who choose not to view images or who use text-only browsers. *See Chapter 11.*

Angle brackets: These are the pointy dealies (< >) that surround HTML tags. *See Chapter 3.*

Attributes: Attributes are a part of HTML tags that provide additional information to the browser. *See Chapter 3.*

AU (file format): AU (or basic AUdio) is the standard file format on Sun computers and is widely recognized on the Web. The quality of an AU file is not as high as the quality of an AIFF file. *See Chapter 12.*

AVI (file format): Audio Video Interleaved (AVI) files combine video and audio in a highly compressed, popular multimedia format. *See Chapter 12.*

Bookmark: A bookmark in Navigator is similar to a bookmark you use to mark a place in a book, except in Navigator you use bookmarks to mark Web pages you want to return to. *See Chapter 2.*

Borders: Table borders act as a visual container for the information within them. Each piece of information is nestled within its own little pod. Also, they serve as a divider between rows and columns so that the information is (usually) more readable. *See Chapter 7.*

Borrowing (code): Borrowing code is a great way to learn how to create effects. You can look at the code, see how it's done, and apply it to your own document. *See Chapter 3.*

Browser: A browser, such as Netscape Navigator, lets you view Web pages after you've created them. Navigator allows you to open Web pages saved on your computer, open Web pages located "out there" on the Internet, and easily view pages you've been working on in Composer. *See Chapter 1.*

Casual types: Casual types refers to the casual Web surfer — you know, people who just skip from site to site following links that interest them. These types often lead a double life, also being decision makers or techies. *See Chapter 4.*

Cell padding: Cell padding refers to the amount of space between text in a cell and the surrounding cell border. Think of cell padding as spreading individual place settings so that each person gets a little more room. *See Chapter 7.*

Cell spacing: Cell spacing refers to the amount of space between individual cells. Think of cell spacing as adding an empty seat between people when they're sitting at the dinner table. *See Chapter 7.*

Cells: Cells are the little open spaces made from intersecting table rows and columns. You can include text, numbers, images, applets — just about anything — in table cells. *See Chapter 7.*

CGI: CGI stands for Common Gateway Interface, and it specifies how programs on the Web server can interact with information submitted through Web pages. *See Chapter 14.*

Clickable areas: Clickable areas are parts of an imagemap that readers click on to link to other information. *See Chapter 11.*

Clickable images: *See* **Imagemaps.** *See Chapter 11.*

Common Gateway Interface: *See* **CGI.** *See Chapter 14.*

Communicator: Communicator is a big Internet toolbox that includes several different tools that, taken together, provide you with a full spectrum of Internet capabilities. *See Chapter 1.*

Compiled: Compiled refers to programs — or in this context, Java applications — in which the individual instructions to the computer are mooshed into one entity. After the Java program is compiled, you can't examine it, tweak it, or fiddle with it. Instead, you have to use it as an individual entity. *See Chapter 13.*

Component Bar: Communicator's Component Bar is a floating button bar that lets you switch between and among Communicator's tools. To switch back and forth between Composer and Navigator, just click the appropriate button. *See Chapter 1.*

Composer: Composer is the Communicator team member in charge of letting you create, edit, save, and preview your Web pages. *See Chapter 1.*

Compression: Compression refers to files being saved in a compact format, which is useful for making the file size smaller. JPG and GIF files are compressed. *See Chapter 10.*

Cookies: Cookies are used by fairly sophisticated Web sites to track information about you. When you visit the site, cookies put information about your preferences at that site on *your* computer and then check out that cookie each time you return to the site. Cookies are also good with milk and are a great source for crumbs in bed (often left by the crumb with whom you share your bed). *See Chapter 5.*

Decision-making types: A decision-making type is a Web page reader who reads because he or she or it needs to make a decision. They want bottom-line information, such as how much something costs, when it can be delivered, or possibly, how it can make them look good. *See Chapter 4.*

Docking: Docking refers to the Communicator Taskbar, which hangs onto the bottom of your screen so that it doesn't get in your way. *See also* **Undocking.** *See Chapter 1.*

Document information: Document information is data about the document, such as its size and date last modified. *See Chapter 15.*

Download: Download means to copy a file from a server onto your local computer. *See Chapter 10.*

Editor: An editor is a tool that lets you create and edit Web pages and sites. Composer is the Communicator editor. Editors are also the people responsible for taking our written drivel and turning it into a great book — thanks, folks! *See Chapter 1.*

Embossed: Embossed refers to how Web table borders appear — that is, lines that appear to be raised slightly from the rest of the page. *See Chapter 7.*

Form: A form is a Web page that contains a collection of places for you (or your reader) to provide and send in information. It's also what you have when you skid gracefully on a banana peel. *See Chapter 14.*

Frames: Frames divide your browser window into multiple parts, each of which can accommodate a separate HTML document. *See Chapter 16.*

Frameset: Also called a layout document, a frameset document sets up the frame structure. *See Chapter 16.*

GIF (file format): An image file format commonly used on the Web. This format is supported by all graphical browsers and supports interlacing and transparent backgrounds. *See Chapter 10.*

Graphical navigation: Graphical navigation is a type of navigation that uses a series of buttons or images, rather than text, as the links. *See Chapter 9.*

Hierarchical organization: Hierarchical organization is a type of Web site organization that ranks sets of topics in order of precedence or according to an existing structure. Hierarchical organization is great for organizing information that easily fits into an outline or into an organizational chart. *See Chapter 9.*

Home page: The home page is usually the starting point for a Web site, usually containing introductory information as well as links to other pages. *See Chapter 9.*

Horizontal line: A horizontal line is a line that you insert into Web pages to serve as a visual break or as an information break. *See Chapter 7.*

Host computer: *See* **Server.** *See Chapter 5.*

HTML: HTML (aka HyperText Markup Language) is what tells browsers what to do with the text, graphics, and other bells and whistles you include in your Web pages. *See Chapter 3.*

HTML document: An HTML document is a Web page — actually all of the codes that make up the Web page. *See Chapter 3.*

HyperText Markup Language: *See* **HTML.** *See Chapter 3.*

Image: An image is any kind of graphic you can imagine — photos, buttons, icons, bullets, lines, drawings, illustrations, cartoons, and so on. In Web pages, images can include a company logo, help establish theme, provide a cool background, serve as navigation, or link to bigger versions of the same picture. *See Chapter 10.*

Imagemap: An imagemap is a single image that includes multiple links to other images, pages, and sites. These are commonly used to show large geographic areas that link to more specific areas, general mechanical gadgets that links to specific gadget parts, and logos and navigation that link to more information. *See Chapter 11.*

Indent: Indent means to move text away from the left margin. Indenting text is handy for setting off or drawing attention to text. *See Chapter 6.*

Interlaced: Interlaced refers to images that appear on-screen in waves rather than in one big chunk. Interlaced images fade onto the screen — that is, the little pixels appear on-screen in waves, with the image appearing progressively clearer as the moments (or minutes, depending on image size) go on. *See Chapter 10.*

Java: Java is a programming language used, among other purposes, to apply fancy effects to Web pages. Java also provides a secure environment with which programs over the Internet can be run. *See Chapter 13.*

Java applet: Java applets are little Java applications that you can easily add to your Web pages. *See Chapter 13.*

JavaScript: JavaScript is a vaguely HTML-ish scripting language developed by Netscape and built into Communicator. You can use it in your Web pages to do cool things like verify form contents and make text appear in the Status bar and make images flash. *See Chapter 15.*

JPG (file format): A highly compressed file format commonly used for images on the Web. This format is great for photographs or other complex images because the compressed file is quite small and, therefore, quick to download. *See Chapter 10.*

Layout document: *See* **Frameset.** *See Chapter 16.*

Line break: A line break is handy for making one line stop and a new line start. It's sort of like starting a new paragraph, only you don't end up with a bunch of blank spaces between the lines. *See Chapter 7.*

Linear organization: Linear organization is a type of Web site organization that presents information sequentially and is especially good for providing instructions or procedures. *See Chapter 9.*

Link: A link is the connection between two Web pages — or, more precisely, a connection from an HTML document to another document or a graphic or anything else on the Internet. Text links appear as blue (usually), underlined text; graphical links usually appear with a border around them. *See Chapter 8.*

Local Web page: A local Web page is a page that's saved on your computer — as opposed to a page from out there on the Internet. *See Chapter 2.*

Location line: The Location line, which is located at the top of your Navigator window, is the easiest place to enter a Web address for a file you want to open. *See Chapter 2.*

Logical (page parts): Logical page parts are the elements that make up a page — for example, paragraphs, headings, lists, footers, and so on. *See Chapter 3.*

MPEG (file format): Moving Pictures Experts Group (MPEG) files are an extremely popular video format on the Internet and are rapidly becoming universally accepted for compressed video of all sorts. *See Chapter 12.*

Navigation: Navigation refers to the links or sets of links (often called *navigation menus*) you include throughout your Web site to let people wander through your site in an orderly manner. *See Chapter 9.*

Navigation menus: A set of links that appear consistently throughout a Web site. These sets of links let readers navigate through the Web site pages and to other information on the Web. *See Chapter 9.*

Navigator: Navigator is the Communicator team member in charge of letting you view (or browse, or navigate, we suppose) your Web pages. *See Chapter 1.*

Nesting: Putting one set of tags inside another set of tags. *See Chapter 3.*

Nonbreaking spaces: These are spaces that keep a word from wrapping onto the next line. *See Chapter 7.*

onMouseOut: `onMouseOut` is a funny abbreviation for when the mouse pointer moves away from something. It has nothing to do with exterminating rodents. *See Chapter 15.*

onMouseOver: `onMouseOver` is a funny abbreviation for when the mouse pointer moves over something. It has nothing to do with skateboarding over a rodent — accidentally, of course. *See Chapter 15.*

Pixel: Pixels are those itty-bitty dots you can see on your computer screen if you moosh your face up close to it. Pixels are used to measure the physical size of Web page elements, such as images. *See Chapter 10.*

Publishing (to a server): Publishing to a Web server means to copy all the HTML documents and associated files to a computer that will then send them out on request to anyone who wants them. *See Chapter 5.*

QT (file format): QuickTime is a format for audio and video, originally popularized on Apple Macintosh computers but now commonly recognized on other systems. *See Chapter 12.*

Readers: Readers refers to the people who access, read, and use your Web sites. *See Chapter 4.*

Reference: A reference is more or less a note to the browser telling it to show an image file (or applet, or JavaScript, or whatever) along with the other page elements. The result is that the referenced element appears to be part of the page, even though it's located in a separate file. *See Chapter 10.*

Reloading: Reloading a file means to update a file that's already open in Navigator to reflect changes you've made in Composer. *See Chapter 2.*

Resizing: Resizing means to make an image physically larger or smaller. You want to resize images to decrease their file size and, therefore, make the image download faster. *See Chapter 10.*

Scanning: Scanning means to take a hard copy version of the image and make it into a computer file. *See Chapter 10.*

Scripting language: A scripting language is a watered-down programming language (eek!) that lets you write instructions — a script — to tell the Web browser or HTML document how to behave. *See Chapter 15.*

Search engine: A search engine is a computer program that sends out "spiders" or "crawlers" that do nothing all day but sniff out new Web addresses. After search engines sniff out a new address, they catalog it in a database, thereby making it available to people who use the search engines. *See Chapter 17.*

Server: The server (or *host computer* or *Web server*), which is actually a program running on a computer on the Internet or on an intranet, sits around all day waiting for people to request Web pages that have been stored on it. When requests come in, the server serves the Web pages. *See Chapters 5 and 14.*

Sound: An audible something-or-other that you can add to Web pages. Like video, these files also require an enormous amount of file space and take forever to download. *See Chapter 12.*

Table: A table is just a grid of rows and columns that intersect to form cells, which are the places where you include information. Tables are also handy for holding meetings, serving dinner, or putting pretty placemats. *See Chapter 7.*

Tags: Tags are the codes you can enter into your HTML documents that determine what each page element is, determine to some extent what the page elements look like, and provide references to additional information. *See also* **HTML.** *See Chapter 3.*

Techie types: Techie types are Web page readers who look for how-to information or new information that they can learn from. *See Chapter 4.*

Template: A template is a master HTML document of sorts that you can use as a starting point to create Web pages. Generally, these templates contain most of the formatting and layout you want, and all you have to do is fill in the blanks with information. *See Chapter 5.*

Textual navigation: Textual navigation is a type of navigation that uses words, rather than images, as the links. *See Chapter 9.*

Thumbnail: A thumbnail is a small image that links to a larger version of the same image. These are handy because they take practically no time to download, let readers choose whether to view the larger version, and take up very little space on the page. *See Chapter 11.*

Tiled: Tiled refers to how background images appear on the page. The first image appears in the upper-left corner, and then multiple copies are tiled (placed side by side) to fill the entire browser window. You can also get a long skinny image to tile vertically — that is, stack one on top of another — to fill a browser window. *See Chapter 10.*

Transparent (image backgrounds): Transparent images are ones in which the image's background matches the browser's background color. The result is that the images become more interesting because they're not limited to looking square or rectangular. *See Chapter 10.*

Undocking: Undocking refers to releasing the Communicator Taskbar from the bottom of the screen and letting it float as an individual window. *See also* **Docking.** *See Chapter 1.*

Uniform Resource Locator: *See* **URL.** *See Chapter 8.*

Upload: Upload means transfer documents from your computer to a server. This is the process of putting your Web pages "out there" on the Web. *See Chapter 19.*

URL: Also called a Uniform Resource Locator, a URL is essentially an address on the Web. URLs (pronounced You-R-Ell) are kind of like street addresses. Just as every house has its own address, every Web page also has its own address. *See Chapter 8.*

WAV (file format): WAVe files are the most common sound file format on Windows computers and are occasionally recognized on other systems. *See Chapter 12.*

Web page: A Web page is a document that appears to the reader as a single entity. It can include things like text, graphics, links, Java Applets, JavaScript, and style sheets. *See Chapters 1 and 2.*

Web server: _See_ **Server.** _See Chapters 5 and 14._

Web site theme: Web site theme refers to the colors, formatting, background, and images that work together to make your Web pages one cohesive unit. _See Chapter 4._

Webbed organization: Webbed organization is a type of Web site organization that provides multiple links between pages. This type is somewhat unstructured; however, because it gives readers lots of link options, readers can freely roam to the topics of their choice. _See Chapter 9._

Widget: Widget is the technically savvy sounding term for form elements, such as checkboxes, radio buttons, input areas, and buttons. _See Chapter 14._

Wizard: In the context of this book, a Wizard is a clever set of Netscape Web pages that asks you questions, lets you fill in information, lets you choose formatting and colors, and — like magic — creates the Web page for you. The Wizard is great for newbie Web page authors; you just fill in the information, and the Wizard spits out the Web page. And, for experienced Web page authors, the Wizard provides a great starting page that you can add to and modify as you want. _See Chapter 5._

Wrap: Wrap refers to how text is aligned with images. For example, an image can appear on a line with text that wraps (continues on) the next line. _See Chapter 10._

WYSIWYG editor: Also called a What-You-See-Is-What-You-Get editor, a WYSIWYG editor lets you see a page's layout and design as you're creating it. _See Chapter 1._

Appendix B

About the CD

ere's some of what you can find on the *Netscape Composer For Dummies* CD-ROM:

- AT&T WorldNet Service, a popular Internet service
- AppletAce, a free Java applet development tool
- BBEdit Lite, a freeware text editor for Mac OS computers that is useful for HTML editing
- Earshot sound effects sampler for Mac OS and Windows
- GraphicConverter, a way-cool shareware program for Mac OS
- HomeSite, a somewhat more sophisticated, high-end HTML editor for Windows
- HTMLPad, an easy-to-use shareware HTML editor for Windows
- Iconographics, a graphics library sampler for Mac OS and Windows
- Paint Shop Pro, a great shareware graphics program for Windows

System Requirements

Make sure your computer meets the minimum system requirements listed below. If your computer doesn't match up to most of these requirements, you may have problems using the contents of the CD.

- A PC with a 486 or faster processor, or a Mac OS computer with a 68030 or faster processor.
- Microsoft Windows 3.1 or later, or Mac OS system software 7.5 or later. Some programs require Windows 95.
- At least 8MB of total RAM installed on your computer. For best performance, we recommend that Windows 95-equipped PCs and Mac OS computers with PowerPC processors have at least 16MB of RAM installed.

- At least 40MB of hard drive space available to install all the software from this CD. (You'll need less space if you don't install every program.)

- A CD-ROM drive — double-speed (*2x*) or faster.

- A sound card for PCs. (Mac OS computers have built-in sound support.)

- A monitor capable of displaying at least 256 colors or grayscale.

- A modem with a speed of at least 14,400 bps.

If you need more information on the basics, check out *PCs For Dummies,* 4th Edition, by Dan Gookin; *Macs For Dummies,* 5th Edition, by David Pogue; *Windows 95 For Dummies,* 2nd Edition, by Andy Rathbone; or *Windows 3.11 For Dummies,* 3rd Edition, by Andy Rathbone (all published by IDG Books Worldwide, Inc.).

How to Use the CD Using Microsoft Windows

To install the items from the CD to your hard drive, follow these steps.

1. **Insert the CD into your computer's CD-ROM drive, and close the drive door.**

2. **Windows 3.*x* (that is, 3.1 or 3.11) users: From Program Manager, choose File⇨Run.**

   Windows 95 users: Click the Start button, and click Run.

3. **In the dialog box that appears, type** D:\SETUP.EXE.

   Most of you probably have your CD-ROM drive listed as drive D under My Computer in Windows 95 or the File Manager in Windows 3.1. Type the proper drive letter if your CD-ROM drive uses a different letter.

4. **Click OK.**

   A license agreement window appears.

5. **Because we're sure that you'll want to use the CD, read through the license agreement, nod your head, and then click the Agree button. After you click Agree, you'll never again be bothered by the license agreement window.**

   From here, the CD interface appears. The CD interface lets you install the programs on the CD without typing cryptic commands or using yet another finger-twisting hot key in Windows.

6. **For more information about a program, click the program's name.**

   Be sure to read the information that's displayed. Sometimes a program may require you to do a few tricks on your computer first, and this screen will tell you where to go for that information, if necessary.

7. **To install the program, click the appropriate Install button. If you don't want to install the program, click the Don't Install button to return to the previous category screen.**

   After you click an install button, the CD interface drops to the background while the CD begins installation of the program you chose.

   When installation is done, the interface usually reappears in front of other opened windows. Sometimes the installation will confuse Windows and leave the interface in the background. To bring the interface forward, just click once anywhere in the interface's window.

   After installation is complete, you will return to the last window you viewed — the installation screen for the program you just installed. To go back to the list of programs in the category you're viewing, click Don't Install.

8. **To install other items, repeat Steps 6 and 7.**

9. **When you finish installing programs, click the Quit button to close the interface.**

   You can eject the CD now. Carefully place it back in the plastic jacket of the book for safekeeping.

To run the Earshot SFX sound files library, you need to keep the CD inside your CD-ROM drive. This is a Good Thing. Otherwise, you would need to install a very large chunk of the program to your hard drive space, which may keep you from installing other software.

How to Use the CD Using a Mac OS Computer

To install the items from the CD to your hard drive, follow these steps.

1. **Insert the CD into your computer's CD-ROM drive, and close the drive door.**

   In a moment, an icon representing the CD appears on your Mac desktop. Chances are, the icon looks like a CD-ROM.

2. **Double-click the CD icon to show the CD's contents.**

3. **Double-click on the Read Me First icon.**

   This text file contains information about the CD's programs and any last-minute instructions you need to know about installing the programs on the CD that we don't cover in this appendix.

4. **To install most programs, just drag the program's folder from the CD window and drop it on your hard drive icon.**

5. **To install AT&T WorldNet Service and other larger programs, open the program's folder on the CD, and double-click the icon with the words "Install" or "Installer."**

   After you install the programs that you want, you can eject the CD. Carefully place it back in the plastic jacket of the book for safekeeping.

What You'll Find

Here's a summary of the software on this CD. If you use Windows, the CD interface helps you install software easily. (If you have no idea what I'm talking about when I say "CD interface," flip back to the section, "How to Use the CD Using Microsoft Windows," earlier in this appendix.)

If you use a Mac OS computer, you can enjoy the ease of the Mac interface to quickly install the programs.

AT&T WorldNet Service, from AT&T

For Windows and Mac OS. In case you don't have an Internet connection, the CD includes sign-on software for AT&T WorldNet Service, an Internet Service Provider.

For more information and updates on AT&T WorldNet Service, visit the AT&T WorldNet Web site: http://www.att.com/worldnet.

If you're an AT&T long-distance residential customer, please use this registration code when prompted by the account registration program: L5SQIM631.

If you use another long-distance phone company, please use this registration code when prompted: L5SQIM632.

If you have an Internet Service Provider, please note that AT&T WorldNet Service software makes changes to your computer's current Internet configuration and will probably replace your current provider's settings.

AppletAce, from Macromedia, Inc.

For Windows 95 and Mac OS. AppletAce is a free Java applet development tool. A Java-based version for all platforms is available on the CD. Check out `http://www.macromedia.com/software/appletace/` on the World Wide Web for a full description.

Note: To use AppletAce, your PC or Mac OS computer must be able to run Java programs outside your Web browser. For Macintosh and compatibles, we recommend that you download and install the Macintosh Runtime For Java (MRJ), available on the World Wide Web at `http://applejava.apple.com/`. Mac OS users should see the `Read Me First` file on the CD for additional information. Because Java is a new programming language, you might experience some odd behavior or other problems with Java-based programs like AppletAce. After installing AppletAce, be sure to read the `AppletAceDoc.html` and `README.TXT` files located in the `Program Files\Macromedia\AppletAce` folder (Windows 95) or in the `AppletAce` folder (Mac OS).

BBEdit Lite 4.0, from Bare Bones Software

For Mac OS. BBEdit Lite 4.0 is a Macintosh freeware text editor with powerful features that make creating HTML scripts for your Web pages easy.

The commercial version of this program, BBEdit 4.0, has stronger HTML editing features. We've included a demo version of BBEdit 4.0 on the CD. This demo is fully-featured but cannot save files.

Earshot SFX Sampler, from DXM Productions

For all operating systems. Earshot SFX is a sound effects library sampler. Check out `http://www.earshotsfx.com/` on the World Wide Web for a full description.

GraphicConverter, from Lemke Software

For Mac OS. GraphicConverter is a shareware graphics viewing and editing tool. A version for Macintosh is available on the CD. Check out `http://www.lemkesoft.de/us_contents.html` on the World Wide Web for a full description.

HomeSite, from Allaire Inc.

For Windows 95. HomeSite is a shareware HTML editing tool. A version for Windows 95 is available on the CD. Check out `http://www.allaire.com/products/homesite/overview.cfm` on the World Wide Web for a full description.

HTMLPad, from Intermania Software

For Windows. HTMLPad is a shareware, text-based HTML editing tool. A version for Windows 95 is available on the CD. Check out `http://www.intermania.com/htmlpad/index.html` on the World Wide Web for a full description.

Iconographics Sampler, from Iconographics Design

For all operating systems. Iconographics Sampler is a graphics library sampler. Check out `http://www.iconographics.com/` on the World Wide Web for a full description. The Icongraphics Sampler files are located in the `ICONOG` folder on the CD.

Paint Shop Pro, from JASC Inc.

For Windows. Paint Shop Pro is a shareware graphics viewing and editing tool. Versions for Windows 3.1 and Windows 95 are available on the CD. Check out `http://www.jasc.com/pspdl.html` on the World Wide Web for a full description.

Web Pages from this book

For all operating systems. Sample Web pages from this book let you experiment with the images, code, and effects described in the book. Check out README.HTM in the CDFILES folder on the CD for a full description.

If You've Got Problems (Of the CD Kind)

We tried our best to compile programs that work on most computers with the minimum system requirements. Alas, your computer may differ, and some programs may not work properly for some reason.

The two likeliest problems are that you don't have enough memory (RAM) for the programs you want to use or you have other programs running that are affecting installation or running of a program. If you get error messages like Not enough memory or Setup cannot continue, try one or more of these methods, and then try using the software again:

- ✔ **Turn off any antivirus software that you have on your computer.** Installers sometimes mimic virus activity and may make your computer incorrectly believe that it is being infected by a virus.

- ✔ **Close all running programs.** The more programs you're running, the less memory you have available to other programs. Installers also typically update files and programs. So if you keep other programs running, installation may not work properly.

- ✔ **If you are trying to use AppletAce, be sure that your computer has software installed that can run Java-based programs.** (See the description on AppletAce in "What You'll Find.")

- ✔ **Have your local computer store add more RAM to your computer.** This is, admittedly, a drastic and somewhat expensive step. However, if you have a Windows 95 PC or a Mac OS computer with a PowerPC chip, adding more memory can really help the speed of your computer and allow more programs to run at the same time.

If you still have trouble installing the items from the CD, please call the IDG Books Worldwide Customer Service phone number: 800-762-2974 (outside the U.S.: 317-596-5261).

Index

AT&T WorldNet℠ Service

A World of Possibilities...

Thank you for selecting AT&T WorldNet Service — it's the Internet as only AT&T can bring it to you. With AT&T WorldNet Service, a world of infinite possibilities is now within your reach. Research virtually any subject. Stay abreast of current events. Participate in online newsgroups. Purchase merchandise from leading retailers. Send and receive electronic mail.

AT&T WorldNet Service is rapidly becoming the preferred way of accessing the Internet. It was recently awarded one of the most highly coveted awards in the computer industry, *PC Computing*'s 1996 MVP Award for Best Internet Service Provider. Now, more than ever, it's the best way to stay in touch with the people, ideas, and information that are important to you.

You need a computer with a mouse, a modem, a phone line, and the enclosed software. That's all. We've taken care of the rest.

If You Can Point and Click, You're There

With AT&T WorldNet Service, finding the information you want on the Internet is easier than you ever imagined it could be. You can surf the Net within minutes. And find almost anything you want to know — from the weather in Paris, Texas — to the cost of a ticket to Paris, France. You're just a point and click away. It's that easy.

AT&T WorldNet Service features specially customized industry-leading browsers integrated with advanced Internet directories and search engines. The result is an Internet service that sets a new standard for ease of use — virtually everywhere you want to go is a point and click away, making it a snap to navigate the Internet.

When you go online with AT&T WorldNet Service, you'll benefit from being connected to the Internet by the world leader in networking. We offer you fast access of up to 28.8 Kbps in more than 215 cities throughout the U.S. that will make going online as easy as picking up your phone.

Online Help and Advice
24 Hours a Day, 7 Days a Week

Before you begin exploring the Internet, you may want to take a moment to check two useful sources of information.

If you're new to the Internet, from the AT&T WorldNet Service home page at www.worldnet.att.net, click on the Net Tutorial hyperlink for a quick explanation of unfamiliar terms and useful advice about exploring the Internet.

Another useful source of information is the HELP icon. The area contains pertinent, time saving information-intensive reference tips, and topics such as Accounts & Billing, Trouble Reporting, Downloads & Upgrades, Security Tips, Network Hot Spots, Newsgroups, Special Announcements, etc.

Whether online or off-line, 24 hours a day, seven days a week, we will provide World Class technical expertise and fast, reliable responses to your questions. To reach AT&T WorldNet Customer Care, call **1-800-400-1447**.

Nothing is more important to us than making sure that your Internet experience is a truly enriching and satisfying one.

Safeguard Your Online Purchases

AT&T WorldNet Service is committed to making the Internet a safe and convenient way to transact business. By registering and continuing to charge your AT&T WorldNet Service to your AT&T Universal Card, you'll enjoy peace of mind whenever you shop the Internet. Should your account number be compromised on the Net, you won't be liable for any online transactions charged to your AT&T Universal Card by a person who is not an authorized user.*

*Today, cardmembers may be liable for the first $50 of charges made by a person who is not an authorized user, which will not be imposed under this program as long as the cardmember notifies AT&T Universal Card of the loss within 24 hours and otherwise complies with the Cardmember Agreement. Refer to Cardmember Agreement for definition of authorized user.

Minimum System Requirements

IBM-Compatible Personal Computer Users:
- IBM-compatible personal computer with 486SX or higher processor
- 8MB of RAM (or more for better performance)
- 15–36MB of available hard disk space to install software, depending on platform
  (14–21MB to use service after installation, depending on platform)
- Graphics system capable of displaying 256 colors
- 14,400 bps modem connected to an outside phone line and not a LAN or ISDN line
- Microsoft Windows 3.1x or Windows 95

Macintosh Users:
- Macintosh 68030 or higher (including 68LC0X0 models and all Power Macintosh models)
- System 7.5.3 Revision 2 or higher for PCI Power Macintosh models: System 7.1 or higher for all 680X0 and non-PCI Power Macintosh models
- Mac TCP 2.0.6 or Open Transport 1.1 or higher

- 8MB of RAM (minimum) with Virtual Memory turned on or RAM Doubler; 16MB recommended for Power Macintosh users
- 12MB of available hard disk space (15MB recommended)
- 14,400 bps modem connected to an outside phone line and not a LAN or ISDN line
- Color or 256 gray-scale monitor
- Apple Guide 1.2 or higher (if you want to view online help)
  If you are uncertain of the configuration of your Macintosh computer, consult your Macintosh User's guide or call Apple at 1-800-767-2775.

Installation Tips and Instructions

- If you have other Web browsers or online software, please consider uninstalling them according to the vendor's instructions.
- If you are installing AT&T WorldNet Service on a computer with Local Area Networking, please contact your LAN administrator for setup instructions.
- At the end of installation, you may be asked to restart your computer. Don't attempt the registration process until you have done so.

IBM-compatible PC users:
- Insert the CD-ROM into the CD-ROM drive on your computer.
- Select *File/Run* (for Windows 3.1*x*) or *Start/Run* (for Windows 95 if setup did not start automatically).
- Type *D:\setup.exe* (or change the "D" if your CD-ROM is another drive).
- Click *OK*.
- Follow the onscreen instructions to install and register.

Macintosh users:
- Disable all extensions except Apple CD-ROM and Foreign Files Access extensions.
- Restart Computer.
- Insert the CD-ROM into the CD-ROM drive on your computer.
- Double-click the *Install AT&T WorldNet Service* icon.
- Follow the onscreen instructions to install. (Upon restarting your Macintosh, AT&T WorldNet Service Account Setup automatically starts.)
- Follow the onscreen instructions to register.

Registering with AT&T WorldNet Service

After you have connected with AT&T WorldNet online registration service, you will be presented with a series of screens that confirm billing information and prompt you for additional account set-up data.

The following is a list of registration tips and comments that will help you during the registration process.

I. Use one of the following registration codes, which can also be found in Appendix B of *Netscape Composer For Dummies*. Use L5SQIM631 if you are an AT&T long-distance residential customer or L5SQIM632 if you use another long-distance phone company.
II. During registration, you will need to supply your name, address, and valid credit card number, and choose an account information security word, e-mail name, and e-mail password. You will also be requested to select your preferred price plan at this time. (We advise that you use all lowercase letters when assigning an e-mail ID and security code, since they are easier to remember.)
III. If you make a mistake and exit or get disconnected during the registration process prematurely, simply click on "Create New Account." Do not click on "Edit Existing Account."
IV. When choosing your local access telephone number, you will be given several options. Please choose the one nearest to you. Please note that calling a number within your area does not guarantee that the call is free.

Connecting to AT&T WorldNet Service

When you have finished installing and registering with AT&T WorldNet Service, you are ready to access the Internet. Make sure your modem and phone line are available before attempting to connect to the service.

For Windows 95 users:
- Double-click on the *Connect to AT&T WorldNet Service* icon on your desktop.
  OR
- Select *Start, Programs, AT&T WorldNet Software, Connect to AT&T WorldNet Service.*

For Windows 3.1*x* users:
- Double-click on the *Connect to AT&T WorldNet Service* icon located in the AT&T WorldNet Service group.

For Macintosh users:
- Double-click on the *AT&T WorldNet Service* icon in the AT&T WorldNet Service folder.

Choose the Plan That's Right for You

The Internet is for everyone, whether at home or at work. In addition to making the time you spend online productive and fun, we're also committed to making it affordable. Choose one of two price plans: unlimited usage access or hourly usage access. The latest pricing information can be obtained during online registration. No matter which plan you use, we're confident that after you take advantage of everything AT&T WorldNet Service has to offer, you'll wonder how you got along without it.

Explore our AT&T WorldNet Service site at http://www.att.com/worldnet.

IDG Books Worldwide, Inc., End-User License Agreement

5. **Limited Warranty.**

   (a) IDGB warrants that the Software and Software Media are free from defects in materials and workmanship under normal use for a period of sixty (60) days from the date of purchase of this Book. If IDGB receives notification within the warranty period of defects in materials or workmanship, IDGB will replace the defective Software Media.

   (b) IDGB AND THE AUTHORS OF THE BOOK DISCLAIM ALL OTHER WARRANTIES, EX-PRESS OR IMPLIED, INCLUDING WITHOUT LIMITATION IMPLIED WARRANTIES OF MERCHANTABILITY AND FITNESS FOR A PARTICULAR PURPOSE, WITH RESPECT TO THE SOFTWARE, THE PROGRAMS, THE SOURCE CODE CONTAINED THEREIN, AND/OR THE TECHNIQUES DESCRIBED IN THIS BOOK. IDGB DOES NOT WARRANT THAT THE FUNCTIONS CONTAINED IN THE SOFTWARE WILL MEET YOUR REQUIREMENTS OR THAT THE OPERATION OF THE SOFTWARE WILL BE ERROR FREE.

   (c) This limited warranty gives you specific legal rights, and you may have other rights that vary from jurisdiction to jurisdiction.

6. **Remedies.**

   (a) IDGB's entire liability and your exclusive remedy for defects in materials and workmanship shall be limited to replacement of the Software Media, which may be returned to IDGB with a copy of your receipt at the following address: Software Media Fulfillment Department, Attn.: *Netscape Composer For Dummies,* IDG Books Worldwide, Inc., 7260 Shadeland Station, Ste. 100, Indianapolis, IN 46256, or call 800-762-2974. Please allow three to four weeks for delivery. This Limited Warranty is void if failure of the Software Media has resulted from accident, abuse, or misapplication. Any replacement Software Media will be warranted for the remainder of the original warranty period or thirty (30) days, whichever is longer.

   (b) In no event shall IDGB or the authors be liable for any damages whatsoever (including without limitation damages for loss of business profits, business interruption, loss of business information, or any other pecuniary loss) arising from the use of or inability to use the Book or the Software, even if IDGB has been advised of the possibility of such damages.

   (c) Because some jurisdictions do not allow the exclusion or limitation of liability for conse-quential or incidental damages, the above limitation or exclusion may not apply to you.

7. **U.S. Government Restricted Rights.** Use, duplication, or disclosure of the Software by the U.S. Government is subject to restrictions stated in paragraph (c)(1)(ii) of the Rights in Technical Data and Computer Software clause of DFARS 252.227-7013, and in subparagraphs (a) through (d) of the Commercial Computer–Restricted Rights clause at FAR 52.227-19, and in similar clauses in the NASA FAR supplement, when applicable.

8. **General.** This Agreement constitutes the entire understanding of the parties and revokes and supersedes all prior agreements, oral or written, between them and may not be modified or amended except in a writing signed by both parties hereto that specifically refers to this Agreement. This Agreement shall take precedence over any other documents that may be in conflict herewith. If any one or more provisions contained in this Agreement are held by any court or tribunal to be invalid, illegal, or otherwise unenforceable, each and every other provision shall remain in full force and effect.

CD-ROM Installation Instructions

Important: Before you use the CD, refer to the "About the CD" appendix for additional system requirements and essential instructions.

The following steps tell how to get the CD running under Microsoft Windows. *If you use a Mac OS computer,* please see the Read Me First document on the CD for quick instructions on how to install the contents of the CD.

Windows users have a colorful interface program that makes it easy to install the software on the CD. To start the interface in Windows:

1. **Insert the CD into your computer's CD-ROM drive, and close the drive door.**

2. **Windows 3.*x* (that is, 3.1 or 3.11) users: From Program Manager, choose File⇨Run. Windows 95 users: Click the Start button, and click Run.**

3. **In the dialog box that appears, type** D:\SETUP.EXE, **and click OK. Type the proper drive letter if your CD-ROM drive uses a different letter.**

   A license agreement window appears.

4. **Read the license agreement, and then click the Agree button.**

   The CD interface appears.

5. **For more information about a program, click the program's name.**

6. **To install the program, click the appropriate Install button. If you don't want to install the program, click the Go Back button.**

7. **To install other items, repeat Steps 5 and 6.**

8. **When you finish installing programs, click the Quit button to close the interface.**

For additional instructions about the programs on the CD, please see the "About the CD" appendix located in the back of the book.

IDG BOOKS WORLDWIDE REGISTRATION CARD

Visit our
Web site at
http://www.idgbooks.com

ISBN Number: 0-7645-0075-9

Title of this book: Netscape Composer™ For Dummies®

My overall rating of this book: ❏ Very good [1] ❏ Good [2] ❏ Satisfactory [3] ❏ Fair [4] ❏ Poor [5]

How I first heard about this book:

❏ Found in bookstore; name: [6] _____

❏ Advertisement: [8]

❏ Word of mouth; heard about book from friend, co-worker, etc.: [10]

❏ Book review: [7] _____

❏ Catalog: [9]

❏ Other: [11]

What I liked most about this book:

_____
_____

What I would change, add, delete, etc., in future editions of this book:

_____
_____

Other comments:

_____

Number of computer books I purchase in a year: ❏ 1 [12] ❏ 2-5 [13] ❏ 6-10 [14] ❏ More than 10 [15]

I would characterize my computer skills as: ❏ Beginner [16] ❏ Intermediate [17] ❏ Advanced [18] ❏ Professional [19]

I use ❏ DOS [20] ❏ Windows [21] ❏ OS/2 [22] ❏ Unix [23] ❏ Macintosh [24] ❏ Other: [25]_____

(please specify)

I would be interested in new books on the following subjects:

(please check all that apply, and use the spaces provided to identify specific software)

❏ Word processing: [26]

❏ Data bases: [28]

❏ File Utilities: [30]

❏ Networking: [32]

❏ Other: [34]

❏ Spreadsheets: [27]

❏ Desktop publishing: [29]

❏ Money management: [31]

❏ Programming languages: [33]

I use a PC at (please check all that apply): ❏ home [35] ❏ work [36] ❏ school [37] ❏ other: [38] _____

The disks I prefer to use are ❏ 5.25 [39] ❏ 3.5 [40] ❏ other: [41]_____

I have a CD ROM: ❏ yes [42] ❏ no [43]

I plan to buy or upgrade computer hardware this year: ❏ yes [44] ❏ no [45]

I plan to buy or upgrade computer software this year: ❏ yes [46] ❏ no [47]

Name: _____ Business title: [48] _____ Type of Business: [49]

Address (❏ home [50] ❏ work [51]/Company name: _____)

Street/Suite# _____

City [52]/State [53]/Zip code [54]: _____ Country [55]

❏ **I liked this book!** You may quote me by name in future
IDG Books Worldwide promotional materials.

My daytime phone number is _____

IDG
BOOKS
WORLDWIDE

THE WORLD OF
COMPUTER
KNOWLEDGE®

❑ YES!

Please keep me informed about IDG Books Worldwide's World of Computer Knowledge. Send me your latest catalog.